How Free Can Religion Be?

How Free Can Religion Be?

Randall P. Bezanson

University of Illinois Press
Urbana and Chicago

Manufactured in the United States of America
♾ This book is printed on acid-free paper.
C 5 4 3 2 1

Library of Congress Cataloging-in-Publication Data
Bezanson, Randall P.
How free can religion be? / Randall P. Bezanson.
p. cm.
Includes bibliographical references and index.
ISBN-13: 978-0-252-03112-0 (cloth : alk. paper)
ISBN-10: 0-252-03112-1 (cloth : alk. paper)
1. Church and state—United States. 2. Freedom of religion—
United States.
I. Title.
KF4865.B49 2006
342.7308′52—dc22 2005031439

Contents

Preface

When an author writes a book, she or he often has ideas and objectives that are important to the book but hardly obvious to the reader. At least that is the case with this book, and so I take this brief occasion at the very beginning to touch on a few points in order to help the reader.

The purpose of this book is not to convince anyone about one view, and certainly not about my own view, of the best approach to the religion guarantees or the proper meaning to be given religious freedom or non-establishment. My hope is only to educate and enlighten. I thus offer no answers, only questions and alternative ways of addressing them. In this sense the book is, in aspiration at least, a written Socratic dialogue, inviting the reader into the interesting, often entertaining, and deeply challenging world of the religion guarantees of the First Amendment, the Supreme Court Justices who populate that world, and the able lawyers who argue cases before the Supreme Court.

This is not a book written just for scholars or lawyers or students, but also—indeed more so—for interested people of all religions or no religion who seek to explore the fundamental questions raised by the twin guarantees of freedom to exercise religion and freedom from government laws that respect an establishment of religion. At the base level, the questions are philosophical, sociological, and spiritual, not legal. But we will witness the way in which they are addressed and given meaning over time by the United States Supreme Court—meaning that, while concrete in a given case, is far from fixed or clear or free from controversy.

I have previously written (and claim no originality then or now) that there are no answers in constitutional law, but only questions and good arguments.

This is perhaps peculiarly true of the religion guarantees. So my aim is to introduce the questions and arguments and to place responsibility for reaching conclusions in the hands of the reader—or perhaps a group of readers sitting around a table with coffee and fine wine after dinner, discussing and debating the meaning of religion in America. Nothing would please me more.

I should also say a word or two about my choice of "stories," or cases. The cases I have selected span the history of the Supreme Court's experience with the religion guarantees, from the late 1800s to the present. I have not picked the cases simply because they are famous ones (though many are) or reach desirable results (as we will see, they may not). I have, instead, selected cases that serve effectively to present the relevant issues, both in the cases themselves and beyond the cases to other fact settings or eras or contexts. I have selected the cases with a view to the three, largely chronological, stages of the Supreme Court's jurisprudence and shifting alliances; but in most other respects the cases selected were those I judged to be the best Socratic instruments by which to discuss the issues and ideas raised by the religion guarantees.

Finally, I must thank the people who have helped me with the book: Jonathan Wilson and Lisa Williams, who assembled endless amounts of raw material about each of the cases; my late colleague Alan Widiss, and my colleague Bill Buss, with whom I have taught seminars on the religion clauses and from whom I have learned much; Zachary Taylor Shultz, who read and commented upon the full text from the perspective both of law and religion; my wife, Elaine, who did her best to make me write in the active voice; and, of course, my students in the many courses I have taught at the University of Iowa and in a special seminar/tutorial at the University of Arizona in the fall of 2004. All these people, and others, have made it painless, enjoyable, and indeed great fun to write this book. I am deeply grateful for that.

Introduction

Thomas Jefferson believed that the freedom of religion was the most important of all the rights conferred in the first ten amendments to the Constitution, commonly called the Bill of Rights. The First Amendment begins with the religion guarantees. "Congress shall make no law respecting an establishment of religion, or prohibiting the free exercise thereof." It then turns to freedom of speech, press, and the right peaceably to assemble. Perhaps Jefferson felt that without the individual's freedom of conscience on matters religious, there could be no freedom in the political and social realms. He may also have believed that without an enforced distance between the state and the organized religious institutions, no secular government devoted strictly to earthly matters of social and political organization could exist. Jefferson voiced such beliefs, though we will, of course, never know precisely what he meant by them.

We do know that many who came to America did so to escape religious persecution. They tended to gather in colonies of like-minded believers and set up colonial governments. Some preserved religious liberty for all believers. Others established government-supported churches and taxed everyone to support that church. Some enforced religious devotion and attendance at church, whatever the individual's preferences regarding religion. Among the various colonies and their various practices, however, virtually none blinked at enforced tithes through taxation. The most liberal colonies enforced tithes (taxes for the support of churches) but allowed the individual to designate the church to which the tithe would be directed. Everyone was religious—not really, but they said so—so the freedom attained consisted mostly of allowing each to chose his or her own religious course, but not to chose nonreligion over religion. And by religion the colonists meant Christianity.

Progress, it seems, took place in small steps. By the time of the Revolution and the later drafting and ratification of the Constitution (and then, two years later, the Bill of Rights), further change had occurred. Part of the change was philosophical. With the influence of people like John Locke, Jean-Jacques Rousseau, and others, there was a greater appreciation of the importance of reason in constructing the body politic. Organized government could be thought of as a compact among men (and women) based on reason, by which society could be organized to protect and maximize the interests of all through the delegation of limited powers to a government. The government and its powers were to be constructed on reason and limited to the realms of reason; realms of faith and religion were to be assigned elsewhere, reserved to the private sphere yet separated off from government and disabled from dictating or controlling government. Such a separation of reason and faith was deemed essential to a government that preserved individual freedom and individual democratic control of the polity. Restricting government to its own sphere of reason and limited powers, moreover, was seen as essential to preserving the sphere of faith and religious freedom. This was the foundation of the secular democratic state in which individual freedom of conscience could be preserved.

But it was but an imperfect vision. At the time of the revolution, many of the colonies still had healthy established and state-supported—even modestly state-enforced—churches. Tithes for religion, and even a preferred religion, continued to be enforced in many colonies. When the Constitution was ratified, there was a general concern about religious freedom and the limitation of it by such tithing practices, but the concern was general and vague. When the Bill of Rights was drafted, the Virginia Bill for Religious Freedom and Madison's famous Remonstrance (which we will consider in detail when we look at *Everson v. Board of Education*) were widely known and had struck a chord. Legally enforced tithes (or taxes) to support a single approved church were broadly disfavored.

Yet the First Amendment religion guarantees were drafted in frustratingly general and ambiguous language that prevented their being tied to any particular practice or view. First, the amendment provided that "*Congress* shall make no law respecting an establishment of religion, or prohibiting the free exercise thereof." Only Congress (and, implicitly, the federal government enforcing federal law) was bound by the amendment. The states were left to their own devices on matters of religious liberty. Many states adopted their own, variously worded, religion guarantees in their constitutions, but these were not controlled by or enforced by federal authority. And many states, like Massachusetts, continued to have established churches, tithes enforced for specific churches, tithes for religion in general, and laws against certain religions well into the nineteenth century. It would not be until the adoption of the Fourteenth Amendment after the Civil War that the religion guarantees of the First Amendment became applicable to the states, and not until 1947 that the Supreme Court fully enforced them against the states.

Second, even with respect to the federal government the wording of the First Amendment religion guarantees was downright unclear. It did not expressly prohibit a legally favored religion. It did not prohibit tithes or taxes for religion, nor state support for religion. Instead, it prohibited any law "respecting an establishment of" religion. This language might at once be broader or narrower than a prohibition of favored churches or tithes enforced by law. The record of the drafting and debates leading up to the adoption of the specific language of the First Amendment sheds precious little light on the subject. It is clear that the drafters wanted to prohibit the new federal government from designating one official national church and taking steps, through taxation or otherwise, to support and enforce that church. And it is clear that the federal government was prohibited from doing so for two reasons: because an established national church would be inconsistent with religious freedom and the separation of religion from secular government and, perhaps more important, because the shape of the relationship between religion and government was to be firmly left to the respective states, with no interference from the new federal government whose encroachments were widely feared.

The meaning of the second religion guarantee, the free exercise clause, was clearer, though not without ambiguity. It declared in sweeping and absolute language that "Congress shall make no law . . . prohibiting the free exercise" of religion. The prohibition was, of course, limited to Congress and the federal government; states were left unfettered to bar free exercise of some or all religions (though none chose the latter course). Religion, at that time, was a widely understood term: Christianity. But the meaning of "exercise" of religion was a different matter. Few would argue in the debates surrounding ratification of the First Amendment that an "exercise" free from government control included any, or at least many, *actions and practices* dictated by one's religious beliefs. There was general agreement that "exercise" included beliefs and expression of beliefs, and that it generally excluded actions. The debate was about whether a few "actions," like church attendance, refusing to take oaths that conflicted with religious beliefs, and the like, were also included as free "exercises."

We will say much more about these matters, and many others, in the stories that follow. The point made here is simply that the religion guarantees were born of a complex stew of untested political theory; fear of unlimited central government; universal acceptance of Christianity; uncertain ideas of individual liberty and the makings of secular democratic government; and very ambiguous language. It would be first left to the evolution of political values in the nation and, then, to the Supreme Court to give more concrete meaning to the language of the First Amendment.

It is on the Supreme Court's contributions to this process that we will principally focus. We will witness the Supreme Court's understanding of the nation's and the Constitution's history, the intention of the framers, the practices under the Constitution, and evolving public and cultural understandings. We will see and evaluate the use to which the Supreme Court puts these historical perspectives in interpreting and enforcing the religion guarantees, beginning in the latter half of the nineteenth century. We will follow the shifting sands of judicial theory through a series of cases that sometimes present new—and sometimes revisit old—problems: the Mormon Church's claimed belief in polygamy; state support for religious schools; the teaching of evolution and creationism in public schools; claims for exemption from compulsory education laws for the Amish, and from drug laws for a Native American religion; rights of free speech and equal access and treatment by religious groups in colleges and public primary and secondary schools; school vouchers; and so on.

Our journey through these cases and issues will be divided into three parts, which roughly reflect the three stages through which the Supreme Court has traveled so far. The first stage, which I call "The Old Time Religion: Separation of Church and State," reflects the essential ingredients of the separation philosophy developed and enforced over the first one hundred or so years of the Court's involvement in religious issues, from the mid-1800s to the mid-1900s. This is the "old time religion" by which the establishment and free exercise clauses were defined and interpreted as a coherent whole, based on the view that preserving separation of church and state was the most important, and thus the primary, means of assuring the individual's religious freedom. It set up a regime in which religious exercise and religious institutions were on their own, unable to seek government financial or other assistance. Being on its own, however, meant that religion was free to follow its own course without impediment from government.

The second stage, which I call the "Time of Testing," covered the years roughly spanning the 1960s through the 1980s. During this stage, cases arose that mightily tested the will and endurance of a Supreme Court unanimously committed, at first, to a separationist vision of the religion guarantees. But in cases involving exemption of the Old Order Amish children from compulsory education laws, state aid in the form of textbooks, equipment, and special education services for children in religious schools—as well as cases challenging school prayer, property tax exemptions for churches, the teaching of evolution in public schools—the separationists had to defend results that appeared increasingly mean-spirited and hostile to religion and the exercise of religious liberty by individuals. To avoid such results, the "wall of separation" between church and state was made increasingly porous, ultimately riddled with exceptions that began to undermine the basic premises and principles of separation. New definitions of the ambiguous terms of the First Amendment were discovered, new interpretations of history were offered, and new theories about the meaning of religion guarantees began to surface, though largely in dissenting opinions.

The third stage I call "The New Awakening." It is a new awakening in the sense that the emerging new theories of the religion guarantees moved from dissenting opinions to majority opinions for the Supreme Court, and over the roughly fifteen-year period from the late 1980s to the present, the new theories have begun to congeal into a fairly coherent approach to the religion guarantees that is in some respects new and in others old. It is an approach that partakes partly of the original separation theory, by which religion could not claim exemption from generally applicable laws governing religious conduct as opposed to belief. Yet it consists also of a new idea that "establishment" should be understood to permit, indeed to encourage, government support for religion, as long as it does not discriminate among religions in doing so. In this way the freedom to exercise religion is fostered, not just allowed, at the hands of the political branches of government, not the courts. This approach is a new awakening in the sense that it is responsive to, or at least corresponds with, the emergence in the same period of renewed religious activity, fervor, fundamentalism, and political activism.

This book follows the course of history. But it is not a work of history. Instead, it is a book about current and timeless ideas concerning religion and religious liberty in the United States. The issues raised in the cases—even the oldest of cases—are far from relics of history. They are likely to arise again and again, often meeting different receptions each time around. This is because the meaning of the Constitution is not fixed but is constantly in motion. The most recent ideas do not replace the old; instead, they often give way to the old when the old reasserts itself in new garb. It is in this sense that it is often said, as I often say to my students, that there are no answers in constitutional law. There are just good arguments.

This book, then, is neither a history nor a compendium of legal answers. It is, instead, a set of questions and arguments, a written Socratic dialogue, with me on one side, the reader on the other. Its subject is the place of religion in America—the proper relation of church and state, and the role of individual liberty of conscience and belief, with regard to that most universal question of all for humans: who are we and why are we here?

STAGE I

The Old Time Religion: Separation of Church and State

We begin at the beginning. Not the beginning of religion or the religion guarantees in America, but the beginning of the Supreme Court's interpretations of the meaning of the religion guarantees, interpretations that, as we will see, draw heavily on the English, colonial, and constitutional history of the guarantees that "Congress shall make no law respecting an establishment of religion, or prohibiting the free exercise thereof."

While those words, in the form of Article I of the Bill of Rights, were made part of the Constitution in 1791, it would not be until almost one hundred years later, in 1878, that the Court began in earnest to give judicial meaning to the ambiguous language of the First Amendment. And a full-fledged theory of the twin religion guarantees (applicable to both Congress and the states) would not be first articulated until 1947. The cases we will survey in this part are foundational, upon which the wall of separation between church and state was erected. The first involves the Mormons' claimed right to practice polygamy as part of their religious beliefs and marks the boundaries of the free exercise guarantee. The second involves public transportation of students to religious schools and gives meaning and primacy to the prohibition of laws respecting an establishment of religion.

It is from these cases that the command of separation of church and state was given legal force.

STORY 1

God's Law or Caesar's? The Free Exercise of Religion

Reynolds v. United States, 98 U.S. 145 (1878)

The First Amendment says, "Congress shall make no law respecting an establishment of religion or prohibiting the free exercise thereof. . . ." The Constitution seems to point to a relationship between the secular state and religion, one in which the state can't have a favored or official religion, and one in which the individual is guaranteed the right freely to exercise his or her religion.

Does this mean that religion must be entirely private and free of state influence, even supportive state influence? Or does it mean that government can promote religion—but must not prefer one religion to another?

Does the free exercise clause guarantee the individual the freedom to "exercise" his or her religion, like the free speech clause guarantees the individual the right to hold beliefs and act on them by speaking them to others? If religious conduct and belief are protected by the free exercise right, how far does that protection extend? Does it include the right to attend church, to publicly display one's religion, to an exemption from compulsory education laws, to create religious schools outside the public school system, to refuse modern medicine, to consume alcohol or drugs as part of religious activities, to kill in the name of religion?

Does it include the right to have more than one wife—to engage in polygamy—free from the law's prohibition? That is the question posed by the *Reynolds* case, decided in 1878. The *Reynolds* case involved the federal government's power to outlaw polygamy in the face of Mormon religious belief (at the time) that polygamy was permissible and, indeed, a required religious practice under basic Church doctrine. George Reynolds chose the law of his religion over the law of his government. Was he entitled to do so by the free exercise guarantee? If so, would that make the government an unwitting and unwilling party to his actions? How should we resolve struggles between the individual believer and the government?

George Reynolds's story involves the nature of religious belief, the emergence of a new and socially threatening religion, and the life and beliefs of an important member of the Mormon Church. It was a national controversy played out over many years in contentious disputes in the national press and in the House, Senate, and the Executive Branch, as well as in the courts. Indeed, it involves a struggle for secular control over a territory and, later, the state of Utah, which was believed by many, including presidents, to have come under the dominion and control of a church that would, if allowed to persist, effectively own the property, control the branches of state government, make the laws, organize the society, and set its social, political, and economic rules and laws in accordance with the doctrines of the Mormon faith.

* * *

George Reynolds was born on New Year's Day, 1842, in the Marylebone District of Central London.[1] He was born into a middle-class London family, his father a master tailor on Regent Street. George was a precocious boy with "an assiduous desire to learn"[2] who, with the help of his maternal grandmother, was able to attend primary school at the North London Collegiate School, where he excelled. In 1851, at age 9, he first became acquainted with Mormonism, through a maid of his grandmother's. He attended services and, after a time, attempted baptism, but was not allowed to do so for lack of his parents' permission.

At age 12, George was sent to Paris for further education, studying French and classical literature and continuing his interest in mathematics, science, geography, history, and astronomy. He also continued his interest in Mormonism. Upon his return to England in 1856 at age 14, he finally succeeded in getting baptized in the Mormon Church. The next year he was ordained a deacon.

For the next few years, George worked as an apprentice for his father and then as a cashier. But his commitment was to the Mormon Church. At age 18, in 1860, he was ordained as an elder and frequently preached around London.

---

1. The following brief account of George Reynolds's life and his involvement in the famous polygamy case is drawn from a PhD dissertation by Bruce Arthur Van Orden, "George Reynolds: Secretary, Sacrificial Lamb, and Seventy," (1986) (Provo: Brigham Young University).

2. *Id.* at 2.

The next year, over his father's strenuous objections, he answered the call for a full-time mission in the Mormon Church. His mission brought him to service in the European Mission, where he served as an elder, a full-time minister, head of a mission in London, secretary to the London Conference, and finally, as secretary to the president of the European Mission and as emigration clerk, responsible for arranging the emigration of Mormons from England and throughout Europe to America and then to the "Mormon Zion" in Utah. During his three years' service as emigration clerk (1862–65), between twenty-five hundred and four thousand Mormons emigrated each year, notwithstanding the ongoing civil war in America.

George Reynolds immigrated to America from Liverpool on May 20, 1865. He arrived in New York twelve days later and then spent a few days arranging for the transportation by train of about twelve hundred other emigrants to Wyoming and Nebraska, from where they would proceed to Salt Lake City by wagon. Reynolds arrived in Salt Lake City on July 5, 1865. Mormon officials with whom and for whom he had worked in England and Europe promptly introduced Reynolds to the president of the Church, Brigham Young, and to Heber Kimball, the first counselor to the president.

During his first few weeks in Salt Lake City, George Reynolds married Polly (his sweetheart from England who had emigrated earlier), found housing, and began work as a clerk in a mercantile company in Salt Lake City. By the end of the year, Brigham Young called Reynolds to work in the office of the president where, for the rest of his career, he occupied various positions of administrative and religious importance in the Church. Reynolds had been highly recommended for his administrative skill, financial experience, and unyielding loyalty to the Mormon Church and its leaders. He also began writing religious and other articles for Church periodicals and newspapers and undertook more serious study of the Church's history and tenets. These were literary undertakings that would lead, by the end of his life in 1909, to the publication of 15 books, 264 articles in religious periodicals, and roughly 150 newspaper articles. Among the books would be the first "scholarly" investigations of the Mormon Church, of the Book of Mormon, and of the history of the lost tribes of Israel who, under Church doctrine, had come from Jerusalem to the Americas following Jesus' death.

When George Reynolds arrived in Salt Lake City, change was afoot. Following the Civil War, many of the Union soldiers remained with the army and traveled west to help open the western frontier. The influx of manpower to Utah lent strength to the federal presence there and to the federal government's efforts to contain the growing influence of the Mormon Church in the Utah Territory. The conflict between the federal government and the

Church had been building for many years, and it would build rapidly between 1865 and October 1874, when Reynolds would be indicted for the crime of polygamy. The conflict involved a wide variety of issues, including land ownership, control of mineral resources, and the exercise of government power, but politically the signal issue marking the conflict was polygamy, a practice firmly embedded in the core beliefs of the Mormon religion and widely practiced in Utah by the members of the Mormon Church.

The Church first publicly acknowledged polygamous practices in 1852, and antagonism toward the Mormons grew throughout the entire country during the 1850s. Both the Republican and Democratic parties campaigned against polygamy in the late 1850s, and petitions for statehood by the citizens of Utah in the early 1860s met with failure, in part, at least, because of the continuing practices in the Church. In July 1862, the Morrill antipolygamy law was enacted by Congress and signed by President Lincoln, who thereafter left the act's prohibitions laying in desuetude as he became fully occupied by the Civil War. The Mormons in Utah took advantage of the hiatus and performed many new polygamous marriages.

Prosecutions of polygamists increased after the Civil War, but they almost always proved unsuccessful, as the Church kept no (or did not admit to having) records, and witnesses to the ceremonies could not be found. Criminal trials thus faltered for lack of evidence. There was increasing political pressure to do something about polygamy, however, both at the federal level and from within Utah from the "ring of gentiles," the politically active members of the non-Mormon population who wanted the practice stopped and, perhaps as important, wanted the political power and governmental influence of the Church restrained. Many bills to strengthen the Morrill Act were introduced in Congress but failed to pass. A major problem in Utah was that the territorial courts where prosecutions were held were often controlled by the Church, which had a heavy hand in appointing the territorial judges and selecting jurors. Finding a jury willing to convict was difficult.

It was not until 1874, in the wake of failed prosecutions launched by James McKean, a zealous antipolygamy crusader appointed Chief Justice of the Utah Territory by President Grant, that a bill was finally passed giving the United States district courts exclusive civil and criminal jurisdiction over polygamy cases and assuring that the juries would have representation from the gentile community as well as from the Mormon population. McKean immediately launched a grand jury, and U.S. Attorney William Carey began seeking indictments against polygamists and then prosecuting them. High-level Church officials were among those prosecuted. But the lack of evidence caused by the absence of Church records and witnesses continued to create problems. Most of the polygamous marriages were claimed to precede the Morrill Act and thus were beyond the reach of the law.

With the federal authorities frustrated, the political controversy building, and the Church experiencing great stress, Brigham Young and his Church authorities decided to find a way to resolve the matter of polygamy for good. They believed that the practice, as a central tenet of the Mormon religion, was protected against legal prohibition by the First Amendment of the United States Constitution, which guaranteed the "free exercise" of religion in the United States. Negotiations were thus begun between Church authorities and U.S. Attorney Carey, and in October 1874, the parties agreed to a "test case" in which the Church would provide the evidence of a polygamous marriage and would challenge the constitutionality of the Morrill Act's prohibition, in exchange for which the pending prosecutions brought against Church authorities, including Brigham Young, would be dropped.

A few months earlier, on August 3, 1874, George Reynolds had decided, with his wife Polly's agreement, to enter into a polygamous marriage with Amelia Shofield.[3] Reynolds believed that his action was required by the "Law of the Lord" and necessary to "escape condemnation and His displeasure. . . ."[4] Unbeknownst to him at the time, George Reynolds would soon provide the Church with its "test case." As Reynolds wrote in his diary:

> On the evening of Wednesday, Oct. 21st, [1874,] I, accompanied by my wife Amelia visited bro Edwin Dowden, on my return, whilst passing the south side of the Templee Block I met bro Cannon who informed me (in substance) that it had been decided among the brethren of the President's Council to bring a test case of the law of 1862 (Anti-Polygamy Act) before the court and that it had been decided to present my name before the grand jury.[5]

Reynolds later wrote, "I was asked to step to the front. I willingly complied and afforded the prosecution such information with regard to my marriages and the names of important witnesses as I thought could prove the facts desired."[6]

For reasons that are not altogether clear, the agreement between Carey and the Church leadership broke down: Carey did not dismiss pending prosecutions, and indeed brought others. Whatever the reason for the breakdown, an indictment against George Reynolds was obtained. The trial at-

3. Reynolds had previously married five other women, all deceased at the time of the marriages and all cousins, it appears, in a practice approved by the church and through which the man would have the women as wives in the afterlife.

4. Van Orden at 58.

5. *Id.* at 59, citing George Reynolds's journal, Vol. 5, Oct. 16, 1874.

6. *Id.* at 3–4, citing autobiographical sketch of George Reynolds.

tracted national press attention. President Grant ordered Gen. Benjamin Cowen, the Assistant Secretary of the Interior, to observe the trial.

During the trial, the prosecution called Reynolds's wife Amelia to testify. She admitted the marriage, apparently relying on the (by then) broken agreement between Carey and the Church. George Reynolds was convicted of polygamy. Because the agreement was breached, Reynolds's lawyers changed course and, instead of simply challenging the constitutionality of the Morrill Act on appeal, they also challenged the legality of the grand jury on procedural grounds. They were successful in their challenge; Reynolds's conviction was reversed. The constitutional issue was left unresolved.

Peace did not prevail for long, however, as the prosecutors could bring the charges again. There had only been a reversal of a conviction, not a jury verdict of not guilty. George Reynolds was indicted a second time on October 30, 1875. The trial once again attracted national attention and stirred national controversy. This time Reynolds was represented by three very prominent and experienced attorneys. In the course of jury selection, the defense tried to disqualify three jurors, all apparently "gentiles," who admitted to having an opinion on the matter but claimed an ability to decide on the facts and law. The judge denied the objection and allowed the jurors to sit. The prosecution, in turn, challenged two jurors, both Mormon, who admitted believing in polygamy but said they would follow the law as instructed by the judge. The court struck those jurors from the panel. Controversy swirled.

In the second trial, the Church's records were not made available to the prosecution, as the agreement was no longer being followed, and none of the witnesses to the polygamous marriage, whose names Reynolds had originally supplied to the prosecutors in the first trial, could recall the marriage. The prosecution had no alternative but to try to have Amelia Reynolds's testimony from the first trial admitted in the second. She was thus subpoenaed, but she could not be found and did not appear. This allowed the prosecution to introduce her earlier testimony and achieve a conviction. It took the jury two hours to return with a guilty verdict. On December 21, 1875, the court sentenced George Reynolds to two years imprisonment at hard labor in the federal prison in Detroit, Michigan.

Reynolds appealed his conviction to the Territorial Supreme Court, which affirmed the conviction on June 13, 1876. In October 1876, Reynolds's case was appealed to the Supreme Court of the United States. Due to a backlog, the appeal was originally scheduled for February 1878. It was thereafter delayed at the request of Reynolds's lawyers until October 1878, and then further delayed a final time until November 14, 1878, in order to await the arrival of Justice Stephen J. Field from California, without whom the prominent and much-watched case might split with a 4-4 vote of the Court. All nine members of the Supreme Court were thus present for the arguments, which were heard over two days (November 14–15, 1878). Transcripts of arguments were not kept during that period in the Court's history, but we know from the Court's opinion that a number of procedural issues, including the admissibility of Amelia Reynolds's testimony from the first trial, were raised. The principal issue for the parties and for the Court, however, was the constitutionality of the Morrill Act's prohibition of polygamy in light of the First Amendment's guarantee that individuals enjoy freedom to exercise their religion.

Following the oral argument, the Court took an initial vote in the case. According to the notes of Chief Justice Morrison Waite, the vote on November 16 was 5-4: five justices voted to uphold Reynolds's conviction, and four, including Waite, voted to reverse it. The basis upon which the votes rested was not recorded. But by the time the case was decided and the opinion issued on January 6, 1879, the Court was unanimous in affirming George Reynolds's conviction and rejecting his freedom of religion claim. Shortly after the opinion was issued, however, the Court did grant Reynolds's plea that his imprisonment not be at hard labor.

It is clear from the Court's opinion that the matter that most attracted the Justices' attention was the freedom of religion claim. The opinion rather quickly disposed of the other procedural claims Reynolds's lawyers made and devoted most of its attention to the constitutional issue. Chief Justice Waite wrote the opinion. The portion devoted to the freedom of religion claim is worthy of extended quotation:

> [A]t the time of his second marriage [George Reynolds] was, and for many years had been, a member of the Church of Jesus Christ of Latter-Day Saints, commonly called the Mormon Church, and a believer in its doctrines; that it was an accepted doctrine of that church "that it was the duty of male members of said church, circumstances permitting, to practice polygamy; . . . that this duty was enjoined by different books which the members of said church believed to be of divine origin, and among others the Holy Bible, and also that the members of the church believed that the practice of polygamy was directly enjoined upon male members thereof by the Almighty God, in a revelation to Joseph Smith, the founder and prophet of said church; that the failing or refusing to practice polygamy by such male members of said church, when circumstances would admit, would be punished, and that the penalty for such failure and refusal would be damnation in the life to come." He also proved "that he had received permission from the recognized authorities in said church to enter into polygamous marriage; . . . that Daniel H. Wells, one having authority in said church to perform the marriage ceremony, married the said de-

fendant on or about the time the crime is alleged to have been committed, to some woman by the name of Schofield, and that such marriage ceremony was performed under and pursuant to the doctrines of said church."

[T]he question is raised, whether religious belief can be accepted as a justification of an overt act made criminal by the law of the land.

The word "religion" is not defined in the Constitution. We must go elsewhere, therefore, to ascertain its meaning, and nowhere more appropriately, we think, than to the history of the times in the midst of which the provision was adopted. The precise point of the inquiry is, what is the religious freedom [that] has been guaranteed.

Before the adoption of the Constitution, attempts were made in some of the colonies and States to legislate not only in respect to the establishment of religion, but in respect to its doctrines and precepts as well. The people were taxed, against their will, for the support of religion, and sometimes for the support of particular sects to whose tenets they could not and did not subscribe. Punishments were prescribed for a failure to attend upon public worship, and sometimes for entertaining heretical opinions. The controversy upon this general subject was animated in many of the States, but seemed at last to culminate in Virginia. In 1784, the House of Delegates of that State having under consideration "a bill establishing provision for teachers of the Christian religion," postponed it until the next session, and directed that the bill should be published and distributed, and that the people be requested "to signify their opinion respecting the adoption of such a bill at the next session of assembly."

This brought out a determined opposition. Amongst others, Mr. Madison prepared a "Memorial and Remonstrance," which was widely circulated and signed, and in which he demonstrated "that religion, or the duty we owe the Creator," was not within the cognizance of civil government. At the next session the proposed bill was not only defeated, but another, "for establishing religious freedom," drafted by Mr. Jefferson, was passed. In the preamble of this act religious freedom is defined; and after a recital "that to suffer the civil magistrate to intrude his powers into the field of opinion, and to restrain the profession or propagation of principles on supposition of their ill tendency, is a dangerous fallacy which at once destroys all religious liberty," it is declared "that it is time enough for the rightful purposes of civil government for its officers to interfere when principles break out into overt acts against peace and good order." In these two sentences is found the true distinction between what properly belongs to the church and what to the State.

In a little more than a year after the passage of this statute the convention met which prepared the Constitution of the United States. Of this convention Mr. Jefferson was not a member, he being then absent as minister to France. As soon as he saw the draft of the Constitution proposed for adoption, he, in a letter to a friend, expressed his disappointment at the absence of an express declaration insuring the freedom of religion, but was willing to accept it as it was, trusting that the good sense and honest intentions of the people would bring about the necessary alterations. Five of the States, while adopting the Constitution, proposed amendments. Three—New Hampshire, New York, and Virginia—included in one form or another a declaration of religious freedom in the changes they desired to have made, as did also North Carolina, where the convention at first declined to ratify the Constitution until the proposed amendments were acted upon. Accordingly, at the first session of the first Congress the amendment now under consideration was proposed with others by Mr. Madison. It met the views of the advocates of religious freedom, and was adopted. Mr. Jefferson afterwards, in reply to an address to him by a committee of the Danbury Baptist Association, took occasion to say: "Believing with you that religion is a matter which lies solely between man and his God; that he owes account to none other for his faith or his worship; that the legislative powers of the government reach actions only, and not opinions,—I contemplate with sovereign reverence that act of the whole American people which declared that their legislature should 'make no law respecting an establishment of religion or prohibiting the free exercise thereof,' thus building a wall of separation between church and State." Coming as this does from an acknowledged leader of the advocates of the measure, it may be accepted almost as an authoritative declaration of the scope and effect of the amendment thus secured. Congress was deprived of all legislative power over mere opinion, but was left free to reach actions [that] were in violation of social duties or subversive of good order.

Polygamy has always been odious among the northern and western nations of Europe, and, until the establishment of the Mormon Church, was almost exclusively a feature of the life of Asiatic and of African people. At common law, the second marriage was always void, and from the earliest history of England polygamy has been treated as an offence against society.

By the statute of 1 James I, the offence, if committed in England or Wales, was made punishable in the civil courts, and the penalty was death. As this statute was limited in its operation to England and Wales, it was at a very early period re-enacted, generally with some modifications, in all the colonies. In connection with the case we are now considering, it is a significant fact that on the 8th of December, 1788, after the passage of the act establishing religious freedom, and after the convention of Virginia had recommended as an amendment to the Constitution of the United States the declaration in a bill of rights that "all men have an equal, natural, and unalienable right to the free exercise of religion, according to the dictates of conscience," the legislature of that State substantially enacted the statute of James I, death penalty included, because, as recited in the preamble, "it hath been doubted whether bigamy or poligamy be punishable by the laws of this Commonwealth." From that day to this we think it may safely be said there never has been a time in any State of the Union when polygamy has not been an offence against society, cognizable by the civil courts and punishable with more or less severity. In the face of all this evidence, it is impossible to believe that the constitutional guaranty of religious freedom was intended to prohibit legislation in respect to this most important feature of social life.

In our opinion, the statute immediately under consideration is within the legislative power of Congress. It is constitutional and valid as prescribing a rule of action for all those residing in the Territories, and in places over which the United States have exclusive control. This being so, the only question which remains is, whether those who make polygamy a part of their religion are excepted from the operation of the statute. If they are, then those who do not make polygamy a part of their religious belief may be found guilty and punished, while those who do, must be acquitted and go free. This would be introducing a new element into criminal law. Laws are made for the government of actions, and while they cannot interfere with mere religious belief and opinions, they may with practices. Suppose one believed that human sacrifices were a necessary part of religious worship, would it be seriously contended that the civil government under which he lived could not interfere to prevent a sacrifice? Or if a wife religiously believed it was her duty to burn herself upon the funeral pile of her dead husband, would it be beyond the power of the civil government to prevent her carrying her belief into practice?

So here, as a law of the organization of society under the exclusive dominion of the United States, it is provided that plural marriages shall not be allowed. Can a man excuse his practices to the contrary because of his religious belief? To permit this would be to make the professed doctrines of religious belief superior to the law of the land, and in effect to permit every citizen to become a law unto himself. Government could exist only in name under such circumstances.

[W]hen the offence consists of a positive act which is knowingly done, it would be dangerous to hold that the offender might escape punishment because he religiously believed the law which he had broken ought never to have been made. No case, we believe, can be found that has gone so far.

Upon a careful consideration of the whole case, we are satisfied that no error was committed by the court below.

Judgment affirmed.

The opinion of the Court was clear, fully reasoned, and comprehensive—a strong opinion written by a strong Court. Chief Justice Morrison Waite was from Ohio, appointed following the Civil War by President Grant, who had been actively involved in the polygamy issue and who had been sufficiently interested in the Reynolds trial to have a government representative attend it. Next was the most senior Justice, Nathan Clifford, an able but not distinguished Justice, originally from Maine and appointed before the war by President Buchanan. The next three Justices were Lincoln appointees: Noah H.

Swayne from Ohio, Samuel F. Miller, a physician and lawyer from Iowa, and Stephen J. Field from California. The Justices appointed by President Grant were William Strong of Pennsylvania, Joseph P. Bradley of New Jersey, and Ward Hunt of New York. The final justice, appointed by President Rutherford B. Hayes, was John Marshall Harlan of Kentucky. In the annals of the Supreme Court, this Court was a remarkable one; it had to be, given its task of judging during the Civil War and through the highly contentious period of Reconstruction in the South. Three of the Justices—Miller, Field, and Harlan—would take their places among the very most influential and respected Justices in the Supreme Court's history. The strength of the Court's opinion, addressing one of the most public and contentious national issues of the day, accounts for the fact that to this day the *Reynolds* opinion is regularly cited and quoted by the Supreme Court, even if its reasoning is not fully followed.

What, precisely, was the Court's reasoning? First, the Court accepted the fact that Reynolds married his second wife as a religious act, and that polygamy was an obligation imposed on Reynolds by his Mormon faith. Therefore, if Reynolds's religious act fell within the "free exercise of religion" guaranteed by the Constitution, the law could not reach it.

Second, the First Amendment religion guarantees must be read together: "Congress shall make no law respecting an establishment of religion, or prohibiting the free exercise thereof. . . ." Together these guarantees set the boundary between religion and government—Jefferson's wall of separation between church and state.

Third, the law prohibiting polygamy is not an "establishment" of religion, for while a regulation or tax visited on many religions but not on a favored sect or belief would be an establishment by government of the favored religion, the polygamy law is not of this sort. It does not operate to favor other religions, but sets a standard of conduct for all people of all religions and for all people, religious or not.

Fourth, the law is not one prohibiting the free exercise of religion, for the freedom to exercise religion under the First Amendment consists of freedom to believe and, presumably, to express one's belief, but not to engage in conduct, or overt acts. In rendering unto Caesar what is Caesar's, and to God what is God's, the Constitution makes Caesar's domain overt acts, and God's domain belief and expression of belief.

Polygamy, the Court says, is an overt act, not a belief or an expression of belief (as by speech), and thus Reynolds's act, though done out of religious conviction and indeed religious duty, is not protected by the Constitution as an exercise of religion. It can be engaged in only at the mercy of government—only, that is, when government chooses not to prohibit the act. And even then, if government chooses to exempt a religious act from a general prohibition in order to prefer one religion to others, the prohibition against establishment of religion would likely foreclose the exemption, just as imposing a tax only on those who failed to attend church would violate the establishment clause.

Fifth, and finally, the government's prohibition of polygamy was constitutional because it applied to everyone and thus did not favor religious over nonreligious acts. Of equal importance, the law's effect was social, not religious: polygamy had always been "odious" in Western societies; it was an offense against society, as it rejected the institution of monogamous marriage and upset the laws about property, inheritance, and family. Therefore, even if the law were born of "moral" and in some sense "religious" ideas, those ideas were also considered foundational and valid rules of civilized society, and thus secular and not sectarian in nature.

The *Reynolds* case raises virtually the full panoply of questions under the religion guarantees of the First Amendment. In the background of the case is the establishment clause issue: the Mormon Church was exercising broad government and public power in the Utah Territory. Would an exemption from the polygamy law facilitate that exercise of power, and thus constitute a forbidden "law respecting an establishment of religion"? Would it do so because the purpose or effect of such an exemption would be to aid Mormonism over other religions, or to prefer religious beliefs to beliefs based on ideology or philosophy?

If so, would this be a sufficient reason for a court to deny a claimed exemption under the guarantee of religious freedom in the First Amendment—with establishment clause concerns winning out over claims of religious freedom? Indeed, even without a religious purpose, would an exemption for Mormons be invalid because of the government-like power already being exercised by the Church in Utah Territory, raising concern that religion and religious institutions unduly influence government and thus undermine government's legitimacy in a religiously pluralistic secular state? Or is the establishment guarantee intended to protect religion from government, thus undermining the independence of religious institutions and beliefs? If so, the exemption question would look a good deal different.

The case also raises questions about the meaning of religion, religious beliefs, religious duties, and the relation between qualifying religious beliefs and resulting practices. These are very difficult questions, none of which the Court probed with any earnestness, preferring instead to assume that Mormonism is a religion, that polygamy is a qualifying belief required by or central to Mormonism, and that Reynolds validly felt or had a duty, at least "when circumstances would permit," to enter into a polygamous second marriage. But these assumptions can easily be questioned. Was polygamy in fact a central tenet of the Mormon belief, distinguishable in its centrality from attending church, which is a "duty" in a sense but not, perhaps, a central one? After the *Reynolds* case and other legal developments, the Mormon Church changed its teachings about polygamy. Does this mean that polygamy was not really a sufficiently central belief to be protected by the free exercise guarantee, or instead that the later change was an instance of continual revelation? And what about the fact that the Church's expressed duty to engage in polygamy applied only when "circumstances permit"? Does this make the duty a qualified and thus less central one? Would the fact that polygamy was (like human sacrifices or self-immolation) illegal mean that "circumstances do not permit," and thus no religious exercise is prohibited by enforcement of the law?

Moreover, the Court avoided—or closed its eyes to—the difficult questions of government purpose presented in the *Reynolds* case. The Court's opinion concludes that the Morrill Act's purpose was secular—preservation of the institution of monogamous marriage and associated property laws—and that its prohibition of polygamy was generally applicable to all people of whatever religious persuasion. But this is little more than bald artifice. The prohibition of polygamy in the Morrill Act was occasioned by the Mormons. It was born of a national controversy fueled by religious passions and driven by a concern that the valuable mineral resources in the Utah Territory would be controlled by an evil religious sect, the Church of Jesus Christ of Latter-day Saints, a Christian sect whose beliefs scandalized all other Christian denominations. The act was passed to control the Mormon Church and to deny one of its central tenets, polygamy. The Morrill Act and the one passed later amid increasing agitation nationally about the Mormons—the act that made the federal court prosecution of Reynolds possible—were intended to stop the Mormons' accretion of power by launching a wave of criminal prosecutions brought by federal prosecutors and judges appointed by President Grant and authorized by Congress.

The antipolygamy law, in other words, was not a secular law in purpose; it was intended to discriminate against the Mormons. Should motive and purpose matter under the religion guarantees? The answer is far from clear. But the Supreme Court, these days at least, seems to think that motive and purpose matter. In 1993, the Supreme Court considered the constitutionality of an ordinance enacted by the city of Hialeah, Florida, which barred ritual animal sacrifice.[7] The law applied generally to all ritual sacrifices, religious or not. But that was not enough to make it constitutional, because the

7. *Church of the Lukumi Babalu Aye, Inc. v. Hialeah*, 113 S.Ct. 2217 (1993).

law was enacted with the purpose of targeting the Santeria religion, which engaged in animal sacrifice as part of its doctrine and practice. "If the object of a law," the Court said, "is to infringe upon or restrict practices because of their religious motivation," is animated by "animosity to the Santeria adherents and their religious practices," and by its "own terms target[s] this religious exercise . . . ," it violates the free exercise guarantee.[8] The Morrill Act would seem to fit the Court's description quite nicely.

The *Reynolds* Court either chose to deny the political reality surrounding the case or chose for other reasons to consider the motive or purpose of the Morrill Act constitutionally irrelevant, at least as long as the act, in its effect (though not in its purpose), applies to everyone, not just the targeted religious group, and could be rationalized as serving a secular purpose. What reason might the *Reynolds* Court have had for intentionally avoiding the law's motive and purpose? One reason, voiced by the Court in some other contexts, is that one can never know for sure what the purpose or motive of a law is, given that it is voted upon by hundreds of members of the House and Senate and approved by the president. With so many people involved, it is likely that there is a mind-numbing array of actual motives and purposes, some benevolent and some not. And it would be unthinkable, and probably unconstitutional, to call the president and all of the members of Congress to a trial to testify about their actual or "real" motive. A related reason is more practical, but even more telling. If a law that otherwise might appear to be general in its application and related to a legitimate end were to be invalidated because of its motive or purpose, what is there to stop the legislature from simply reenacting the very same law, avoiding all reference to illicit purpose? If there is nothing to stop such a result, what is the point of invalidating the law on grounds of bad motive or purpose in the first place?

The questions of the meaning of "establishment" of religion, of religion itself and qualifying religious belief, and of purpose and motivation, are all very important and difficult ones. There are no obvious answers, and as we will discover in future stories, the Supreme Court has vacillated in its answers over time. The *Reynolds* Court was largely able to avoid answering these questions

8. The Court added the qualification that in a rare case, such a law might be valid if it were necessary to achieve the most compelling of valid government purposes and were narrowly tailored to advance only that interest. Justices Blackmun and O'Connor expressed the view that even in such a rare case, the law, motivated by religious discrimination, would nevertheless be invalid. Either view, of course, is different from the *Reynolds* Court's view that the Morrill Act was secular and general in application and in no way intended to discriminate against religion, thus raising no free exercise or establishment clause difficulty by virtue of its purpose.

by simply assuming that Reynolds's claims were valid, and concluding, in the face of reality, that the government's purpose was secular and legitimate.

But even with such assumptions, the Court said, Reynolds lost because his religious "exercise" was conduct, an overt act, and not just belief and expression of belief. It was therefore not protected by the free exercise clause and the Constitution's idea of individual religious liberty, because God's business is only belief and its expression. Conduct is Caesar's, or the United States government's, business. This is the final, and in the end the most decisive, basis upon which the Court's decision rested. Is the distinction between belief and its expression on the one hand, and overt acts on the other, a sound one in light of the text of the First Amendment, of its historical meaning and purpose, and of logic, religious principle, and government necessity?

Let's start with the text and meaning of the First Amendment. It provides that government "shall make no law prohibiting the free exercise of religion." The *Reynolds* Court restricts this individual right to belief and speech, and not conduct. Is this a sensible construction of the terms of the guarantee? The free speech guarantee, located also in the First Amendment, guarantees freedom of "speech." Notably, when "speech" and belief were intended, the framers found a word so limited. Yet in the religion clause free "exercise" of religion was used. In light of the difference in language, it seems wrong to say, as the Court did, that "exercise" means simply "belief and speech." By its own definition "exercise" connotes action, conduct, overt acts. Had the framers wanted the religion guarantee to be limited to belief and speech they could have used terminology like freedom of conscience, freedom to believe and express belief. Indeed, earlier drafts of the amendment did just that, but they were ultimately rejected in favor of "exercise." In light of this, can "exercise" reasonably be limited to belief and speech? The Court has interpreted the free "speech" guarantee to include not just speaking and writing, but conduct as well, when that conduct, like the burning of a flag, is, or is part of, expression of a belief. So is it reasonable to construe "exercise" even more narrowly than "speech," excluding conduct from the meaning of "exercise" when it is not excluded from the meaning of "speech"?

Apart from the text and its interpretation, does it make sense from a religious or governmental or practical viewpoint to restrict free exercise to belief and speech? Religion is not just about belief and speech. At its core, religion rests on belief, to be sure, but sharing and exercising that belief through communal activities are also usually necessary: building a church; attending services (and needing excuses from school or work, from time to time, to do so); engaging in missionary activities and proselytizing; wearing prescribed clothing. These all fall into the category of overt acts or conduct, not just belief and speech.

The religion guarantees were adopted to assure that individuals could freely *practice* their religion and that the state could not cripple disfavored sects and prefer or mandate others. In light of this, can the religion guarantees be sensibly read to exclude these and other activities from constitutional protection? Could a town prohibit the construction of any building that would hold more than twenty people, except for stores, theaters, and the city hall? Churches would effectively be barred under such a rule. Would the law be constitutional because building a church and attending it is conduct, not belief, and is thus not protected by the freedom to exercise religion? Would the establishment clause thus be the only recourse by which the law could be challenged, requiring an argument that because the law prohibits churches, just like the Morrill Act prohibited polygamy, it discriminates against religion, thus "establishing" nonreligion? Like the polygamy prohibition, which is not restricted to a particular religion, the hypothetical law is likewise not restricted to churches; it applies to any other gathering place or pool hall or the like, and it serves traffic, aesthetic, and land-use planning purposes, not religious ones. We would perhaps ask too much of the establishment guarantee to rely on it in this case.

Finally, and at a practical level, is a rule excluding all overt acts from protection as "exercises of religion" necessary for the conduct of government? The Court in *Reynolds* so stirringly and absolutely declares that "government could exist only in name" were an exemption granted. Does such a bright line comport with common sense? The answer is almost certainly not. Could a city permit a church to serve wine in communion without a liquor license, in the interest of the free exercise of religion by those receiving communion? If another city chose to prohibit communion wine because no church can qualify for a liquor license under the general liquor laws, should the churches affected and their members be able to claim an exemption under the free exercise guarantee, at least when their religion requires wine and prohibits the more common substitute of grape juice? Would compelling government to give an exemption cripple government, "permit[ting] every citizen to become a law unto himself," as the Court put it, and setting up a situation in which "Government could exist only in name . . . "?

What about a church claiming a right to hire its religious employees based on their religion, and thus to be exempt from the general civil rights law that prohibits discrimination in hiring based on religion? What about zoning variances and special parking rules for churches, or the extension of tax exemptions to churches and to religious individuals donating to their churches? These are all acts, not just belief and expression of belief in the sense of speech. Can they be excused from general legal requirements in the name of free exercise of religion? Would government be fatally undermined were it to execute these acts voluntarily (*as it now does*)? If government were not voluntarily to excuse religious actors or extend benefits to them (on the terms applied to similar nonreligious activities), would it undermine the operation and legitimacy of secular government to require exemptions in the name of free exercise?

If, on the other hand, we reject the bright and fixed boundary the *Reynolds* Court drew between conduct and belief and speech, where *do* we draw the line? Does the question turn on how important the conduct is to the religious doctrine and beliefs of the actor? Does it depend on the importance of the government interest in applying its general legal rule without exception, as perhaps with murder versus zoning laws? Is it both, with the answer being a product of balancing the religious belief and practice against the government's interest in regulating or collecting taxes, for example? Just how do such considerations get weighed in the balance? And who does the weighing? Must the balancing be done by a court, since judges are smart and independent and thus able to judge the bona fides of Church doctrine and religious conviction? Or can government decide, on its own, to waive a general rule in the interests of religious believers and religious institutions? Can the democratic political process be trusted to be even-handed and fair-minded in such matters? Does granting government the power to make such voluntary accommodations threaten the legitimacy of government itself (in the minds of nonbelievers, perhaps), making government subject to the pressures religion can bring to bear as a special interest group? Would it also perhaps undermine religion's independence from government, making religious institutions fight in the partisan political system to obtain and protect their advantages?

These questions, in part, bring us back full circle to the establishment guarantee and what Jefferson's wall of separation between church and state should be understood to mean.

* * *

The *Reynolds* case is an important case of lasting significance for the law of religious freedom in the United States. It introduced the basic concepts that even today animate the Supreme Court's interpretation of the religion guarantees: the idea of preference or discrimination against religion by government; of separation of church and state; of a law's general applicability; of secular purpose; of religion and religious belief stemming from religious duty; and, most important to the *Reynolds* case, of belief versus conduct. Each of these concepts, it turns out, has had a troubled history in the jurisprudence of the Supreme Court, a history that we will witness in many of the cases discussed in the stories that lie ahead.

We might finally ask whether the *Reynolds* case would be decided the same way today. At one level, that of political reality, it is hard to imagine a different result, even in a climate in which sexual mores and social conventions and attitudes are rapidly changing. But at a different level the Court might have a more difficult time explaining its decision, for today the Court is more focused on motive or purpose, not just on general applicability of a law that restricts religious practice; and as we will soon see, the Court has not toed the bright line between belief and conduct. Given this, it is hard to see how the Court could escape the obvious—indeed the blatant and discriminatory—religious purpose behind the Morrill Act's prohibition of polygamy in the Territories, much less the later laws that made Reynolds's prosecution in federal court possible. These laws were indeed general laws applied to everyone, but in name only: no other religion practiced polygamy, and prosecutions for polygamy were the hook with which the legal system gained purchase in its effort to limit the power of the Mormon Church. Would a law prohibiting a central tenet of Islam on purportedly secular moral grounds, though affecting only Muslims, be constitutional today?

In *Reynolds,* Caesar won. It would not always be so.

STORY 2

The Wall of Separation: "No law respecting an establishment of religion . . ."

Everson v. Board of Education, 330 U.S. 1 (1947)

The religion guarantees, the Supreme Court often says, are complementary. Yet the clauses are also distinct. The "exercise of religion" is a different thing than an "establishment of religion." Many people believe that the two guarantees are as often in tension (if not in conflict) as they are complementary. And often as not, the way the Court has avoided the tension in specific cases has simply been to use one guarantee as the dominant tool for analysis, leaving the other as a shadow in the background. How does the Court choose?

In the *Reynolds* case the Supreme Court judged George Reynolds's claim of religious freedom to enter a polygamous marriage under the free exercise clause of the First Amendment. Polygamy is an act, not simply a belief, and thus the free exercise guarantee did not protect it. Had the Court decided otherwise—had it decided that polygamy was, like wine at communion, a constitutionally protected exercise of religion—would carving an exception from the general law against polygamy have violated the establishment clause because the law would then formally favor the Mormon religion?

In the *Everson* case, which will be the focus of this story, the Court judged the constitutionality of a law providing bus transportation equally to children in private religious schools and to children in public schools under the establishment clause of the First Amendment. Does the use of tax funds to assist students in religious schools constitute a "law respecting the establishment of religion"? If so, couldn't the religious school students claim that the law discriminated against them because they attend religious school and therefore prohibited their "free exercise of religion"?

In *Reynolds* the Court escaped the establishment clause question by relying on the free exercise clause. In *Everson* it did the opposite, choosing the establishment clause. Why did the Court make these choices?

Through the *Everson* case we will explore the answer to this question by giving definition to the establishment clause. What is an establishment of religion? Is it a state-designated church, like the Church of England? Is it instead an action by the state that indicates a preference for, or support of, a church, like an exemption for Mormon polygamy, thus signaling an endorsement—a message of preference—by government of a religious belief? Is it a commitment of public resources to a religious organization or institution, like bus transportation to Catholic schools? Or is an establishment of religion much broader in scope, encompassing also a preference by government for religion over nonreligion, as when every president ends the State of the Union speech with "God Bless America"?

How should the Court go about deciding the answer to these questions? The Court might consider the text of the First Amendment—"Congress shall make no law respecting an establishment of religion"—to be definitive, and where the text is unclear leave the unresolved questions to the political branches of government without constitutional constraint. We might also look at history, including the intention of the drafters, or framers, of the Bill of Rights, or the public attitudes and practices at the time the Bill of Rights was ratified, or the English and colonial experiences before the Constitution was ratified. Should history bind the Court, or just guide it, in deciding what the Constitution means? Since history is by definition always old and the Constitution's text is almost always incomplete and ambiguous, perhaps the Supreme Court Justices, mindful of both but bound by neither, should decide cases based upon logic, reason, wisdom, and experience. After all, they are given life tenure, they are all very smart and accomplished and experienced in the world, and they are paid to do something.

* * *

In 1941, the state of New Jersey passed a law providing that children attending religious schools, like children attending public schools, should be reimbursed for the cost of public bus transportation to and from school.[1] In

1. The law extended the benefits to all schoolchildren at nonprofit schools as well as those at public schools, providing that "[w]henever in any district there are children living remote from any schoolhouse, the board of education of the district may make rules and contracts for the transportation of such children to and from school, including the transportation of school children to and from school other than a public school, except such school as is operated for profit in whole or in part."

the Township of Ewing, New Jersey, the law would require, as a practical matter, provision of bus transportation to students in the public schools and in the Catholic schools serving the township area.

On September 21, 1942, the Board of Education of the Township of Ewing, in Mercer County, New Jersey, adopted the following resolution in conformance with the 1941 law:

> The Transportation Committee recommended the Transportation of Pupils of Ewing to the Trenton High and Pennington High and Trenton Catholic Schools, by way of public carriers as in recent years. On motion of Mr. R. Ryan, seconded by Mr. French, the same was adopted.
>
> C. G. Latham, District Clerk

Ewing did not have school buses, so it instead relied on the public bus system, reimbursing students for the cost of daily bus fare from their homes to the public or Catholic school that they attended. The daily round-trip bus fare was $.20, or $.22 if a transfer was needed. For the fall semester of 1942, the Board paid a total of $8,034.95 under the resolution, of which $357.74 was paid to the parents of students attending parochial schools. Twenty-one students attending parochial schools received transportation assistance, sixteen at parochial high schools and five at parochial grade schools. The average reimbursement for the semester was about $18.00 per student.

Arch R. Everson was a resident and taxpayer of Ewing Township and also executive vice president of the New Jersey Taxpayers' Association. Following the board's payment of the reimbursements for the fall semester of 1942, Everson brought a suit as a taxpayer against the Board of Education of Ewing Township, challenging the constitutionality of the payments under the First Amendment. He met with initial success, with the trial court striking down the payments to nonpublic school students under the state constitution. On appeal, the New Jersey Court of Errors and Appeals reversed, holding that the statute and the reimbursements under it violated neither the New Jersey Constitution nor the United States Constitution. Everson appealed to the Supreme Court of the United States, which heard the case in November 1946 and issued its opinion on February 10, 1947.

The Supreme Court that decided the Everson case was a relatively young Court, with no one having served as a Justice for more than ten years. Seven of the Justices were appointed by President Franklin Roosevelt, and two by President Harry Truman. Four would be considered among the most respected Justices in the history of the Court (Black, Douglas, Frankfurter, and Jackson). Justice Hugo Black, a former senator from Alabama who gained a reputation as a First Amendment absolutist, wrote the opinion of the Court for the five-Justice majority. With him in the majority were Justices Stanley Reed from Kentucky; William O. Douglas from Washington; Frank Murphy from Michigan; and Fred Vinson from Kentucky, appointed by President Truman and later to become Chief Justice. The Justices in dissent were, in order of seniority, Felix Frankfurter, a former Harvard Professor from Massachusetts; Robert Jackson from New York, who also served (while a Justice) as the Chief Prosecutor in the Nuremberg Trials following World War II; Wiley Rutledge from Iowa, who had been the dean at the Iowa Law School; and Harold Burton, a republican from Ohio appointed by President Truman.

We will begin with the majority opinion written by Justice Black. *Everson* is the first case comprehensively to address the establishment clause. Justice Black's job, then, is to give meaning to the clause. He does so by beginning his opinion with history. Indeed, Justice Black begins and ends his opinion with history. For him, the historical record is sufficiently clear about the purpose of the establishment clause, and the meaning of an establishment of religion, that little else is needed.

Justice Black, for the Court:[2]

The New Jersey statute is challenged as a "law respecting an establishment of religion." The First Amendment . . . commands that a state "shall make no law respecting an establishment of religion, or prohibiting the free exercise thereof." These words of the First Amendment reflected in the minds of early Americans a vivid mental picture of conditions and practices which they fervently wished to stamp out in order to preserve liberty for themselves and for their posterity.

A large proportion of the early settlers of this country came here from Europe to escape the bondage of laws which compelled them to support and attend government-favored churches. The centuries immediately before and contemporaneous with the colonization of America had been filled with turmoil, civil strife, and persecutions, generated in large part by established sects determined to maintain their absolute political and religious supremacy. With the power of government supporting them, at various times and places, Catholics had persecuted Protestants, Protestants had persecuted Catholics, Protestant sects had persecuted other Protestant sects, Catholics of one shade of belief had persecuted Catholics of another shade of belief, and all of these had from time to time persecuted Jews. In efforts to force loyalty to whatever religious group happened to be on top and in league with the government of a particular time and place, men and women had been fined, cast in jail, cruelly tortured, and killed. Among the offenses for which these punishments had been inflicted were

2. In addition to substantial editing, footnotes and authorities cited in the text have been deleted.

> such things as speaking disrespectfully of the views of ministers of government-established churches, nonattendance at those churches, expressions of non-belief in their doctrines, and failure to pay taxes and tithes to support them. These practices of the old world were transplanted to and began to thrive in the soil of the new America. The very charters granted by the English Crown to the individuals and companies designated to make the laws which would control the destinies of the colonials authorized these individuals and companies to erect religious establishments which all, whether believers or non-believers, would be required to support and attend. An exercise of this authority was accompanied by a repetition of many of the old world practices and persecutions. Catholics found themselves hounded and proscribed because of their faith; Quakers who followed their conscience went to jail; Baptists were peculiarly obnoxious to certain dominant Protestant sects; men and women of varied faiths who happened to be in a minority in a particular locality were persecuted because they steadfastly persisted in worshiping God only as their own consciences dictated. And all of these dissenters were compelled to pay tithes and taxes to support government-sponsored churches whose ministers preached inflammatory sermons designed to strengthen and consolidate the established faith by generating a burning hatred against dissenters.

It should be noted that Justice Black's history focuses not on 1789, when the Constitution was ratified, or 1791, when the Bill of Rights, including the First Amendment, was ratified, but instead on the European and English history of government-established churches and the experience in the colonies, which was likewise marked by frequent state-sanctioned churches, though accompanied by less brutal enforcement mechanisms.

Justice Black's history is good history. It is, however, just one aspect of the historical record that could be relied upon. It discovers meaning in the history leading to the Constitution, not in the words and intentions of the framers of the First Amendment, or in the debates leading to its drafting and ratification. As we will see in the *Everson* opinions (and, more clearly, in the subsequent cases), the historical perspective chosen often has a decisive impact on the result reached in a case.

> These practices [of established churches, taxes to support tithes to favored churches, compelled attendance, and the like] became so commonplace as to shock the freedom-loving colonials into a feeling of abhorrence. The imposition of taxes to pay ministers' salaries and to build and maintain churches and church property aroused their indignation. It was these feelings which found expression in the First Amendment. No one locality and no one group throughout the Colonies can rightly be given entire credit for having aroused the sentiment that culminated in adoption of the Bill of Rights' provisions embracing religious liberty. But Virginia, where the established church had

> achieved a dominant influence in political affairs and where many excesses attracted wide public attention, provided a great stimulus and able leadership for the movement. The people there, as elsewhere, reached the conviction that individual religious liberty could be achieved best under a government which was stripped of all power to tax, to support, or otherwise to assist any or all religions, or to interfere with the beliefs of any religious individual or group.

Here Justice Black has taken a critical turn in his opinion. The English and Colonial history aroused "sentiments" that resulted in the religion guarantees of the Bill of Rights, and Virginia's experience in eliminating its established church is illustrative of the general "sentiments" in the nation when the Bill of Rights was finally added to the Constitution.

What were these "sentiments"? They were, Justice Black says, the desire to strip government of all power to tax, to support, or otherwise to assist any or all religions. This is a very strong and absolute statement, one which would prohibit teachers from excusing students from school for religious reasons; prohibit private schools from substituting for public ones; and disallow property tax exemptions to churches, charitable deductions for gifts to one's church, giving "vouchers" with which students could choose their school, and government support for religious social service organizations like Alcoholics Anonymous. It would also prohibit government from supporting or assisting religion in general, as by special zoning rules for churches. Does Justice Black's account of history support such an extreme and indeed hostile definition of a prohibited "establishment" of religion by government?

And why should Virginia, among all the colonies and new states, be considered illustrative of the meaning of a clause of the Constitution? Virginia was, in fact, not representative. Its favored church was Anglican; in other colonies it was Catholic or Lutheran or Baptist. In Rhode Island there was no established church. In Massachusetts the established church was more dominant than in Virginia. As it turned out, Virginia acted against government taxation and support at a particularly convenient time, leading up to the drafting and ratification of the Bill of Rights, and the principal figures in the Virginia action were James Madison and Thomas Jefferson, both of whom played an important, though not singular or decisive, role in the drafting of the religion clauses. But these two men were not always of one mind on the meaning of "establishment," and even if they had been, should the definition of a term in the Constitution turn on the agreed meaning by two people when many other framers participated in the debate and drafting, and people from all the states participated in its ratification?

Finally, it should be observed that at the time of ratification of the Bill of Rights, the First Amendment applied only to Congress and the federal government, not to the states, many of which continued established church practices for nearly a hundred years. Should Virginia's views on "non-establishment" be seen as reflecting anything more than its rule for federal, or national, establishments, the constraints of which left the states free from federal interference in following their own very different courses? These are questions we should keep in mind as we consider the history and logic of Justice Black's opinion.

Justice Black now turns quite specifically to Virginia and to Thomas Jefferson and James Madison.

> The movement toward this end reached its dramatic climax in Virginia in 1785–86 when the Virginia legislative body was about to renew Virginia's tax levy for the support of the established church. Thomas Jefferson and James Madison led the fight against this tax. Madison wrote his great Memorial and Remonstrance against the law. In it, he eloquently argued that a true religion did not need the support of law; that no person, either believer or non-believer, should be taxed to support a religious institution of any kind; that the best interest of a society required that the minds of men always be wholly free; and that cruel persecutions were the inevitable result of government-established religions. Madison's Remonstrance received strong support throughout Virginia, and the Assembly postponed consideration of the proposed tax measure until its next session. When the proposal came up for consideration at that session, it not only died in committee, but the Assembly enacted the famous "Virginia Bill for Religious Liberty" originally written by Thomas Jefferson. The preamble to that Bill stated among other things that:
>
> > Almighty God hath created the mind free; that all attempts to influence it by temporal punishments, or burthens, or by civil incapacitations, tend only to beget habits of hypocrisy and meanness, and are a departure from the plan of the Holy author of our religion who being Lord both of body and mind, yet chose not to propagate it by coercions on either . . . ; that to compel a man to furnish contributions of money for the propagation of opinions which he disbelieves, is sinful and tyrannical; that even the forcing him to support this or that teacher of his own religious persuasion, is depriving him of the comfortable liberty of giving his contributions to the particular pastor, whose morals he would make his pattern.
>
> And the statute itself enacted "That no man shall be compelled to frequent or support any religious worship, place, or ministry whatsoever, nor shall be enforced, restrained, molested, or burthened, in his body or goods, nor shall otherwise suffer on account of his religious opinions or belief. . . ."
>
> [T]he provisions of the First Amendment, in the drafting and adoption of which Madison and Jefferson played such leading roles, had the same objective and were intended to provide the same protection against governmental

intrusion on religious liberty as the Virginia statute. . . . Most of [the new States also provided] similar constitutional protections for religious liberty. . . .

The meaning and scope of the First Amendment, preventing establishment of religion or prohibiting the free exercise thereof, in the light of its history and the evils it was designed forever to suppress, have been several times elaborated by the decisions of this Court. . . . The broad meaning given the Amendment by these earlier cases has been accepted by this Court in its decisions concerning an individual's religious freedom. . . . There is every reason to give the same application and broad interpretation to the "establishment of religion" clause. The interrelation of these complementary clauses was well summarized in a statement of the Court of Appeals of South Carolina, quoted with approval by this Court, in *Watson v. Jones*, 13 Wall. 679, 730, 20 L.Ed. 666: "The structure of our government has, for the preservation of civil liberty, rescued the temporal institutions from religious interference. On the other hand, it has secured religious liberty from the invasions of the civil authority."

Justice Black has now concluded his history lesson. The history he outlines is sound. The conclusions he draws from it are reasonable. But his view, in the end, will not prevail, as we will see in later stories. This does not mean that he was wrong in his conclusions; many scholars agree with him. But his view reflects a couple of facts we have noticed. The history Justice Black relies upon is not all of the history that might be considered relevant, such as, for example, the history of the exact choice of wording in the establishment clause, which somewhat vaguely prohibits a law "respecting an establishment of religion." The conclusions he draws are arguably much broader than the history itself would require. The objection to general taxes as a means of collecting tithes for support of preferred churches, for example, is not the same thing as a reimbursement to students for bus transportation to their chosen schools, secular and sectarian alike. Finally, the statute actually enacted in Virginia (as opposed to the broad rhetoric accompanying it) was restricted to prohibiting individuals from having to "frequent or support any religious worship, place, or ministry." The *statute*, in other words, was clearly not a broad and absolute prohibition of any government support for religion, financial or otherwise.

But Justice Black nevertheless presses on, seizing the opportunity to interpret and give meaning to the establishment clause, which until then had not been thoroughly addressed by the Court. And in giving the clause definition, Justice Black wrote perhaps the most expansive and "absolutist" definition ever attempted by the Court.

The "establishment of religion" clause of the First Amendment means at least this: Neither a state nor the Federal Government can set up a church. Neither can pass laws which aid one religion, aid all religions, or prefer one religion over another. Neither can force nor influence a person to go to or to remain away from church against his will or force him to profess a belief or disbelief in any religion. No person can be punished for entertaining or professing religious beliefs or disbeliefs, for church attendance or non-attendance. No tax in any amount, large or small, can be levied to support any religious activities or institutions, whatever they may be called, or whatever form they may adopt to teach or practice religion. Neither a state nor the Federal Government can, openly or secretly, participate in the affairs of any religious organizations or groups and vice versa. In the words of Jefferson, the clause against establishment of religion by law was intended to erect "a wall of separation between Church and State."

With this paragraph, Justice Black set out in the broadest and most definitive terms the meaning of an establishment—any government support or preference for a religion or religion versus nonreligion, and any special tax for religion, or use of tax funds to support religion, or any involvement in "the affairs" of any religious organizations or vice versa. In the view of many, Justice Black thus leapt beyond all of the history he had relied upon and set up an apparently impregnable "wall of separation" between church and state under the auspices of the establishment clause.

But Justice Black's work was not done. He had to decide upon the constitutionality of the reimbursement scheme in the *Everson* case, a scheme alleged to represent a use of tax revenues to support a religion and its practice—the attendance by Catholic children in parochial schools. The New Jersey law appeared, in other words, rather clearly to "aid one religion, aid all religions, or prefer one religion over another . . . [and to be a] tax in any amount, large or small, . . . levied to support any religious activities or institutions. . . ."

Justice Black's remaining job was difficult not because he judged the New Jersey law to be unconstitutional, but for precisely the opposite reason. Justice Black had to explain why the law did *not* in fact breach his "wall of separation between church and state."

We must consider the New Jersey statute in accordance with the foregoing limitations imposed by the First Amendment. . . . New Jersey cannot consistently with the "establishment of religion" clause of the First Amendment contribute tax-raised funds to the support of an institution which teaches the tenets and faith of any church. On the other hand, other language of the amendment commands that New Jersey cannot hamper its citizens in the free exercise of their own religion. Consequently, it cannot exclude individual Catholics, Lutherans, Muhammadans, Baptists, Jews, Methodists, Non-believers, Presbyterians, or the members of any other faith, because of their faith, or lack of it, from receiving the benefits of public welfare legislation. While we do not mean to intimate that a state could not provide transportation only to children attending public schools, we must be careful, in protecting the citizens of New Jersey against state-established churches, to be sure that we do not inadvertently prohibit New Jersey from extending its general State law benefits to all its citizens without regard to their religious belief.

Measured by these standards, we cannot say that the First Amendment prohibits New Jersey from spending tax raised funds to pay the bus fares of parochial school pupils as a part of a general program under which it pays the fares of pupils attending public and other schools. It is undoubtedly true that children are helped to get to church schools. There is even a possibility that some of the children might not be sent to the church schools if the parents were compelled to pay their children's bus fares out of their own pockets when transportation to a public school would have been paid for by the State. The same possibility exists where the state requires a local transit company to provide reduced fares to school children including those attending parochial schools, or where a municipally owned transportation system undertakes to carry all school children free of charge. Moreover, state-paid policemen, detailed to protect children going to and from church schools from the very real hazards of traffic, would serve much the same purpose and accomplish much the same result as state provisions intended to guarantee free transportation of a kind which the state deems to be best for the school children's welfare. And parents might refuse to risk their children to the serious danger of traffic accidents going to and from parochial schools, the approaches to which were not protected by policemen. Similarly, parents might be reluctant to permit their children to attend schools which the state had cut off from such general government services as ordinary police and fire protection, connections for sewage disposal, public highways and sidewalks. Of course, cutting off church schools from these services, so separate and so indisputably marked off from the religious function, would make it far more difficult for the schools to operate. But such is obviously not the purpose of the First Amendment. That Amendment requires the state to be neutral in its relations with groups of religious believers and non-believers; it does not require the state to be their adversary. State power is no more to be used so as to handicap religions, than it is to favor them.

Justice Black sets out two arguments for his conclusion that the New Jersey law is constitutional. Both are strong arguments. First, he says, to exclude the Catholic children from the school transportation program could be seen as a discrimination against them based on their religious beliefs, a violation of their free exercise rights *and* a violation of the establishment guarantee's prohibition of discrimination *against* as well as in favor of a religion or religion in general. In making this argument Justice Black has set up a tension between the establishment guarantee and the individual's right to exercise religion under the First Amendment. The two clauses, in other words, are not always complementary; instead, they conflict. When they do, the ordinary rules of the establishment clause, voiced so ardently and absolutely just a few paragraphs before, are suspended in favor of free exercise interests of the children.

The difficulty with this, of course, is that the Court's opinion does not say that New Jersey *must* provide the bus transportation—just that it can if it wishes. Yet if the exclusion of the Catholic children would discriminate against them based on their religion, in violation of the free exercise guarantee, it is hard to see how New Jersey could be given the choice. The dissenting opinion, as we will see, bores in hard on this point.

Justice Black's second argument is that the tax funds and government support of the Catholic children's transportation were directed not to the Catholic schools, and not to the substance of the education program in the schools, but instead to the children directly. The children, in other words, made the choice of which school to attend, unimpeded by the costs of transportation. The tax was not, in short, expenditure in support of religion or a religion, but was instead in support of student safety. But does this distinction between money going directly to a church, or to an individual with the purpose of allowing that person to attend the church, a sound one? Is it a formalism—perhaps a necessary one—much like the distinction in the *Reynolds* polygamy case, between belief and overt acts?

Surely giving all people a government payment in order that religious people could make contributions to their churches would be a violation of the establishment guarantee, wouldn't it? Yet giving people a tax deduction for their contributions, and thus in reality relieving them of a tax they would otherwise owe on the income thus contributed, is the same thing, but we take it for granted today. Isn't this a distinction without a difference? The purpose of the tax deduction is, in part, to help churches in their good works and in their religious activities. The purpose of the New Jersey bus reimbursement law was to support religious schools by making attendance at them cheaper, safer, and more convenient. And the same result could be achieved by giving the money to the church in both cases, and then requiring the church to refund part of the members' contributions or to reimburse the children for their bus transportation. Should it matter which form the aid takes if the effect and purpose of the aid is the same?

> This Court has said that parents may, in the discharge of their duty under state compulsory education laws, send their children to a religious rather than a public school if the school meets the secular educational requirements which the state has power to impose. It appears that these parochial schools meet New Jersey's requirements. The State contributes no money to the schools. It does

not support them. Its legislation, as applied, does no more than provide a general program to help parents get their children, regardless of their religion, safely and expeditiously to and from accredited schools.

The First Amendment has erected a wall between church and state. That wall must be kept high and impregnable. We could not approve the slightest breach. New Jersey has not breached it here.

Affirmed.

The *Everson* case was decided by a 5-4 vote, with four Justices dissenting. The main dissent was written by Justice Jackson and is followed by Justice Rutledge's separate dissent. Two things are interesting about the dissents. The first is the different use of history. Second and more striking is that the dissent largely agrees with the establishment clause principle so ardently and absolutely set out by Justice Black in the majority opinion. The dissenting Justices simply do not believe that Justice Black followed his own history or his own rule; instead, he constructed a purely formal and historically unwarranted rule to justify allowing state support of religion under a guarantee that is intended to prohibit it.

Mr. Justice *Jackson*, dissenting.

I find myself, contrary to first impressions, unable to join in this decision. I have a sympathy, though it is not ideological, with Catholic citizens who are compelled by law to pay taxes for public schools, and also feel constrained by conscience and discipline to support other schools for their own children. Such relief to them as this case involves is not in itself a serious burden to taxpayers and I had assumed it to be as little serious in principle. Study of this case convinces me otherwise. The Court's opinion marshals every argument in favor of state aid and puts the case in its most favorable light, but much of its reasoning confirms my conclusions that there are no good grounds upon which to support the present legislation. In fact, the undertones of the opinion, advocating complete and uncompromising separation of Church from State, seem utterly discordant with its conclusion yielding support to their commingling in educational matters. The case which irresistibly comes to mind as the most fitting precedent is that of Julia who, according to Byron's reports, "whispering 'I will ne'er consent,'—consented."

* * *

It is of no importance in this situation whether the beneficiary of this expenditure of tax-raised funds is primarily the parochial school and incidentally the pupil, or whether the aid is directly bestowed on the pupil with indirect benefits to the school. The state cannot maintain a Church and it can no more tax its citizens to furnish free carriage to those who attend a Church. The prohibition against establishment of religion cannot be circumvented by a subsidy, bonus or reimbursement of expense to individuals for receiving religious instruction and indoctrination. . . .

Of course, the state may pay out tax-raised funds to relieve pauperism, but it may not under our Constitution do so to induce or reward piety. It may spend funds to secure old age against want, but it may not spend funds to secure religion against skepticism. It may compensate individuals for loss of employment, but it cannot compensate them for adherence to a creed.

It seems to me that the basic fallacy in the Court's reasoning, which accounts for its failure to apply the principles it avows, is in ignoring the essentially religious test by which beneficiaries of this expenditure are selected. A policeman protects a Catholic, of course—but not because he is a Catholic; it is because he is a man and a member of our society. The fireman protects the Church school—but not because it is a Church school; it is because it is property, part of the assets of our society. Neither the fireman nor the policeman has to ask before he renders aid "Is this man or building identified with the Catholic Church?" But before these school authorities draw a check to reimburse for a student's fare they must ask just that question, and if the school is a Catholic one they may render aid because it is such, while if it is of any other faith or is run for profit, the help must be withheld.[3]

To consider the converse of the Court's reasoning will best disclose its fallacy. That there is no parallel between police and fire protection and this plan of reimbursement is apparent from the incongruity of the limitation of this Act if applied to police and fire service. Could we sustain an Act that said police shall protect pupils on the way to or from public schools and Catholic schools but not while going to and coming from other schools, and firemen shall extinguish a blaze in public or Catholic school buildings but shall not put out a blaze in Protestant Church schools or private schools operated for profit? That is the true analogy to the case we have before us and I should think it pretty plain that such a scheme would not be valid.

Justice Jackson is taking an easy way out of the case here. He is relying strictly on the law's de facto discrimination in favor of one religion. But while the *fact* of the law's narrow incidence to Catholic children is beyond dispute in the case, the truth is that the text of the New Jersey Act is not so limited, and Justice Black was addressing the constitutionality of a law that applied generally, including all religious schools. Justice Jackson and Justice Black are making arguments that pass each other as ships in the night.

---

3. Author's note. The act does not mention only Catholic schools; it provides assistance to all nonprofit private schools, whatever the religion or even if not religious. But in fact the only students who are reimbursed are students attending Catholic schools (and, of course, the local resolution mentioned Catholic schools by name), a situation characteristic of many—indeed most—private school assistance programs, even to this day.

In the end, however, Justice Jackson acknowledges this and broadens his dissent to address also laws that apply generally but include within them benefits for religion and religious institutions and practices.

> The Court's holding is that this taxpayer has no grievance because the state has decided to make the reimbursement a public purpose and therefore we are bound to regard it as such. I agree that this Court has left, and always should leave to each state, great latitude in deciding for itself, in the light of its own conditions, what shall be public purposes in its scheme of things. It may socialize utilities and economic enterprises and make taxpayers' business out of what conventionally had been private business. It may make public business of individual welfare, health, education, entertainment or security. But it cannot make public business of religious worship or instruction, or of attendance at religious institutions of any character. There is no answer to the proposition that the effect of the religious freedom Amendment to our Constitution was to take every form of propagation of religion out of the realm of things which could directly or indirectly be made public business and thereby be supported in whole or in part at taxpayers' expense. That is a difference which the Constitution sets up between religion and almost every other subject matter of legislation, a difference which goes to the very root of religious freedom and which the Court is overlooking today. This freedom was first in the Bill of Rights because it was first in the forefathers' minds; it was set forth in absolute terms, and its strength is its rigidity. It was intended not only to keep the states' hands out of religion, but to keep religion's hands off the state, and above all, to keep bitter religious controversy out of public life by denying to every denomination any advantage from getting control of public policy or the public purse. Those great ends I cannot but think are immeasurably compromised by today's decision.
>
> This policy of our Federal Constitution has never been wholly pleasing to most religious groups. They all are quick to invoke its protections; they all are irked when they feel its restraints. This Court has gone a long way, if not an unreasonable way, to hold that public business of such paramount importance as maintenance of public order, protection of the privacy of the home, and taxation may not be pursued by a state in a way that even indirectly will interfere with religious proselyting.
>
> But we cannot have it both ways. Religious teaching cannot be a private affair when the state seeks to impose regulations which infringe on it indirectly, and a public affair when it comes to taxing citizens of one faith to aid another, or those of no faith to aid all. If these principles seem harsh in prohibiting aid to Catholic education, it must not be forgotten that it is the same Constitution that alone assures Catholics the right to maintain these schools at all when predominant local sentiment would forbid them. . . . Many groups have sought aid from tax funds only to find that it carried political controls with it.

> [T]he great purposes of the Constitution do not depend on the approval or convenience of those they restrain.

On the question of general programs of support that include religious institutions within them, Justice Jackson makes two related arguments, both resting on the history Justice Black has recounted, but both employing that history to different ends. The first argument is that the use of tax funds to support religion presents a special problem under the Constitution, a problem different from police protection or fire protection or crossing guards near schools. Money is fungible; it cannot be traced and therefore can find its way to support the religious mission itself. A fire truck doesn't do that.

The second argument is related, at least by way of justification for the special scrutiny of programs that involve tax funds benefiting religious institutions. It is that the establishment clause was designed to assure the autonomy and independence of religion and religious institutions from the government, and likewise to assure that secular government is free from influence by religious institutions. To channel tax funds to religious institutions is to compromise that independence: it makes religion dependent upon government in some measure, and thus less able to resist it; and it signals religion's influence brought to bear on government. Indeed, it is beyond dispute, as Jackson observes, that the New Jersey law, though general in application and available to private nonprofit and nonreligious schools, was the work of the organized churches and religious interests in the political process.

Independence, then, and not greed, avarice, or tax reduction, was the principle underlying the "wall of separation" between church and state. This theme was taken up in considerable historical detail in the dissenting opinion of Justice Rutledge.

> Mr. Justice *Rutledge,* with whom Mr. Justice *Frankfurter,* Mr. Justice *Jackson* and Mr. Justice *Burton* agree, dissenting.
>
> The [First] Amendment's purpose was not to strike merely at the official establishment of a single sect, creed or religion, outlawing only a formal relation such as had prevailed in England and some of the colonies. Necessarily it was to uproot all such relationships . . . to create a complete and permanent separation of the spheres of religious activity and civil authority by comprehensively forbidding every form of public aid or support for religion.
>
> No provision of the Constitution is more closely tied to or given content by its generating history than the religious clause of the First Amendment. In the documents of the times, particularly of Madison, who was leader in the Virginia struggle before he became the Amendment's sponsor, but also in the writ-

ings of Jefferson and others and in the issues which engendered them is to be found irrefutable confirmation of the Amendment's sweeping content.

[Madison's Memorial and] Remonstrance stirr[ed] up a storm of popular protest [in Virginia and] killed the Assessment Bill. . . . With this, the way was cleared at last for enactment of Jefferson's Bill for Establishing Religious Freedom. Madison promptly drove it through in January of 1786, seven years from the time it was first introduced. This dual victory substantially ended the fight over establishments, settling the issue against them.

The next year Madison became a member of the Constitutional Convention. Its work done, he fought valiantly to secure the ratification of its great product in Virginia as elsewhere, and nowhere else more effectively. Madison was certain in his own mind that under the Constitution "there is not a shadow of right in the general government to intermeddle with religion" and that "this subject is, for the honor of America, perfectly free and unshackled. The Government has no jurisdiction over it. . . ."

Ratification thus accomplished, Madison was sent to the first Congress. There he went at once about performing his pledge to establish freedom for the nation as he had done in Virginia. Within a little more than three years from his legislative victory at home he had proposed and secured the submission and ratification of the First Amendment as the first article of our Bill of Rights.

All the great instruments of the Virginia struggle for religious liberty thus became warp and woof of our constitutional tradition, not simply by the course of history, but by the common unifying force of Madison's life, thought and sponsorship. As the Remonstrance discloses throughout, Madison opposed every form and degree of official relation between religion and civil authority. For him religion was a wholly private matter beyond the scope of civil power either to restrain or to support. Denial or abridgment of religious freedom was a violation of rights both of conscience and of natural equality. State aid was no less obnoxious or destructive to freedom and to religion itself than other forms of state interference. "Establishment" and "free exercise" were correlative and coextensive ideas, representing only different facets of the single great and fundamental freedom.

In no phase was he more unrelentingly absolute than in opposing state support or aid by taxation. Not even "three pence" contribution was thus to be exacted from any citizen for such a purpose. Tithes had been the life blood of establishment before and after other compulsions disappeared. Madison and his coworkers made no exceptions or abridgments to the complete separation they created. Their objection was not to small tithes. It was to any tithes whatsoever. "If it were lawful to impose a small tax for religion the admission would pave the way for oppressive levies." Not the amount but "the principle of assessment was wrong." And the principle was as much to prevent "the interference of law in religion" as to restrain religious intervention in political matters. In this field the authors of our freedom would not tolerate "the first experiment on our liberties" or "wait till usurped power had strengthened itself by exercise, and entangled the question in precedents." Nor should we.

* * *

The funds used here were raised by taxation. The Court does not dispute nor could it that their use does in fact give aid and encouragement to religious instruction. It only concludes that this aid is not "support" in law. But Madison and Jefferson were concerned with aid and support in fact not as a legal conclusion "entangled in precedents." Here parents pay money to send their children to parochial schools and funds raised by taxation are used to reimburse them. This not only helps the children to get to school and the parents to send them. It aids them in a substantial way to get the very thing which they are sent to the particular school to secure, namely, religious training and teaching.

Believers of all faiths, and others who do not express their feeling toward ultimate issues of existence in any creedal form, pay the New Jersey tax. When the money so raised is used to pay for transportation to religious schools, the Catholic taxpayer to the extent of his proportionate share pays for the transportation of Lutheran, Jewish and otherwise religiously affiliated children to receive their non-Catholic religious instruction. Their parents likewise pay proportionately for the transportation of Catholic children to receive Catholic instruction. Each thus contributes to "the propagation of opinions which he disbelieves" in so far as their religions differ, as do others who accept no creed without regard to those differences. Each thus pays taxes also to support the teaching of his own religion, an exaction equally forbidden since it denies "the comfortable liberty" of giving one's contribution to the particular agency of instruction he approves.

New Jersey's action therefore exactly fits the type of exaction and the kind of evil at which Madison and Jefferson struck.

* * *

No one conscious of religious values can be unsympathetic toward the burden which our constitutional separation puts on parents who desire religious instruction mixed with secular for their children. They pay taxes for others' children's education, at the same time the added cost of instruction for their own. Nor can one happily see benefits denied to children which others receive, because in conscience they or their parents for them desire a different kind of training others do not demand.

But if those feelings should prevail, there would be an end to our historic constitutional policy and command. No more unjust or discriminatory in fact is it to deny attendants at religious schools the cost of their transportation than it is to deny them tuitions, sustenance for their teachers, or any other educational expense which others receive at public cost. Hardship in fact there is which none can blink. But, for assuring to those who undergo it the greater, the most comprehensive freedom, it is one written by design and firm intent into our basic law.

* * *

Two great drives are constantly in motion to abridge, in the name of education, the complete division of religion and civil authority which our forefathers made. One is to introduce religious education and observances into the public schools. The other, to obtain public funds for the aid and support of various private religious schools. In my opinion both avenues were closed by the Constitution. Neither should be opened by this Court. The matter is not one of quantity, to be measured by the amount of money expended. Now as in Madison's day it is one of principle, to keep separate the separate spheres as the First Amendment drew them; to prevent the first experiment upon our liberties; and to keep the question from becoming entangled in corrosive precedents. We should not be less strict to keep strong and untarnished the one side of the shield of religious freedom than we have been of the other.

The judgment should be reversed.

Separation of church and state, Justice Rutledge says, requires utter independence, and that independence is a necessary prerequisite to individual religious freedom. Government support for religion will, history proves, inevitably lead to competition among sects for influence and authority and assistance, and will therefore ultimately lead to favored religions, the existence of which will necessarily limit the individual's freedom to exercise his or her own personal religious beliefs. In this way the establishment clause's wall of separation can be reconciled with the free exercise guarantee of religious liberty. Indeed, the separation enforced by the establishment clause is primary and cannot be overridden by a claim that separation yields a restriction on the individual's freedom to exercise religion. This, at any rate, is the dissenting opinions' view, based on history.

Given that this strong dissenting view rests on the very history and principles Justice Black called on in the majority opinion, how do we understand Justice Black's view? How do we reconcile his allowing the government funding, yet setting an apparently high and impregnable wall separating church and state? There are two possibilities. This first is that Justice Black agreed with the dissent's general view; he just left a little flexibility at the joints. Independence must be assured, but just a little government assistance won't do any harm, and denying it would look mean-spirited. This is the point of Justice Jackson's reference to Lord Byron's Julia who, "saying 'I will ne'er consent,'—consented."

The second possibility is that Justice Black saw religious liberty—the free exercise guarantee—as primary and the establishment guarantee as secondary in importance under the First Amendment. The primary purpose of the Constitution was individual religious liberty. Limiting (but not flatly prohibiting) government support for religion was important to religious freedom, but when the two guarantees clashed, as when bus transportation to parochial schools would breach the absolute separation of church and state, establishment clause concerns should give way to the children's interest in practicing their religion by going to religious schools. At least this is true for Justice Black when the aid is limited in amount, is part of a general program, and is directed to the children rather than directly to the religious institutions.

There is yet a third possibility, which would not manifest itself until late in the twentieth century. The third view is that "we are a religious people," as the Court would say a few years after *Everson,* and there is nothing in the First Amendment establishment guarantee that forecloses government support for or indeed financial assistance to religious institutions as long as the support or assistance goes to all religious institutions equally. The purpose of the establishment guarantee was to prohibit government from discriminating *among* religions, for such discrimination would indeed threaten religious liberty. But nothing in the history of oppression or in the nature of religious freedom prohibits government from actively supporting all religions.

Indeed, the establishment clause applied only to the United States government, and not to the states. And following the ratification of the Bill of Rights, states remained free to have established churches, taxes devoted to churches only, and the like. And many states used their freedom to do just that. This could have two consequences in *Everson.* First, while the establishment clause finally became applicable to the states following the Civil War, it would not be historically unreasonable even today to leave states greater breathing room given the states' prior practice and the ambiguity surrounding the establishment clause's "incorporation" into the liberty guaranteed by the Fourteenth Amendment. Second, the states' practices after 1791 were arguably indicative of their views toward the meaning of "establishment" as used in the First Amendment. After all, the states had been the agencies of ratification of the Constitution and, two years later, the Bill of Rights. If so, that meaning was certainly not strict separation.

Viewing history and the text of the Constitution from this different perspective could yield a very different view of the prohibition of laws "respecting an establishment of religion." It might be expressed this way: In modern society, at least, no institution can exist without government support, for the tentacles of government have extended everywhere, from taxation, zoning, and education, to welfare, private charity, job discrimination, and restrictions on freedom of speech, including religious speech. In such an environment, it can be argued, a rule against any amount or form of assistance to religion would condemn religious institutions to prolonged but inevitable death. Religion and religious institutions play an essential role in civilized and organized society: they provide and enforce values of civility, and by placing faith in a higher power they afford a perspective that enables the social order to function without constant anarchy and discord. Thus, tax benefits to churches, deductions for tithes, tuition support for private schools through vouchers, provision of books and educational materials for private religious schools, excused absences at school or work for religious holidays, and all variety of other forms of positive support and encouragement for religion are perfectly permissible should the state choose to provide them. Whether and how to accommodate religion through exemptions from general laws or support for religious activities is up to the state as long as the accommodation or support is equally available to all religions—and accommodations need not be given at all.

This is a radically different view of the establishment guarantee than any of the Justices voiced in the *Everson* case. For them, establishment was primary, and the only question was whether to make any exceptions, even narrow and limited, to the "wall of separation" that guaranteed religion its own separate sphere and thus assured its freedom and independence, and the freedom of individuals to make their own choices about religion. All of the Justices held the same, fairly coherent theory of the religion guarantees: nonestablishment was necessary to, and thus compatible with, religious freedom; free exercise of religion was a guarantee of the individual's freedom to believe, not to act, and thus was dependent on a secular government that could visit no benefits or burdens on a religious belief, or make public rights, such as voting or holding property or receiving benefits, dependent on one's religious belief. This is what came to be called the separationist view. The dissenters in *Everson* were strict separationists. Those in the majority were separationists who believed the Constitution requires government to be neutral in its relation to religion. Government may not favor religion or a religion, but it may extend limited support to religion as long as the support is part of a general program of support to nonreligious organizations as well, the program serves strictly secular public purposes (like children's safety when going to school), and the support goes to the individual, who can then freely choose to spend it for religion or not.

As we will see, the strict separationists had a rule that could be easily applied. But it yielded such distasteful results—as it would have done in *Everson,* and as it would if property tax exemptions for churches were prohibited—that it could never gain the support of a majority of the Supreme Court. The "neutrality" separationists, however, met a better fate. For many years following the *Everson* decision, the prevailing view of the religion guarantees was that reflected in *Reynolds* and *Everson:* religious exercise includes beliefs but generally not overt acts; and government and religion must be separate, but separation is not breached by extending support or benefits to religious practice or institutions as part of a neutral and generally applicable government program. The neutrality view nevertheless reflected a general view of separation of church and state that held sway for over a hundred years: in the interest of individual freedom and harmony in the operation of government and the social order, religion and government should occupy their own—and largely separate—spheres.

It would not be until the 1990s that a revolution in thinking about the religion guarantees would clearly emerge, and the separationists would, remarkably, virtually disappear from the Supreme Court. In their place would be Justices with a range of views based on the primacy of the freedom to exercise religion; the secondary importance of non-establishment; and with the rise in religious fervor, political demands that religion and religious institutions are an interest in the political system that deserves its due, just as all other special interests deserve.

But before we get to that account, we will trace the path of the law in the middle distance as the Supreme Court struggles mightily to manage its rule of neutrality under the free exercise and establishment clauses.

STAGE II The Time of Testing

The bitter pill of *Reynolds*'s and *Everson*'s rules of strict separation—even with the somewhat qualified "neutrality" exception crafted by the *Everson* majority—soon became increasingly difficult for the Court to swallow. Neutrality required that any support for religion in the form of assistance or, as often, exemption from general laws like the prohibition on polygamy, take the form of a general and secular law, and that the support or exemption goes to the individual rather than a church. Free exercise, moreover, applied only to belief and expression, not religious conduct.

Not long after *Everson,* cases arose that would challenge the tight constraints imposed by the Court's wall of separation. We will consider three of these cases: the Amish claim to exemption from compulsory education laws (*Yoder*); the fundamentalist Christians' claim that teaching evolution in public schools violates their religious liberty and undermines their faith (*Epperson*); and the claim by believers and nonbelievers alike that school prayer "establishes" religion (*Engle*). These three "stories" will be presented in reverse chronological order, which may appear a bit awkward to some. My judgment, however, is that this order best accomplishes the purposes of the book, for it permits us first to focus on the free exercise challenges to the Court's neutrality and separation regime, then to move to the establishment guarantee challenges, and finally to view both guarantees together as a source of tension in the separationist view.

In answering the claims presented in *Yoder, Epperson,* and *Engle,* the Supreme Court had to delve deeper into the history and meaning of the religion guarantees and in the process reexamine, adjust, and modify the relatively simple regime of separation of church and state crafted in the *Reynolds* and *Everson* cases. To some observers, the wall of separation would appear to crumble; to others, it would become impregnable. Most important for us, signs of dramatically different interpretations of the religion guarantees—the precursors of even further and radical changes to come—would emerge from the adjusting and modifying worked by the Court.

STORY 3

The Amish Conundrum: The Conflict between Free Exercise and Non-establishment

Wisconsin v. Yoder, 406 U.S. 205 (1972)

Can the recognition of an exemption from a law in the name of freedom to exercise religion amount to a preference for a religion that violates the prohibition against government establishing religion? Is this especially likely when the exemption is restricted to only one religion and, furthermore, is granted because the religion "earned" it by its tradition of obedience to law, self-sufficiency, passivity, and embrace of the core values in American society? If a religion that is thoroughly domesticated in the larger social order is entitled, by that fact, to special status, can that be described in any other terms than an establishment of religion?

Our story is about the meaning of religion and religious "exercise." It is about the extension of free exercise from matters of belief and expression in the *Reynolds* case to overt acts and, indeed, to pervasive patterns of conduct in the adherents' community. It is about direct clashes between the establishment clause and the free exercise guarantee, and the extent to which the "wall of separation" can withstand such pressure.

Our story is about the Old Order Amish.

* * *

In early January 1964, four families moved into the hilly and fertile dairy-farming area around New Glarus, Wisconsin. They were Old Order Amish families who had purchased about one thousand acres of farmland in the countryside around New Glarus, beginning what would become a colony of twenty-five or thirty Amish families. They purchased the land with cash, having sold their farms in the Hazeltine-Independence area of Iowa.

Their reason for moving was religious freedom. The families, including the family of Adin Yutzy, who would become one of the parties in the *Yoder* case in the Supreme Court, had been engaged in a prolonged conflict with school authorities in Iowa. The conflict involved dress in public-school physical education, and education beyond the eighth grade.

The Old Order Amish are part of the Mennonite tradition that grew out of the Anabaptist movement during the Protestant Reformation. Mennonites believed that baptism and admission into the Church should be reserved only for adults, a view deemed heretical by other Protestant sects. The Mennonites were persecuted and many were killed in seventeenth-century Europe because of their beliefs, and as a result many fled to America beginning in the late 1600s, originally settling in Pennsylvania. Among them were the Old Order Amish.

The Amish formed in Switzerland in the late 1600s, splitting off from the Mennonite Church. The Amish believe that their religion dictates an entire way of life in conformance with the Biblical admonition in Romans 12:2: "Be not conformed to this world but be transformed by the renewal of your mind." They believe in leading a plain life free of luxury and technology unrelated to basic human needs, a life devoted to farming, community, and sustenance that minimizes distractions from the life of the renewed mind devoted to God. They wear plain, black clothes and do not use cars or many other technologies related to modern life. They shun dancing, movies, public displays of self, competition for power, drinking, and other manifestations of modern culture.

The Amish are very devoted to education, having been among the founders of the idea of popular education in the sixteenth century. But they believe education should be limited to reading, writing, and mathematics, skills necessary to a basic life devoted to God. They reject the teaching of modern subjects based on modern culture, values, and styles of living, such as psychology, history, art, literature, and sociology. The Amish thus willingly send their children to public schools only through the eighth grade, where education is largely limited to the basic skills unattended by modern values and perspectives. After the eighth grade they generally continue their children's education in the "Word" and in Amish values through work and community guidance of their elders, or in Amish schools, taught by Amish teachers educated only to the eighth grade level in the public schools. In 1964—and indeed in 1971 when the *Yoder* case was heard in the Supreme Court—it was said that no Amish person in the United States had ever been convicted of a felony, and none had relied in any way on public welfare. "They're producing better citizens than the rest of us," said Rev. Dean M. Kelley, Director of Civil and Religious Liberties for the National Council of Churches, in 1969. "Maybe we should try their kind of education instead of trying to make them conform to our sort of pot-smoking system."[1]

New Glarus was located about forty miles southwest of Madison, Wisconsin, in the southern reaches of some of the most beautiful dairy-farming land in the Midwest. In 1964, the town of New Glarus had a population of about twelve hundred. It was a small, rural farming town founded in 1845 with the help of the Swiss government "to provide refuge for starving Swiss mountaineers from the Glarus region of Switzerland."[2] The vast majority of the population were of Swiss descent. It was perhaps partly because of an affinity with the Swiss that the four Amish families selected New Glarus as their new home.

The main reason for the families' move, however, was the conflict that had arisen in Iowa, which, like most states, had a compulsory education law. The Iowa law required education until age 18, and while it permitted private schools to satisfy the law, Iowa required the teachers in private schools to be certified and trained at the college level, and the state also prescribed required curricula for private schools, including religious schools. The Amish families who years before had settled in the Independence-Hazeltine area in Buchanan County, Iowa, had established their own schools that taught the basic reading, writing, and mathematics skills only, schools in which the students were taught by unaccredited, eighth-grade-educated Amish teachers. The public schools in Buchanan County were unacceptable to the Amish because of the subjects taught beyond the eighth grade and also, in the earlier grades, because of state education requirements of proper dress and competitiveness.

The education authorities in Iowa were unable or unwilling to adapt their requirements to the religious needs of the Amish, as some other states had done. As a result, both sides dug in their heels, and ultimately charges were brought against the parents of the Amish children who refused to attend the public schools. Despite the efforts of Governor Harold Hughes to find a peaceful and amicable resolution of the problem, school officials persisted, Amish parents were fined, and steps were taken forcibly to bring the children to the public schools. As the *Des Moines Register* reported on November 22, 1965, "Screaming Amish school children and their weeping parents today

---

1. George W. Cornell, "Amish Rights, Living, Threatened by Courts," Associated Press, June 21, 1969.

2. "Top Court Expected to Settle Amish Issue Soon," *Capital Times* (Madison, Wis.), Mar. 3, 1972.

fought attempts by school officials to carry the youngsters off to public schools. . . . The children screamed and chanted 'Jesus Loves Me' when school authorities tried to take them from an Amish school. . . . Their bearded fathers dragged a wagon in front of the school to block the bus which came to take the children to schools which the Amish regard as 'Worldly.' "[3]

In light of these difficulties, the Amish families—four at the beginning, followed later by families from Iowa, Ohio, and a few other states—found New Glarus particularly welcoming because of Wisconsin's compulsory education law, which required education only until age 16 and, more important, made generous provision for private and religious schools, which were required to meet only minimal curricular specifications and whose teachers were not required to be certified or specially trained. Amish teachers, in other words, would likely do.

The first few years following the Amish families' settlement in New Glarus were generally cooperative and constructive. The Amish population grew, and their children attended the public schools with a minimum of fuss. Efforts were made to accommodate the Amish children's beliefs with regard to the physical education classes and in other ways beyond the eighth grade. The New Glarus community welcomed the Amish. The town erected hitching bars for the Amish horses and made space for the carriages and wagons in the shopping district. This was, according to Village President Waldo Freitag, "a gesture of good will toward the new arrivals. I feel it is a free country and anyone can settle where they please. I hope [the Amish] co-operate in community matters." Superintendent of schools Roy Habek said, "I do not foresee any points of controversy. We have agreed to try and co-operate fully."[4]

Over time, however, the difficulties posed for the Amish in the public schools became harder to resolve amicably. The problems centered on gym classes, curricular content in the higher grades, and the compulsory education requirement for sixteen-year-olds, which effectively required students to take courses such as biology that involved the study of evolution. Jonas Yoder, a parent of Amish students, explained the problems. "We have nothing against the gym classes themselves, but we don't like what our children would have to wear to class." He added, "we traditionally have read the German Bible and use German in our church services," but the public schools did not offer German to the students. "Basically, public schools are too modern for us," said Wallace Miller, another Amish. "We like things a little more old-fashioned." As for the requirement for sixteen-year-olds, Miller said,

3. "Amish Fight Off Public School Bid," *Des Moines Register* (UPI), Nov. 22, 1965.

4. "First Amish Settle in N. Glarus Area," *Capital Times* (Madison, Wis.), Jan. 18, 1964.

"We don't think there is anything in the Constitution about that." Another Amish father, whose children under age 16 were no longer in public school, said, "They [his children] finished the eighth grade. If [the school officials] want to put us in jail, they'll have to do the chores."

Matters finally reached a point at which compromise and accommodation simply could not work, so in the summer of 1968, the Amish built their first one-room school, and in September, just before the beginning of the school year, thirty-six Amish children, twenty-three of whom were in the first eight grades, withdrew from the New Glarus public schools, with significant, unanticipated consequences for public school funding.[5] Some people would later claim that the abrupt loss of funding was the occasion for the subsequent action against the parents, but the Amish would never take that position and, indeed, they respected the good faith of the school board and the school authorities, even though they disagreed with them.

The legal problem arose with three high-school-age children who had completed eighth grade but who were not yet age 16, and who therefore were required by state law to attend an approved public or private school. The Amish children were Barbara Miller, 15; Frieda Yoder, 15; and Vernon Yutzy, 14. On October 1, 1968, Kenneth Glewin, the New Glarus superintendent of schools, acting in his capacity as truant officer, filed letters of complaint against the parents. On November 16, 1968, the children's three fathers, Jonas Yoder, Adin Yutzy, and Wallace Miller, were criminally charged with the misdemeanor of failing to send their children to high school classes. The three men appeared in Green County court unrepresented by counsel, as the Amish do not believe in hiring lawyers to represent them. They did not at first enter a plea, but indicated belief that the statute under which they were charged was unconstitutional. They would later be represented by counsel affiliated with a nonprofit organization named the Committee for Amish Freedom and would formally challenge the constitutionality of the Wisconsin law.[6]

The trial was held before Green County judge Roger Elmer on April 2, 1969. Trial briefs focusing on the constitutional question had been filed by the parties. Judge Elmer issued his decision in an opinion dated August 15, 1969. In it he noted that persecution of religious minorities was what the guarantees of religious freedom were intended to prevent, and that "[m]an's lack of empathy and perspective, with its resultant self-righteous intolerances and repres-

5. "Amish Open a School," *State Journal* (Madison, Wis.), Sept. 20, 1968.

6. "Charge Amish Fathers for School Violations," *State Journal* (Madison, Wis.), Nov. 21, 1968.

sions directed toward minority religions have not added luster to his composite human nature."

But the judge also observed that the evidence at trial indicated that "[a]n appreciable number of Amish-reared youth may decide to adopt a different faith, join a different church or leave the Amish community to become a part of a different culture in which they must compete with those who have had a high school education." Amish children are "not only children but also individuals congenitally entitled to their own freedoms, each in his own right, each born under the protection of the same constitutional promises." Thus, while the Wisconsin law did "interfere with the freedom of the defendants [fathers] to act in accordance with their religious belief," the state's compulsory education requirement was a reasonable and constitutional exercise of the government's power over public education and served the interests of those children who could make their own (and different) choices about religion and lifestyle. Jonas Yoder, Adin Yutzy, and Wallace Miller were found guilty and fined $5 each.

The three fathers, now represented by a team of lawyers from the Committee for Amish Freedom, appealed the judge's decision to the Wisconsin Supreme Court. On January 8, 1971, the court issued its opinion, ruling 6-1 that the Wisconsin compulsory education law, as applied to the Old Order Amish parents in New Glarus, violated the free exercise guarantee of the First Amendment. "Although education is a subject within the power of the state to regulate," the Court's majority said, "there is not such a compelling state interest in two years of high school compulsory education as will justify the burden it places upon . . . free exercise of [the Amish parents'] religion."

Asked about the decision, Jonas Yoder said, "It was wonderful." He added, "I blame ourselves" for the problems with the New Glarus schools. If the Amish had built a school immediately upon settling in New Glarus, "the trouble wouldn't have happened." Harry Miller said, "I think 90 percent of the people were for us. I hope this is the end of the trouble."[7] In this, Mr. Miller was premature, for the state of Wisconsin promptly filed an appeal with the United States Supreme Court, which granted review of the case on May 24, 1971, and scheduled oral argument for December 8, 1971.

* * *

The Court that heard argument in the Yoder case consisted of only seven Justices. Two members of the Court, Justices Black and Harlan, had just retired, and their replacements, Justices Powell and Rehnquist, had not yet been

7. "Ruling Could Be End of Amish Wanderings," *State Journal* (Madison, Wis.), Jan. 9, 1971.

confirmed and therefore chose not to participate in the Court's decision. The Chief Justice was Warren Burger, appointed by President Nixon. Next, in order of seniority, were William O. Douglas, appointed by President Roosevelt; William Brennan and Potter Stewart, both appointed by President Eisenhower; Byron White, appointed by President Kennedy; Thurgood Marshall, appointed by President Johnson; and Harry Blackmun, the youngest member of the Court, appointed just the year before by President Nixon. Except for Chief Justice Burger and Justice Blackmun, the Court consisted of members of the Warren Court which, during the 1950s and 1960s, had actively and often controversially (though less so in retrospect) interpreted the Constitution to bar racial discrimination, school prayer, coerced confessions, and to extend the rights of equality.

The lawyers arguing the case were John W. Calhoun, the assistant attorney general of Wisconsin, and William B. Ball of Pennsylvania, representing the three Amish fathers.

The arguments began shortly after 10:00 A.M. on Wednesday, December 8, 1971.

Chief Justice Burger: We will hear argument in No. 110, Wisconsin against Yoder and others. Mr. Calhoun.

Mr. Calhoun: Mr. Chief Justice, and may it please the Court.

Respondents here are members of the Old Order Amish religious sect. They . . . object to education of their children in public, private, secular or nonsecular schools beyond a certain point. At the present time the objection is the eighth grade. The trial court noted the problem of the arbitrary eighth grade cutoff in its decision.

Question: The State required attendance in school—what?—through a certain age or a certain grade?

Mr. Calhoun: [T]hrough a certain age. . . . Seven [to] sixteen.

Question: That would mean, would it not, that if you had a remarkable or unusual child who began school when he was four, and whose parents wanted to take him out to pursue his own studies at a point, he'd still have to go to school formally until he was sixteen?

Mr. Calhoun: Well, if he could show . . . achievement equivalent to a high school education at any point, he would be excused from the compulsory attendance law.

Question: So the achievement test is interposed on the arbitrary sixteen [rule], isn't it?

Mr. Calhoun: Yes, there's an area of discretion there to be exercised by the State Superintendent of Public Instruction, Your Honor, and this provides for certain unusual cases, and of course there are exemptions for health problems and handicap and that sort of thing.

Question: Do the Amish have private schools?

Mr. Calhoun: Yes. In many areas they do. And in this particular instance . . . they apparently refused to set up any school which goes beyond the eighth grade. There are no secondary schools in operation by the Amish in Wisconsin, that I know of.

Question: I gather the issue here . . . is not whether the children must go to school. . . . Rather . . . the issue is whether the parents . . . must see to it that the children go to the school? And I take it that it's really a limited issue, constitutionally at least, whether their freedom of religion is violated by requiring them to send their children to school.

Mr. Calhoun: Well, we think there are two issues here, really. First of all, is whether the . . . respondents [parents] may select the time, the extent, and whether or not they will comply with the compulsory school attendance laws. And whether there is, . . . more broadly . . . , a constitutional right to conscientiously object to education.

The Court is trying in its questions to define the precise issue or issues presented in the case. Calhoun would like the case to focus on the children's right to an education, and on the parents' claim to control their children's rights based on the parents' beliefs, which he will then claim can't be limited to religious beliefs, but instead will introduce a new—and dangerous—right conscientiously to object to education, whether on religious grounds or on grounds of moral conviction or philosophical objection.

Question: Yes, but I gather—or am I wrong?—[that] we are not concerned here with whether the children have to go to school, Amish or not; we're concerned with whether Amish parents can be compelled, under threat of criminal [prosecution], to—

Mr. Calhoun: Well, of course we're concerned about the rights of the child to an education. . . . [T]he compelling interest of the State is in the education of the children, and the interest of the child in education is important—vital.

Question: Well, Mr. Calhoun, isn't it true in Wisconsin and in other States that the way to get to the fact that the child is not in school is to get the parents? Isn't that the normal procedure . . . ?

Mr. Calhoun: Well, that's right. It's a question of whether or not they have complied with the law.

Question: Yes, but doesn't the State have to show a compelling interest in this?

Mr. Calhoun: Yes, we think there's a compelling interest in education.
Question: Well, is it enough that it's a compelling interest in education, or does it have to be some other kind of compelling interest?

The definition of the state's interest (or purpose) being served by the compulsory education law will in the end have a decisive impact on the outcome of the case. As we will see, Calhoun will argue that the compelling interest is simply the state's interest in education, an important and traditional interest, but a very broadly defined one. Calhoun's argument is that the state's educational purpose is, by definition, one that applies to all children without exception, for it is an interest in universal education up to a minimum level. The argument has a tautological quality to it, but if the state's action is a product of democratic and broad public will, the goal of universal public education is an end in itself that fits the long history of state involvement in education in this country.

The Amish parents, on the other hand, want the compelling interest to be defined in very specific terms: What is the state's interest in applying the compulsory education law to them, in particular; or in the alternative, what is the compelling interest in requiring education up to age 16, rather than up to eighth grade, or age 15, or age 14? If they can succeed in casting the state's interest in these narrow terms, they will be able to make arguments specific to the Amish, like the argument that their education in the Amish community up to age 16 is every bit as good as the public school's education, and thus, in light of their religious objections, there is no reason to apply the general rule to them.

There are, of course, problems with both views of the state's interest. If the blunt state interest in education is enough to justify the law, then why couldn't the state require any course or any subject it wanted as part of the curriculum—say, basket weaving, or Presbyterianism, or creationism (the subject of a later story)—or set the requirement at age 10 or age 20 rather than age 16, and then claim that the compelling interest in education justifies the law without further inquiry? On the other hand, if each application of the state's general education law must satisfy searching judicial scrutiny in its application to each student, then the system would fall of its own weight and judges would effectively be placed in charge of education in this country. Couldn't a precocious child claim exemption from all math because he or she is very talented at mathematics and will learn it better at home, or couldn't an athletically active and talented child claim exemption from physical education on the ground that it will do him or her no good? Calhoun's argument is that exemptions might well be made in such cases—not by courts in the name of the Constitution, but by professional educators who understand the learning and socializing processes and the specific goals served in a particular school or course.

This is the argument he must make, but the Court presses him hard on it.

Mr. Calhoun: No. I don't think there has to be any other kind of compelling interest, because it is through compulsory education . . . that the interest is implemented. The interest . . . is education.

Question: [But the State] has to have a compelling interest in total compliance, doesn't it? Can you demonstrate that?

Mr. Calhoun: No, I don't think that the compelling interest is . . . in total compliance, necessarily. The question is whether or not the Court can say that the Amish parents have a constitutional right to conscientiously object to education, to sending their children to school.

Here Calhoun holds his ground on the definition of the state's compelling interest, a definition which absolves the state of having to justify each specific application of its law to every individual or group, but he also needs to turn the argument to two other and related points. First, he wants to argue that the Amish parents' free exercise claim can't be limited to claims arising out of religious belief, but will inevitably evolve into a broader, philosophically based right of conscientious exemption that will undermine the state's broad authority at a systematic level and will draw judges into making specific educational choices. Second, he will draw a distinction, as the Court did in the *Reynolds* polygamy case, between belief and overt acts, the latter not being protected by the free exercise guarantee.

Question: Well, . . . does the State challenge that [religious freedom] is [the basis for the Amish parents'] position about education and [their belief in education] is [the] warp and woof [of] their religion?

Mr. Calhoun: What we have said is simply this: the law interferes with [the Amish parents'] freedom to act, but not with their religious belief, as such. And . . . the cases are clear . . . that the freedom to act may be restricted [notwithstanding] the First Amendment, but the freedom to believe may not.

Question: Well, you mean the old polygamy cases?

Mr. Calhoun: That's right, the old Mormon cases—

Question: Is that what we have here?

Mr. Calhoun: Yes, yes. It's as simple as that, and it could be decided that way.

Question: I wish it were. I don't find that that's so.

The *Reynolds* argument, based on the belief/conduct distinction, is obviously not meeting with a welcoming reception. Calhoun needs to make the argument, and he will return to it. But for the moment he decides to return once again to the compelling state interest question.

Mr. Calhoun: But we're saying that there is a compelling interest in education . . . and that this Court and the Congress and the people of this country have manifested this compelling state interest.

Question: I don't see how anyone can challenge that. (Laughing)

Mr. Calhoun: I don't either. . . . It's just as clear as that. . . . The compulsory school attendance law has been in existence for years. [Such requirements] were part of the established church when this country was founded [as a British colony], when the Colonists established the theocratic societies in the pre-Revolutionary days. . . . [W]hen the church became disestablished, the compulsory school attendance laws remained. They remained in a democratic fashion, and they are applied and enacted in a democratic fashion.

[Education] is a positive force . . . for the benefit of society. And it is the Legislature that should determine . . . whether the compulsory school attendance laws are necessary to enact or to obtain the full benefit of education to the individual and society.

This is a good and sophisticated argument. Compulsory education is part of the very democratic political compact, part of the basic structure of the social order. Educational decisions, including what should be taught and how long education of certain types should be required, involve questions that are not judicially ascertainable. A Court must, on such matters, give great deference to educators and, most fundamentally, to choices arrived at through the democratic political process on the state and local levels. Democracy and the authority of the elected branches best fit such decisions, which affect everyone and rest on core values in the culture. Moreover, such decisions can't be dissected or the system will fail and judges will effectively take over education.

Question: We have other cases, of course . . . , where the power and the duty of the State to support education comes into collision with the religion clauses of the First Amendment. Isn't that what we have here?

Mr. Calhoun: [W]hat particular cases do you have in mind?

Question: Well, the recent cases . . . where States were giving support to private schools and that State action was thought to be in conflict with the First Amendment.

Mr. Calhoun: No, I think . . . [those cases involve] an establishment [clause] question, rather than a freedom-of-worship question.

The cases referred to involve government funds being directed to religious schools, which, the Court had held, usually violates the establishment clause of the First Amendment. In the *Yoder* case, however, the question is not whether government aid establishes religion (since the argument is that the government refused to provide aid by denying exemption from the law), but whether *denial* of aid unconstitutionally restricts freedom to exercise religion. Of course, one could argue that the requested exemption for the Amish from Wisconsin's law would represent a benefit conferred only on religion and, in fact, only on a particular religion, and thus would be, in Justice Black's terminology in *Everson,* a law which "aid[s] one religion . . . or prefer[s] one religion over another" in violation of the establishment clause. But if the Amish exemption claim were *judicially* accepted, that would by definition mean (because courts are always right?) that the establishment clause was not violated. Is this reasoning circular? Yes. And unsatisfying.

But that issue is for another day, and other, later, stories. For now, the questioning changes course.

Question: If the Amish could show that their own training in agriculture brought their children at age 16 to the same point, or a higher point of achievement, as compared with those who went to the vocational schools to learn about agriculture, would you be here?

Mr. Calhoun: Well, I'm not sure, because I'm not sure whether that would meet the standards. We probably wouldn't be here. We might be in some other lower court, determining whether there was a reasonable ruling by the administrative bodies, such as the Department of Education, who are experts in this area. But it would not be the same constitutional question. . . .

Now, I've indicated that the compulsory school attendance law, and the ruling of the Wisconsin courts, [considered] in terms of the conscientious objector cases [recently decided in relation to the Vietnam War], present a constitutional right to anyone who has a conscientious objection based on a sincere moral belief to object to education. And we submit that this [broad understanding] would raise havoc with the educational system, not only in Wisconsin but throughout the country. . . . The manner in which a juvenile judge, for example, deals with a dependent child would be affected by the decision of this Court. [I]f it were to say that there is a constitutional right to conscientiously object to education, I feel that would be removing a vital tool from the administration of the law as it related to youth and children.

Calhoun has returned to the argument that the religious claim cannot be confined to traditionally religious belief, but will inevitably expand to broader philosophical and ideological grounds for objection to specific aspects of required education. His reference is to the Court's earlier decisions under the conscientious objection provisions of the selective service law, where conscientious objection was expanded beyond religion to include "a sincere and meaningful belief which occupies in the life of its possessor a place parallel to that filled by . . . God." His argument is a valid, though strictly negative, one. It is also problematic because, as a technical matter, the Court's military service decisions were grounded on a construction of a statute, not on the religion guarantees. Yet it was also clear that the Court's construction of the statute in those cases was guided by what the Constitution would likely require.

But the matter is dropped, and, after a brief question on another point, Calhoun's time is up.

Question: Mr. Calhoun, would your case be any different if instead of age sixteen, it were age 21?

Mr. Calhoun: No, I think we've gotten into the area of reasonableness, Your Honor, and again the line is drawn somewhere, and is reached . . . in the legislative halls and in the testimony of witnesses, who are experts in education. . . . But I don't think the underlying principle is much different.

Mr. Chief Justice Burger: Very well, Mr. Calhoun. Mr. Ball.

Mr. Ball: Mr. Chief Justice, and may it please the Court.

The legal basis for this prosecution is the refusal of these parents on religious grounds to afford the three children in question, at most, two years of high school under a statute which requires not a high school course, not four years of high school, not even one year necessarily, but merely school through age 15. . . .[8]

Now, in terms of the interest the State has in trying to compel these children to attend school beyond the eighth grade, we have to realize that for Frieda Yoder . . . , only one year of schooling was involved, because she was 15 years and 5 months old when the criminal complaint was brought

---

8. Ball adds as a footnote to this statement that, for vocational education, the Wisconsin statute requires training through age 18. But there was no vocational school in Green County where the Amish lived, and so the difference is not relevant to the *Yoder* case.

> against her father. Barbara Miller would have only six months of this State benefit of additional compulsory education, because she was 15 years and 8 months old at the time the criminal complaint was brought.
>
> Now, it is the position of the Amish parents that the application of the statute to them violates their free exercise of religion, and that there has been no showing whatever, no showing at all that non-application of the statute to them violates or creates any substantial danger to any interest of the State of Wisconsin.
>
> Nobody on our side challenges the fact that the compulsory education laws bespeak a compelling State interest.

Ball makes his position very clear that the compelling State interest must be in compulsory attendance between ages 14 and 16 specifically, not in universal compulsory education as a general goal. He will return to that argument later, but first he turns to the religious freedom claim.

> My argument . . . will pursue two points: one, the free exercise claim; and secondly, the question of danger to the interests of the State. . . .
>
> The free exercise point is extremely important. [H]ere we're not talking about one tenet of religion being at stake—for example, observance of the Sabbath, or opposition to military training. We're not talking here about one particular practice, say, studying of the Gospel through speech or press or assembly. We're not talking about one forced exercise, such as the salute to a graven image, or recitation of prayers, or Bible reading. We're talking about a whole complex of religious interests. Religious interests in rights in education, in worship, in parental nurture, in individual religious choice, in vocation, in communal association, with respect to teaching and learning and with respect to privacy. . . .
>
> [I]ndeed, we're talking about . . . the continued existence of the Amish faith community in the United States.

Ball has pressed the Amish free exercise claim in the strongest possible terms. He has emphasized the pervasive significance of the Amish objection to high school in terms of the very existence of the Church and the community. In doing so, he has tried to make it easier for the Court to accept the Amish religious claim without inviting an infinite variety of similar claims by all sorts of religions—claims to freedom from paying taxes, or from the alcohol laws and the serving of wine to minors in communion, and the like. In doing so, he has brought the focus of his argument onto the Amish faith itself and its belief system, but he is, as we will see, quite happy, even eager, to submit his client's beliefs and good faith to the scrutiny of the Court.

Question: And the Amish are in, what, about a dozen or 15 States of the Union . . . ?

Mr. Ball: Yes, about 15, Mr. Justice Stewart. About 50,000 people.

Question: And each Amish community is unique, in a way, there are local variations among them, are there not, and among their—

Mr. Ball: There are slight variations among them. I would say that Old Order Amish are fairly uniform, whether you find them in Lancaster County, Pennsylvania, or . . . in New Glarus, Wisconsin. . . . They follow the same practices and have the same attitudes toward religion, education, children, the simple life, and so on.

Question: [The Old Order Amish] have come down from the Anabaptists, as I understand it.

Mr. Ball: Yes, that is correct.

Question: And these particular people go back to Switzerland in the . . . sixteenth century?

Mr. Ball: They do. They go back to a time in the sixteenth century, Mr. Justice Stewart, when a number of people of the Protestant Reformation sought to return to what they believed to be the Golden Age of Christianity, in the early centuries of Christianity, and to reject the institutional churches, the Catholic Church and the other Protestant Churches; and to do this, to have that life, they believed that their lives had to be governed completely by the Sermon on the Mount. And this would be, therefore . . . , the call to the creating of a community of love, of mutual help, of simplicity, closeness to nature, animals, soil, plants, and so on, turning the other cheek, and extremely importantly, perhaps the most critical point in the understanding of the Amish religion, separation from the world, which they believe . . . was a . . . principle enjoined upon them by the Gospels themselves, where St. Paul . . . says "Do not be conformed to this world."

And so . . . in two ways have [they] sought to separate themselves from the world . . . over the centuries.

First . . . , there has to be a separation from what they consider pride of intellect. That is to say, the higher learning, as they express it. They believe that education's aim should be the life of goodness, not the life of the intellect; the making of a good man, not the making of the good American life. They believe that this life of goodness rejects the world of technical cunning, and instead embraces wisdom. They believe that life is a very short pilgrimage, and that its whole purpose is to get human beings to their salvation in the arms of God.

A question was posed at [trial] . . . by the Deputy Attorney General . . . to Professor John Hostetler . . . , the world's foremost authority on the Amish people. He asked . . . "Isn't it the point of education to help a person to get ahead in the world?" And Doctor Hostetler replied, "It depends on which world."

[T]he aim of education is to get to Heaven. Therefore, [the Amish] reject what many of the rest of us accept in the world of knowledge, and they believe that the education in writing and reading and arithmetic, which a child can acquire up until the time of adolescence, is sufficient education; particularly in view of the fact that Amish life is not concerned with technical and technological achievement and development.

Question: Now, Dr. Hostetler grew up in an Amish community, and he's a Ph.D. . . . [H]ow is that to be explained?

Mr. Ball: It shows that he left the Amish faith; it shows that people can leave the Amish faith; and that the fact that they began in life as Amish children is not necessarily a crippling experience. He later elected to leave the Amish faith. And this is done . . . at the time of adult baptism. At that time, a child, or a young man or woman, must face up to the fact of whether he wishes to live the Amish life or not; and he may refuse to live the Amish life if he wishes to do so. Some do. There are no wholesale departures from the ranks of the Amish people. [W]hile there is some attrition, the community has continued in pretty much the same size over the years.

Question: Is there a belief in elementary education, or just an acceptance of it?

Mr. Ball: Well, they believe that the basic skills are sound and desirable for a child to have. They're quite aware of their citizenship. They believe a person should be able to read and write and communicate.

Question: So there's more than just an acquiescence in that, there's an affirmative acceptance of education?

Mr. Ball: Yes, there's an affirmative acceptance of education to that point.

Question: Mr. Ball, I take it, then, . . . that among consistent adherents to the church there are no professional people, no lawyers, no physicians?

Mr. Ball: That is quite true, Mr. Justice Blackmun.

Question: And yet, they do rely, certainly, on medical knowledge elsewhere, do they not?

Mr. Ball: Yes. [T]heir point of view is not whether medical knowledge is necessarily good for the world; their point of view is one that is simply based upon the fact that they believe that they, themselves, may not pursue the higher learning. . . . But they will seek medical treatment. Right now they are receiving legal help, though they did not seek it. [T]hey would rather suffer, personally, prosecution than make a test case, go into court, and so on. The second element of separation [in the Amish faith] is separation from the ways of the world. The Amish do not want their children, and they do not want themselves, to be exposed to the spirit of luxury, of ostentation, of strife, consumerism, competition, speed, violence, [or] other such elements as are commonly found in our American life.

Therefore, education for them embraces a rejection of the higher learning, and a positive emphasis upon the learning of the agricultural life; it rejects the concept of exposure to and service in the ways of the world; and, when you add to this the factor of adolescence, you will see why an Amish person, whether we would agree with him or not, may not, from a religious point of view, attend school beyond the eighth grade.

The factor of adolescence is extremely basic in Amish religious thinking. It's the time of the starting of life's work; it's meeting the challenges and real responsibilities on the part of young people; it's a very sensitive time when values are formed.

The Amish religion forbids high school, then, because of those three elements, with a tremendous stress on the importance and the opportunity which adolescence creates. [I]f they are placed in [high] school, the record shows that they are going to be . . . exposed to the social life of the school . . . ; they are going to be exposed to a curriculum, much of which they must religiously reject, and much of which is superfluous to their intended life as growing up in the Amish faith community.

The Amish do not maintain any high schools whatever.

Question: That's within your reading-writing premise?

Mr. Ball: Yes, that's correct, Mr. Justice Brennan.

[W]hen you take a child from Amish life at adolescence and place him in a high school, he is naturally going to be exposed to those values which his parents' religion rejects. . . . And this alienation . . . of the child who has been raised, as he has a right to be raised, in the Amish faith community up until adolescence—to be suddenly placed in a high school where there's different dress, different speech, very, very different people, with very, very different backgrounds—this is extremely traumatic . . . and . . . psychologically damaging to such a person.

[A]dolescence is a very important part of this whole thinking of the Amish, that up until the eighth grade, in those earlier years, the chance, or the temptation to become a worldly person, and the imposition of values in another [public elementary] school system [which they often attend and did here], may have far less impact than they will to a child who is beyond adolescence.

Question: From a religious point of view, is this elementary education approach somewhat like that of the Jewish faith, with the—I think it's age 13 when a Jewish child is considered to have become a mature adult? Is there an analogy between the Amish attitude and that of the Jewish faith?

Mr. Ball: Yes. I think it's a quite close analogy, Mr. Chief Justice Burger. And . . . that is well brought out by . . . the brief amicus curiae in this case by the Synagogue Council of America and other related Jewish groups.

Ball's argument on the adolescence point is considerably more complicated than he makes it appear and than the Court allows it to be. To be sure, religion is often grounded in faith and belief, not fact or reason, and part of its exercise consists of hiding or denying facts or other perspectives that would undermine the faith-based system of thought. And the religion guarantees may often protect, in the name of free exercise, the group's ability to deny or hide other facts from the adherents' minds. As we will see in a later story, this is the essence of the argument about evolution in public schools; it is part of the reason for, and religious justification of, private religious schools that the Court has in so many words said the state must allow as an alternative to public schools, in the name of free exercise of religion. Ball's adolescence argument is precisely of this sort: at an age when children are impressionable yet must also make lifelong religious commitments, the Amish should be entitled to remove the children from public schools in order to hide the facts, knowledge, reason, and other perspectives (beliefs, too?) that may undermine their religious beliefs.

Ball's argument is doubly difficult, however, for at heart it has to do with the Amish Church's ability to attract the children into the religious community at a time when, in theory, they are free to reject it and set out on their own. The Amish are asking the state, in effect, to become a party to the Church's effort to hide evil facts and evil knowledge from potential adherents, and to assist the Church in presenting only the Church's view of reality, in order to gain the children's adherence to the sect. To some this will be an offensive and exaggerated way of characterizing Ball's argument, which he dresses up in more attractive garb. But there is a certain cultish quality to the Amish system. Indeed, one might wonder whether the eighth-grade-only educational principle is really an element of the Church's religious belief system, or is rather an effective practice that serves the Church's institutional interests in survival. Ball's claim that rejection of the Amish claim in *Yoder* will mean the end of the Old Order Amish in this country suggests, ironically, that the practice serves an absolutely essential instrumental purpose in the future viability of the Church as an institution. And it does so at the expense of knowledge and thus understanding of the pluralistic society of which the adherents, in the end, are a part.

But Ball has managed to make his argument without getting into these nettlesome matters, and he now turns the argument to the question of the state's interest, which he, of course, wants to characterize as narrow and specific, thus leaving room for individualized challenges. On this definitional question, the Court pretty much lets him have his way.

Mr. Ball (continuing): I would like to come, if I may, in the time that remains, to . . . the danger to the State, which the State has said it is faced with if these Amish children, for religious reasons, are permitted not to attend school through age 15.

One has to ask [why] the State, with its very ample legal research resources, never placed a single witness on the stand, [nor] produced any documentary evidence at all, [not] one scrap of any study which would give color to the charge that the Amish non-attendance threatens some compelling State interest.

The reason, of course, is obvious. The state defined its interest as the general one in universal minimum public education, a goal serving democratic and politically constitutive ends in a democracy and settled upon by democratic, and thus public, consent. In these terms, universal public education by definition requires, and thus justifies, universal applicability of the requirement, and that's the end of the matter. Ball's rhetorical sleight of hand skims over this argument by the state and recasts the state interest question on his terms—as a rule whose application must be justified in each particular instance and thus is subject to challenge in terms of the Amish children and their specific educational achievements and future needs in the Amish community. By this technique Ball gets the issue framed in his terms without having to justify—or even admit—having done so.

Ball continues on his track and, stunningly, the Court seems to sit mute, even transfixed.

All the evidence on that point . . . came from the defense. The State offered really two points: First of all, that Amish non-attendance of two years, one year, six months, whatever it might be, threatens, of all things, the State's establishing and maintaining an educational system. Six judges below, the Wisconsin Supreme Court, denied this fact. Certainly there is no danger of fraud. Very few people could show what the Amish have shown, that is to say, a unique and ancient religious tradition . . . , the obvious nurture and protection of children which takes place in the Amish community, which treasures children, the whole factor of training in life for a useful and productive vocation, and no casting of the children upon the community.

No one else's rights are harmed by virtue of Amish non-attendance.

> And here I'm reminded of Justice Brennan's [statement], "the values of the First Amendment . . . look primarily towards the preservation of personal liberty, rather than towards the fulfillment of collective goals."

This is an apt and good point. But if one looks deeper, it is a bit unclear. Are the interests of personal liberty those of the Amish community and parents, and compulsory education the state's "collective goal," as Ball would have it? Or are the interests in personal liberty the rights of the Amish children, who will have to decide upon their own faith in a few years, and who are being protected from exposure to other ways of thinking by the collective goal of the Amish parents and community? In this sense, by its compulsory education law for *everyone*, including the Amish, the state is protecting the individual interests, and the Amish religious community is serving the collective interests.

Mr. Ball (continuing): [T]he State action in forcing these children into high school constitutes denial of the free exercise of religion. This, I think, is established in the case, irrespective of what may be thought of the Amish religion. The remaining question then becomes one of a compelling State interest, which means what is the danger to the State, and certainly it is not in the general enforcement or maintenance of an education system.

Now, does [exemption from the compulsory attendance law] deny the child [his or her] free choice? Does it deny the child, as the State says, his right to an education?

There is a national consensus that . . . there is no compelling State interest . . . in State compulsory education laws . . . beyond the 15th birthday. [I]f this is the case in State after State, that the State doesn't feel that a child needs to attend school beyond 15, then it seems to me that these children do not present, in terms of their own right to an education, any danger to any compelling State interest.

We have produced in evidence [a] study . . . by Professor John Hostetler, under a commission from the U.S. Office of Education, of achievements of Amish children in standardized testing, and it reveals that they perform well.

The State has talked loosely about the disease of ignorance in opening the gateways of opportunity to these children. But we introduced positive evidence which shows that Amish education produces good people; we've cited the testimony of Dr. Erickson of the University of Chicago, when we specifically asked him questions concerning Amish education, which he carefully studied. And his comment was,

> The Amish definitely provide for their children of high school age what could be called an education. I would be inclined to say they do a better

> job in this than most of us do. The Amish are in a fortunate position respecting the school which they conduct for children beyond the eighth grade. It is learning by doing—an ideal system. We are learning that current education is detached from the real world and that in the things they talk about the pupils do not become involved or have real responsibility. The lack, in modern education, of a clear connection between learning and doing is responsible for much of the student actions that we have today.

We asked, "What kind of people are these?" And we put the sheriff of Green County on the stand. We asked him question after question . . . about those crimes of violence which are most . . . typically committed by young people today: arson, looting, rape, etc. The sheriff gave these people a complete bill of health. They have never been known for the commission of crime.

Dr. Littell, an authority on the history of the Amish people, has stated that they have not been known to have committed a felony in 250 years on this soil. They are a peaceable people and an asset in our society. Not in terms of gross national product or the building of missiles, but certainly in terms . . . of the goodness that they afford as an example to the rest of our society.

And the Director of Welfare [of Green County] testified that the Amish completely take care of themselves; they do not cast their burden on the community; they do not have people on relief or welfare; they do not have their aged in public homes for the aged.

I think what we are talking about here are really great achievers. They've been in the education business for 300 years. They're the finest natural farmers in the Western Hemisphere.

You go up—Members of the Court, you go up to Lancaster County in Pennsylvania, and if you were to see these people and see them in actuality, you would find young men who are heads of families and managers of large farms, experts in husbandry; you'd find in their women very model women, managers of households, very fine people.

[I]t's quite surprising that these people are singled out as not having an education, denying their people an education. For 300 years these people have performed very well in our society.

The question before the Court, then, is whether the State may destroy—because that's what it will come to if these children are forced into high school—a peaceable, self-sustaining community, 250 years on this soil, on the grounds that the parents in that community cannot refuse to send their children, on account of a clear mandate of their religion, to one or two years of high school.

If the decision of this Court is against the Amish, I fear that many people will feel that this Court has indicted our nation as too ossified, too brittle, too moribund to allow difference, innocent difference, to exist and to flourish in its midst.

The Amish do not come . . . as fearful supplicants to this Court; they come here with confidence, believing in this court as their brothers in justice, in love and goodness, and belief in constitutional liberty.

Thank you.

Mr. Chief Justice Burger: Thank you, Mr. Ball.

Wow! One can sense the Court sitting in rapt attention, not daring to interrupt. Ball's argument is compelling: based on facts in the record; resting on a premise that makes sense, which is that the state has to have some specific compelling interest in applying the law to these children; drawing on history and Amish values to clearly distinguish their claim from any other religious or philosophical claim that might be made, and thus removing the risk of a slippery slope; and finally asserting that the Court's decision will determine the continued existence of the Amish religion itself. This is strong and powerful stuff, stated with logic brought to life by passion. It clearly affected the largely mute Justices.

But do we believe all of it, once we step back from the passion and look coldly at what issues the case presents? Should the refusal to send children to high school be accepted as a free exercise of religion? Refusing to attend high school is an act, not a belief. It is a dramatic act of disobedience in the name of religion. Would exempting the students from high school, and thus from "forbidden knowledge," really square with the demands of a pluralistic and free, self-governing society? Would exempting them only serve to reinforce the power of the Church over the children and thus yield a legally assisted increase in Church control over the religious freedom of the children/adherents? Should the right to free exercise of religion belong to the Church, or to the children? And finally, would granting a special exemption limited to the Old Order Amish religion effectively constitute an establishment of religion, granting it favored legal status by excusing it from obligations owed by us all?

Calhoun has four minutes for rebuttal, a very short time in which to try to resuscitate some of these hard questions from the fog of passion left by Ball's remarkable argument.

Mr. Calhoun: We have absolutely no quarrel with the Amish way of life. In fact, to some of us in the remorseless daily crunch of living, the grass on the Amish side of the fence looks green, and much greener than ours, at times. But I submit that retreat to a simpler era may have had some justification 200 years ago, when Rousseau was extolling the virtues of the Cro-Magnon man, but too much water has gone through the turbines for that kind of position today.

What is needed is more education to cope with the problems of society, more pride in intellect, not less pride. This is what we develop in our educational programs.

The issue in the case is clearly joined in Calhoun's statement: the conflict is between modernity on the one hand, retreat and social isolation on the other. The state is not so much choosing modernity as recognizing it as a fact that cannot be ignored; the state's interest is in preventing through education a self-destructive and socially untenable right to cultural isolationism. And it is protecting the Amish children's right, at least, to make a choice in the matter. Does a religion that believes in the literal truth of the Bible have the right to protect its children from contact with evolution? Does a religion based on evil have the right to keep its children free from knowledge of good? Calhoun continues:

Mr. Calhoun: [W]hat is being taught [in schools] is changing. The worldly courses of language, foreign languages, and the institution of educational television into the elementary grades. These things are objectionable [to the Amish], you see.

Question: Well, haven't some very distinguished educators been very critical of the American system, because it was concentrating on courses like interpersonal relations, community relations, etc., with students who couldn't spell and read adequately and write by the time they get out of high school?

Mr. Calhoun: Education today is undergoing serious study and revision. [M]any experts in the field have written urging reform. . . . [T]here should be organic involvement at the local level in education. . . . [B]ut what this Court should be doing is to encourage that sort of thing; encourage the ferment and the change that's necessary to make education a viable institution.

Calhoun is trying to reemphasize the general social importance of education, a government responsibility for everyone in a democratic society. And he is subtly suggesting that the Court must give great deference to those involved in education with respect to the particular decisions made, or else the Supreme Court will end up judging the relative value of particular courses or curricula as a matter of constitutional law. That's a role the Court should stay far away from.

Question: Mr. Calhoun, do you agree with Mr. Ball's statement that this is absolutely against [the Amish] religion to go to school beyond the elementary school?

Mr. Calhoun: I don't agree with it fundamentally, no. . . . The trial court stated that "Obviously in the long history of this sect it existed in areas when and where there was no such thing as an eighth grade or even school systems of any kind. Just how the eighth grade cutoff point was arrived at was not explained. Age apparently was not the test, nor was the quality of the school system apparently a factor."

Question: Do you deny that it [is] part of their faith that they should not go to public school beyond the eighth grade?

Mr. Calhoun: No. I deny—I say this: that the trial court found that this did not interfere with their religious belief, as such, but with their freedom to act; and that the freedom to act, the restriction on their freedom to act here was a reasonable one which had been imposed since 1642 in this country, that the compulsory school attendance is not a law which has just recently been enforced. We've had it since the beginning of our education system.

Thank you, Your Honors.

Mr. Chief Justice Burger: Very well, Mr. Calhoun. Thank you. Thank you, Mr. Ball. The case is submitted.

Calhoun's final point rested on the belief/conduct distinction the Court had first articulated in the *Reynolds* case. The distinction had largely been *declared* in *Reynolds,* not explained and justified. It was an intuitively sensible and direct way to dismiss the religious exercise claim made by an outcast religious sect on behalf of a radical and socially unacceptable practice, polygamy. Calhoun was right in coming back to the distinction and relying on it, emphasizing its role against the background of unbroken history with compulsory education laws in this country.

By emphasizing the belief/conduct distinction, Calhoun made the Court's decision a bit more difficult in two respects. First, as a legal matter, it would have to overrule this aspect of the *Reynolds* case, and perhaps explain why the distinction wasn't really necessary to reach the conclusion that polygamy could be outlawed. Second, as a practical matter, the Court would have to consider whether the difference in the two cases came down to the facts that the Mormons were then disfavored and reviled, while the Amish were respected and even romanticized, and that polygamy was simply deemed for social rather than legal reasons to be more unacceptable than refusal to obtain an education. To be sure, polygamy was an act that threatened social institutions like marriage and property, and it was morally repulsive to most people. But doesn't exemption from the educational system of the country also threaten important premises of the social and political order? Perhaps the key difference is that the Amish and their practices are not repulsive: farming is good, community is good, and the Amish are peaceful, giving, law-abiding folks. But what about the coercion of ignorance implicit in the Amish practice of rejecting the world and the worldly during adolescence, when the child is most vulnerable and when he or she must make a choice of religion and life? Is coercion, if that's what is involved, any less distasteful than polygamy? Or is ignorance, like polygamy, a means to salvation? On reflection, the distinction between *Reynolds* and *Yoder* may not be as clear as it first appeared.

Many of these questions, and others raised in the argument, appear to have occupied the Justices as they decided the outcome of the case and then crafted their opinion. It was not until May 15, 1972, nearly five months following the oral argument, that the Court's decision was announced. The Court's opinion was written by the Chief Justice, with five of the six other Justices in agreement. Only Justice William O. Douglas dissented.

Mr. Chief Justice *Burger* delivered the opinion of the Court.

The record in this case abundantly supports the claim that the traditional way of life of the Amish is not merely a matter of personal preference, but one of deep religious conviction, shared by an organized group, and intimately related to daily living. That the Old Order Amish daily life and religious practice stem from their faith is shown by the fact that it is in response to their literal interpretation of the Biblical injunction from the Epistle of Paul to the Romans, "be not conformed to this world. . . ." [T]he Old Order Amish religion pervades and determines virtually their entire way of life, regulating it with the detail of the Talmudic diet through the strictly enforced rules of the Church community.

Their way of life in a church-oriented community, separated from the outside world and "worldly" influences, their attachment to nature and the soil, is a way inherently simple and uncomplicated, albeit difficult to preserve against the pressure to conform. Their rejection of telephones, automobiles, radios, and television, their mode of dress, of speech, their habits of manual work do indeed set them apart from much of contemporary society; these customs are both symbolic and practical.

The impact of the compulsory-attendance law on respondents' practice of the Amish religion is not only severe, but inescapable. . . . Compulsory school attendance to age 16 for Amish children carries with it a very real threat of undermining the Amish community and religious practice as they exist today;

they must either abandon belief and be assimilated into society at large, or be forced to migrate to some other and more tolerant region.

The State advances two primary arguments in support of its system of compulsory education. It notes, as Thomas Jefferson pointed out early in our history, that some degree of education is necessary to prepare citizens to participate effectively and intelligently in our open political system if we are to preserve freedom and independence. Further, education prepares individuals to be self-reliant and self-sufficient participants in society. We accept these propositions.

However, the evidence adduced by the Amish in this case is persuasively to the effect that an additional one or two years of formal high school for Amish children in place of their long-established program of informal vocational education would do little to serve those interests. It is one thing to say that compulsory education for a year or two beyond the eighth grade may be necessary when its goal is the preparation of the child for life in modern society as the majority live, but it is quite another if the goal of education be viewed as the preparation of the child for life in the separated agrarian community that is the keystone of the Amish faith.

The State attacks respondents' position as one fostering "ignorance" from which the child must be protected by the State. No one can question the State's duty to protect children from ignorance but this argument does not square with the facts disclosed in the record. Whatever their idiosyncrasies as seen by the majority, this record strongly shows that the Amish community has been a highly successful social unit within our society, even if apart from the conventional "mainstream." Its members are productive and very law-abiding members of society; they reject public welfare in any of its usual modern forms.

It is neither fair nor correct to suggest that the Amish are opposed to education beyond the eighth grade level. What this record shows is that they are opposed to conventional formal education of the type provided by a certified high school because it comes at the child's crucial adolescent period of religious development.

The Amish alternative to formal secondary school education has enabled them to function effectively in their day-to-day life under self-imposed limitations on relations with the world, and to survive and prosper in contemporary society as a separate, sharply identifiable and highly self-sufficient community for more than 200 years in this country. In itself this is strong evidence that they are capable of fulfilling the social and political responsibilities of citizenship without compelled attendance beyond the eighth grade at the price of jeopardizing their free exercise of religious belief.

Aided by a history of three centuries as an identifiable religious sect and a long history as a successful and self-sufficient segment of American society, the Amish in this case have convincingly demonstrated the sincerity of their religious beliefs, the interrelationship of belief with their mode of life, the vital role that belief and daily conduct play in the continued survival of Old Order Amish communities and their religious organization, and the hazards presented by the State's enforcement of a statute generally valid as to others. Beyond this, they have carried the even more difficult burden of demonstrating the adequacy of their alternative mode of continuing informal vocational education in terms of precisely those overall interests that the State advances in support of its program of compulsory high school education. In light of this convincing showing, one that probably few other religious groups or sects could make, and weighing the minimal difference between what the State would require and what the Amish already accept, it was incumbent on the State to show with more particularity how its admittedly strong interest in compulsory education would be adversely affected by granting an exemption to the Amish.

Affirmed.

Mr. Justice *Douglas,* dissenting in part.

It is the future of the student, not the future of the parents, that is imperiled by today's decision. If a parent keeps his child out of school beyond the grade school, then the child will be forever barred from entry into the new and amazing world of diversity that we have today. The child may decide that that is the preferred course, or he may rebel. . . . He may want to be a pianist or an astronaut or an oceanographer. To do so he will have to break from the Amish tradition. . . . It is the student's judgment, not his parents', that is essential if we are to give full meaning to what we have said about the Bill of Rights and of the right of students to be masters of their own destiny. If he is harnessed to the Amish way of life by those in authority over him and if his education is truncated, his entire life may be stunted and deformed. The child, therefore, should be given an opportunity to be heard before the State gives the exemption which we honor today.

[T]he emphasis of the Court on the "law and order" record of this Amish group of people is quite irrelevant. A religion is a religion irrespective of what the misdemeanor or felony records of its members might be. I am not at all sure how the Catholics, Episcopalians, the Baptists, Jehovah's Witnesses, the Unitarians, and my own Presbyterians would make out if subjected to such a test.

In another way, however, the Court retreats when in reference to Henry Thoreau it says his "choice was philosophical and personal rather than religious, and such belief does not rise to the demands of the Religion Clauses." That is contrary to what we held in *United States v. Seeger,* where we were concerned with the meaning of the words "religious training and belief" in the Selective Service Act, which were the basis of many conscientious objector claims. We said:

> Within that phrase would come all sincere religious beliefs which are based upon a power or being, or upon a faith, to which all else is subordinate or upon which all else is ultimately dependent. The test might be stated in these words: A sincere and meaningful belief which occupies in the life of

> its possessor a place parallel to that filled by the God of those admittedly qualifying for the exemption comes within the statutory definition. This construction avoids imputing to Congress an intent to classify different religious beliefs, exempting some and excluding others, and is in accord with the well-established congressional policy of equal treatment for those whose opposition to service is grounded in their religious tenets.[9]

> I adhere to these exalted views of "religion" and see no acceptable alternative to them now that we have become a Nation of many religions and sects, representing all of the diversities of the human race.

What should we make of the *Yoder* case? It is a case that seemed, at the time, to turn the constitutional world of *Reynolds* and *Everson* upside down. Did it? We won't be able to answer that question until part III. Until then, the case should be seen as but one decision among many that we will consider—cases involving school prayer, teaching evolution in public school, school funding, and rights of religious groups to use public facilities—in which the strict separation paradigm of *Reynolds* and *Everson* was put under intense pressure and, as often as not, the Court chose to lower or bend the wall of separation between church and state, yet tried to keep the wall standing.

Yoder, then, does not give us general answers to the dilemmas and puzzles presented by the religion clauses. It instead demonstrates how difficult the problems are and how malleable the judicial standards can become. It demonstrates the art of judicial obfuscation in an opinion that is neither thorough nor fully honest in its reasoning.

- In deciding the case, the Court simply swept aside the rule of *Reynolds,* extending free exercise protection to conduct as well as belief and expression—and extending it a long way, too.
- It simply dismissed out of hand the State's interest in a rule of universal education, opting instead for a regime in which specific applications of the compulsory education requirement could be subject to constitutional challenge and claims for exemption.
- Yet the Court effectively scoffed at the possibility that judges would thus get drawn into the interstices of educational policy and curriculum under the authority of the First Amendment.
- The Court remained mute on the concern that the Amish parents' claim would expand into a more general right of philosophically grounded conscientious objection to education, spawning, for instance, the homeschooling movement.

---

9. *United States v. Seeger,* 380 U.S. 163, 176 (1965).

- It decided on thoroughly tautological grounds that giving an exemption to the Amish, particularly because they are a law-abiding and good religion, would not violate the establishment clause's prohibition of government assistance to one religion over all others, because what free exercise requires, nonestablishment permits.
- And finally it dismissed the relevance, on technical legal grounds, of the inescapable risk that the Amish children's right to free exercise of their chosen religion—their constitutional right to choose their religion—would be rendered a nullity by the authority of their parents and the Church to remove them from public school, and thus from exposure to different and new ideas and facts just as they were approaching maturity.

It was left to Justice Douglas, in lone and partial dissent, to challenge many of these assumptions and conclusions. It was Justice Douglas who said that he would extend the right to claim exemption to all life-governing belief systems, not just religious beliefs in a God. It was Justice Douglas who expressed serious concern about the rights of the largely silent children to make their own choices, as indeed the Amish Church allowed them to do (while denying them much of the knowledge with which such a choice could be made). It was Justice Douglas who worried, though not too much, about the extension of an exemption so selectively that establishment clause concerns might arise. And it was Justice Douglas who, observing and welcoming the rejection of the belief/conduct distinction in *Reynolds*, suggested that in time the *Reynolds* decision itself, and the illegality of polygamy, should be revisited.

In time, as we will see, Justice Douglas's prediction would prove at least premature, and the Court would take a very different turn back in the direction of *Reynolds*. But I do not want us to get ahead of ourselves here. I mention this only to make a final point about what we should make of the *Yoder* case. It is a point that should be stated even at this early stage: The law of the religion guarantees is never absolute, and it is never finally settled. Everything can be reversed, and everything is subject to change at the hands of a good argument. That remains as true today as it was in 1972. The proper meaning and application of the religion guarantees is always debatable. For some, that is a source of frustration. For others, it is the source of life and excitement in the otherwise terse and uncertain language of the First Amendment: "Congress shall make no law respecting an establishment of religion, or prohibiting the free exercise thereof."

Those who are seriously frustrated by uncertainty and change should probably stop here.

But if you do, you will miss a very interesting and provocative journey.

STORY 4

Darwin versus Genesis

Epperson v. Arkansas, 393 U.S. 97 (1968)

By the 1920s, Charles Darwin's "theory" of evolution was broadly accepted in biology as an explanation of the development of species by random variation and natural selection based on scientific evidence. It had never been accepted by the many Christians who believed in the literal truth of the Bible and, specifically, the Genesis story. As evolution was meeting with increasing support, it was also meeting stiffer religious resistance from the creationists.

William Jennings Bryan, famed orator, thrice candidate for president of the United States, and former secretary of state, was a fundamentalist and creationist. More specifically, he believed that the teaching of evolution in public schools throughout the country was corrupting the nation's youth, jeopardizing their moral development by removing God from the creation of life. Whether Darwin's theory was based on science or not didn't matter. It was not the place of the scientific elites to dictate what should be taught in public schools. This was the essence of the campaign he led against the teaching of evolution in public schools.

Bryan's campaign met with considerable success. During the 1920s, more than twenty states considered antievolution laws. Tennessee was one of them. In 1924, and at Bryan's urging, Tennessee enacted the Butler Act, named for its principal proponent, John Washington Butler. The act prohibited "any teacher in any of the Universities, Normals and all other public schools of the State which are supported in whole or in part by the public school funds of the State, to teach any theory that denies the story of the Divine Creation of man as taught in the bible, and to teach instead that man has descended from a lower order of animals." The penalty for violating the act was a fine of from $100 to $500. In signing the act into law on March 21, 1925, Governor Austin Peay described the act as "a distinct protest against an irreligious tendency to exalt so-called science, and deny the Bible in some schools and quarters. . . ."[1]

John Scopes, a biology teacher in Dayton, Tennessee, was recruited by the American Civil Liberties Union to challenge the act. Scopes agreed and, after teaching evolution to his class from one of the main biology texts, was charged with violating the act. William Jennings Bryan then volunteered to help the state of Tennessee in prosecuting Scopes, an offer that was eagerly accepted. The ACLU, in turn, accepted the pro bono (free) services of Clarence Darrow, perhaps the most famous defense lawyer in American history, to defend Scopes.[2]

The Scopes trial, also dubbed the Monkey trial, attracted national attention, pitting the greatest orator against the greatest lawyer in one of the most public and dramatic issues of the day. The judge allowed the trial to descend into a struggle between the Biblical version of creation against Darwin's theory, between faith and science. It was, according to one historian, "a case of fundamentalism versus Modernism, theological truth versus scientific truth, literal versus liberal interpretation of the Bible, Genesis versus Darwin. . . ."[3] From the beginning, the trial was to be but a predicate for an appeal to the United States Supreme Court, challenging the constitutionality of the antievolution law as violative of the First Amendment religion guarantees. At the end of the trial, Darrow asked the jury to convict his client in order to allow an appeal. They did—in nine minutes.

To get to the Supreme Court, Scopes had first to appeal to the Tennessee Supreme Court, which was expected promptly to sustain the constitutionality of the Butler Act and affirm Scopes's conviction. But fate dealt Darrow and the ACLU a different hand. The Tennessee Supreme Court concluded that the act was constitutional, but it reversed Scopes's conviction on a technicality, thus making any further appeal of the case to the United States Supreme Court impossible.

William Jennings Bryan died shortly after the Scopes trial, and with his death the fervor of the antievolution crusade also died. Other states would still enact antievolution laws, including Arkansas in 1928, but it would not be until forty

---

1. Ray Ginger, *Six Days or Forever?* Tennessee v. John Thomas Scopes 7 (1958).

2. Edward J. Larson, *Summer for the Gods: The Scopes Trial and America's Continuing Debate Over Science and Religion* 72 (1997).

3. Sheldon N. Grebstein ed., *Monkey Trial:* The State of Tennessee v. John Thomas Scopes x (1960).

years later that another challenge to the laws would be launched—this time in Arkansas, and not by the ACLU, but by the Arkansas Education Association. Susan Epperson, a biology teacher at Little Rock Central High School, would bring the test case, the objective of which would not be to put Genesis or Darwin on trial, but rather to remove the cloud of an unenforced, and largely unobeyed, criminal law prohibiting teachers in state-supported schools or universities "to teach the theory or doctrine that mankind ascended or descended from a lower order of animals," or "to adopt or use in any such institution a textbook that teaches" the theory.[4] The Arkansas act was adopted by voter initiative, the first initiative act in Arkansas history. The initiative process had been needed because, in the wake of the Scopes trial, the legislature was unwilling (though by the slimmest of margins) to enact a law similar to Tennessee's.

Susan Epperson recounted her experience in an interview with Ray Moore, editor of *The American Biology Teacher,* in 1998.[5]

Question: How did your case begin?

Susan Epperson: I was approached at school one day in the early fall of 1965 by Mrs. Virginia Minor, a fellow teacher at Central representing the Arkansas Education Association [AEA], who asked if I might be interested in being . . . a plaintiff to challenge the constitutionality of the law. . . . I didn't fully understand what they had in mind, but I said I might be interested. When I went home and mentioned it to my husband, he said "Do it!"

A week or two later, I met with Mrs. Minor; Mr. Eugene Warren, the AEA lawyer; and Mr. Forrest Rozzell, Executive Secretary of the AEA, to read a preliminary brief. It was five pages long. Mr. Warren was always careful to explain things to me throughout the process, since legal proceedings were pretty foreign to me. . . . Reading the brief, I saw that it expressed my own thoughts about the situation, and the only reason I could think of for not "signing on" was fear of the controversy and the publicity I knew would come. Up until that day, it had never occurred to me there might be anything I could do to bring about change.

Question: Were you teaching about evolution in your class?

Susan Epperson: Yes, in the sense that any discussion about different phyla and species and everything in-between includes a discussion of their relatedness. Many teachers ignored the law . . . , but others in some places were definitely unable to teach about evolution.

---

4. Initiated Act No. 1, Arkansas Acts 1929.

5. "Editorial: Thanking Susan Epperson," 60 *American Biology Teacher* 642–46 (Nov./Dec. 1998).

I taught evolution near the end of the year. . . . I didn't see how I could teach biology properly without including evolution, so I was faced with the very dilemma outlined in Mr. Warren's brief. I wanted to obey all laws. I also wanted to teach all the important concepts in biology. . . .

Mr. Warren called me early in December to say he was going to file the brief at the courthouse. Knowing there would probably be a story in the paper the next day, I went to my principal, Mr. Harry Carter, to let him know what one of his teachers was up to! He was completely supportive and told me to contact him immediately if I had trouble from anyone in the building. I greatly appreciated that. I was still afraid of the publicity.

Question: How did people respond when you filed the complaint?

Susan Epperson: Most were supportive. Our pastor, a large man, phoned and offered to be my personal bodyguard! Both positive and negative letters came in the mail, some including religious tracts and pamphlets.

Question: The trial, the first one, finally started. It was on April Fools' Day, 1966.

Susan Epperson: Yes. What a day for a trial! In the fall, Mr. Warren had thought this could be handled just by the lawyers, but the State Attorney General wanted to have a trial, and so I got to testify. Not exactly what I had expected when I signed the brief!

Attorney General Bruce Bennett defended the law for the state. He seemed to want to make the trial into a big publicity vehicle. He said that he had witnesses to disprove the validity of evolution and he was ready for a long trial, with many witnesses to testify about how evolution was contrary to the Bible. Mr. Warren, on the other hand, wanted to stick to issues about the law itself, its wording, and whether it was constitutional. . . . We were challenging the law, not religious or scientific ideas.

I was on the stand less than an hour. Mr. Bennett asked about my religious beliefs but Mr. Warren objected and was sustained. At one point Mr. Bennett asked if I had heard of "Nitschky's theory of evolution." I thought he might be referring to the German Philosopher Friedrich Nietzsche, but I didn't know about any such theory anyway. I asked if he would spell "Nitschky" for me. I think Mr. Warren objected at that point. On the next day, the *Gazette* wondered, tongue-in-cheek, if perhaps Mr. Bennett had been referring to the Green Bay Packers' linebacker, Ray Nitsky!

Mr. Warren consistently objected whenever Mr. Bennett tried to ask witnesses about religious beliefs, and judge Murray Reed sustained Warren's objections. After a time, it became clear that Mr. Bennett was running out of questions. I remember seeing him flipping through pages, as if wondering, "What do I do now?" With Judge Reed upholding Warren's objections, the argument was kept on track and the hearing was concluded that same day. The AEA was not attempting to prove or disprove evolution; we were merely trying to determine whether the state had the right to deny our right to teach it.

In May 1966, Judge Reed issued his decision in Susan Epperson's favor. The state promptly appealed to the Arkansas Supreme Court. A year later, in June 1967, without having held any hearing or oral argument, the Arkansas Supreme Court reversed Judge Reed and upheld the Arkansas law. The opinion was, to put it lightly, terse and completely unenlightening—a mere two sentences signed per curiam (for the court) with no justice's name attached to it.

Per curiam.[6]

Upon the principal issue, that of constitutionality, the court holds that Initiated Measure No. 1 of 1928 is a valid exercise of the state's power to specify the curriculum in its public schools. The court expresses no opinion on the question whether the Act prohibits any explanation of the theory of evolution or merely prohibits teaching that the theory is true; the answer not being necessary to a decision in the case, and the issue not having been raised.

The decree is reversed and the cause dismissed.

Ward, J., concurs. I agree with the first sentence in the majority opinion. To my mind, the rest of the opinion beclouds the clear announcement made in the first sentence.

Brown, J., dissents [without opinion].

Susan Epperson then appealed her case to the Supreme Court of the United States, which agreed to hear the case and set it down for oral argument on October 16, 1968. By that time, Bennett, the Arkansas Attorney General, had lost re-election in Arkansas. Oral argument would thus be between Eugene Warren and Don Langston, an assistant attorney general under the newly elected attorney general who, it appears from Langston's argument, was less than fully enthusiastic in his support of the Arkansas law.

The Supreme Court that heard the argument in the *Epperson* case was the full Warren Court in its last term before the retirement of Earl Warren. Chief Justice Warren had led the Court through a period of revolutionary change between 1953 and 1969. He was followed, in order of seniority, by Justice Hugo Black, appointed in 1937; William Douglas, appointed in 1939; John Marshall Harlan, appointed in 1955; William Brennan, appointed in 1956; Potter Stew-

---

6. *State v. Epperson,* 416 S.W.2d 322, 242 Ark. 922 (Ark. 1967).

art, appointed in 1958; Byron White, appointed in 1962; Abe Fortas, appointed in 1965; and Thurgood Marshall, appointed in 1967. Politics aside, it was one of the best Courts ever assembled, in terms of pure intellect.

Chief Justice Warren called on Eugene Warren to begin the argument.

Mr. Warren: Mr. Chief Justice, may it please the Court:

> This case involves the constitutionality of the Arkansas Anti-Evolution Law. Mrs. Susan Epperson, a teacher, and H. H. Blanchard,[7] the father of two would-be learners, challenged the constitutionality of the initiated act 1–F-1926, which was the so-called Monkey Bill or the Anti-Evolution Law.
>
> The challenge was based upon . . . the freedom of speech, the freedom to [speak] and to learn, and the . . . freedom of religion, the question of the establishment clause of the First Amendment.
>
> We have briefed these points as well as we possibly can. We have the benefit of supporting briefs of amicus [curiae]. . . . I shall not burden or impose on the time or the patience of this Court to argue to any great extent the question of the First Amendment freedoms, but I would like to discuss with emphasis, greater emphasis than in our brief, the question of failure of the Act to meet the permissible statutory vagueness [requirements] of the due process clause.

In most cases this would be a treacherous, if not foolish, strategy, for Warren is relying on his briefs to address the First Amendment questions that are at the heart of the case, choosing instead to argue that, independent of the religion clause arguments, the statute is too vague for anyone to understand what behavior is criminal and what is not. The Constitution does not permit such statutes to be applied, as they are unfair to the persons subject to their criminal penalties, and they confer too much discretion on the state and the prosecutor in deciding when and against whom to bring criminal charges.

In electing to follow the strategy of avoiding the religion guarantee questions (unless asked about them by the Court), Warren is manifesting great confidence that he will prevail on those issues—indeed, he is implying that the questions are open and shut, and the Arkansas law is clearly constitutionally invalid. In this, his confidence turns out to be well placed, as we will see.

But in fact the religion clause issues are anything but open and shut: the result might be clear, but the exact reasoning in support of it is very elusive and

7. Blanchard, the parent of two students in Arkansas, also joined the lawsuit at the instance of the AEA, representing the interests of the students in learning about evolution.

tricky, as we will also see. Warren might, in fact, have known this, and decided, in light of the difficulty of explaining the law's unconstitutionality under the establishment clause, that he would give the Court an alternative approach that might avoid those problems. This is likely the reason he chose to place his emphasis in oral argument on vagueness and the due process guarantee rather than separation of church and state under the establishment clause.

Mr. Warren (continuing): From the time that this act was . . . adopted, teachers in Arkansas . . . have been and are genuinely confused and concerned, uncertain as to whether or not the language of the act which forbids the teacher to teach the theory or doctrine that man ascended or descended from a lower form of animal . . . , forbids the teacher to discuss the matter or permit . . . a classroom discussion of the theory, or whether the actual meaning of the act was that the teacher could not teach that the [basis for the] theory had been established or [that] it was true. Mrs. Epperson testified that she did not wish to teach that the theory was true, but simply to explain [it] because [it is] contained in the chapter of the biology book that had been furnished by the local school district. As I understand it, there simply is no biology textbook that . . . doesn't have some reference or some explanation of the theory of the evolution of man.

Judge Reed, the trial judge, commented on [the uncertainty about] the question of whether or not the language of the act permitted a discussion of [evolution in addition to] teaching that the theory is true. We devoted 12 pages in our brief to the Arkansas Supreme Court to a discussion of statutory vagueness . . . , yet the Supreme Court of Arkansas in a two-line opinion held that [the act] was a valid exercise of the power of the state to control the curriculum of the schools.

Question: [T]his statute, as I read it, says that it is unlawful to teach in any university, college, normal public school, and so forth. If it . . . said that it is unlawful to teach children in primary grades one through six [about evolution], would you take the same position under the First Amendment?

Mr. Warren: I would take the same position. . . . I take the position that the [curriculum] of the public schools, even in the elementary grades, is not a matter for ballot, but a matter for the proper education officers.

This is a pretty extreme position for Warren to take in the name of teachers' First Amendment rights, and it is one that he didn't need to take. The problem with his view is that state legislatures specify a great deal of detail about curricula in the compulsory education laws, and then the state education agencies reduce that to even greater detail. So saying that evolution can't be taught in the first six grades is not really all that different from the state saying (as one Justice noted) that a theory of racial inferiority and difference should not be taught. The slipperiness of the First Amendment arguments—here a free speech rather than establishment clause argument—is perhaps one reason that Warren elected to focus on the vagueness argument. And it is to that argument that he promptly tries to return the Court's attention.

Question: So you don't think any lines can be drawn at all depending upon the level of the education, primary versus high school?

Mr. Warren: I must say that I believe that these are matters for educators and not for the ballot. But to go back, when this case was decided by the Supreme Court of Arkansas, [the Court] made the statement in the second line [of its opinion] that we do not decide whether the act forbids the discussion or explanation of the theory or forbids [only teaching that] the theory is true. This in itself condemns the act. It certainly makes it vague. [With] a penal act . . . where conviction requires the dismissal of the teacher from her . . . job, the teacher shouldn't be required to take this gamble.

Question: Is it also a fine?

Mr. Warren: A $500 fine.

Question: Has there been any prosecution under the statute?

Mr. Warren: To my knowledge, there has not been. There have been threats of prosecution. There have been some cases started but I don't think they were ever concluded.

Question: It is evident there is not much danger in the convictions.

Mr. Warren: I don't know, Mr. Justice Black. I can't say there was any danger or not. There was a lot of uncertainty and a lot of fright. . . . In a number of districts in Arkansas, the subject of biology is not even taught. In other districts . . . , because the biology books do have chapters [on evolution], when the teacher reaches the chapter the teacher simply skips it.

[Some teachers apparently announce] that the reading of the chapter is illegal, [perhaps knowing that] the children probably run and read it and get more from that chapter than any other chapter in the book.

The act also forbids the teacher to use a textbook in which the theory is [discussed]. . . . If the act has that sort of meaning, then that means that every school has got to rid its library of all of these books. That's just plain ridiculous. That is book burning at its worst.

[A] teacher couldn't refer a student to the dictionary for fear that the student inadvertently might turn to the page that had the explanation of evolution on it, and then the teacher is subject to dismissal from her position.

We say that the act is clearly vague, clearly unconstitutional.

With that, Warren sat down, reserving the remainder of his time for rebuttal if needed. He had used only about half of the time allotted for his argument. He had managed to stay relatively clear of the substantive constitutional grounds on which his briefs claimed that the law was invalid. He was asked about the free speech argument—that prohibiting the teaching of evolution violated the free speech of the teachers—and he promptly got into trouble. Surely, the Justices' questions asked, teachers are not free to teach whatever they want—math in English class, racial stereotypes to impressionable students. The state and the school boards have much authority even on these particularized matters. As we will see, the establishment clause argument and its scope raise nettlesome questions, too, including the countervailing argument that the fundamentalist parents and students who find evolution upsetting and undermining of their religious beliefs could claim that they are entitled to be free of exposure to the theory. In *Yoder* the Amish would make an argument based on these very premises and succeed. Warren, however, had managed completely to avoid the establishment clause and free exercise issues, perhaps for the best.

While Warren had been successful in his strategy, it probably wasn't all his doing. It seems likely that the Court had made up its mind about the case—that the Justices believed the law violated the establishment clause, and that they didn't need to ask any further about the question. The vagueness argument did interest them, and their questions may well have been attempts to see if the argument would really hold up and serve as a basis for a narrower decision in the *Epperson* case. In the end, though, the vagueness argument probably seemed too evanescent to the Court. It was as much a construct of the Arkansas Supreme Court's opinion, which "ventured no opinion on the act's meaning," as it was a true problem that would apply more generally to other cases. And if the Court were to reverse the Arkansas Supreme Court's opinion on vagueness grounds, there would be nothing to stop the Arkansas court from later construing the act in more specific terms that avoided vagueness but still violated the First Amendment religion guarantees. No good could come from having the case return to the United States Supreme Court if such a decision were rendered by the Arkansas court.

In this sense the Arkansas Supreme Court had been tricky when it simply declared the act valid, without explanation, and then refused to say what the act meant. Perhaps the Arkansas justices thought that they had trapped the Supreme Court into deciding only on vagueness grounds, which the Arkansas court could fix, foreclosing the Supreme Court from striking down the law on establishment clause grounds because the establishment clause argument depended on the meaning of the statute (did it just prohibit teaching the truth of evolution, in which case the law might be constitutional; or did it prohibit any mention of evolution, in which case it wouldn't be?), and the Arkansas court had refused to clarify its meaning.

Perhaps. But if this were their intention, they would be sadly mistaken. As we will see, the Supreme Court of the United States is not easily tricked, and it has no patience for lower courts that appear to be trying to pull a fast one.

The Chief Justice next called on Don Langston, assistant attorney general for Arkansas. Langston was on the staff of the new attorney general, and he wanted to take pains at the very outset of his argument to distance himself and his boss from the former attorney general and, indeed, from the case.

Mr. Langston: May it please the Court, I think it should be noted to start off with, that . . . this action was originated in 1965, prior to the administration of the [current] attorney general. . . . The present administration took over defense of this lawsuit after it was decided by the Supreme Court of Arkansas and was appealed to this court.

Question: What [is] the significance of that?

Mr. Langston: I was just giving you background, Your Honor.

Question: I thought you were telling us your administration doesn't like the statute.

Mr. Langston: No, I am not here prepared to say that, Your Honor.

Question: It might not be too late, you know.

Mr. Langston: [W]e have always interpreted [Arkansas law] to mean that we [must] defend the constitutionality of [Arkansas] statutes [when they are challenged in cases like this.]

I think it should also be noted . . . that the [district court, which found the statute unconstitutional,] filed and rendered what I would call a rather lengthy opinion for a trial court in Arkansas. We have the benefit of its reasoning in this Court.

However, the Supreme Court of Arkansas, which ordinarily and in almost all of its cases renders an opinion with reasons to back it up, has failed—I shouldn't say failed to—but has not filed an opinion which is usually written by one of its justices with reasoning for its decision. They merely issued a per curiam opinion in this case, which they very rarely do.

I don't know why they didn't file a written opinion with reasoning.

Question: Maybe they couldn't.

Mr. Langston: I have heard rumors to that effect.

Langston has disavowed support for the Arkansas Supreme Court's decision in the case; effectively disavowed support for the law by saying he is legally obliged to defend it and (implicitly) that he wouldn't do so otherwise;

applauded the district court judge's opinion striking the law down; and criticized the Arkansas Supreme Court's decision as simply a result based on no expressed reasoning at all. This is hardly a way to start an argument unless you are trying mightily to lose the case—which he probably was. His next statement makes this pretty clear, even if it weren't already.

Mr. Langston (continuing): Of course, the second sentence in the per curiam opinion [refused to clarify the law]. . . . If a case were brought to prosecute a teacher under this act, I would say that the opinion of the Supreme Court, and the [text of] the statute, would be interpreted to mean that to make a student aware of the theory, not to teach whether it was true or untrue, but just to teach that there was such a theory, would be grounds for prosecution under the statute; and the Supreme Court of Arkansas' opinion should be interpreted in that manner.

Question: Should be interpreted to the effect that it is a criminal offense for a teacher to make a student aware that there is such a theory?

Mr. Langston: That is correct, Your Honor. In our opinion "teach" means to make the student aware that there is such a theory, not whether it is true or untrue.

Question: So you think we should take the Arkansas statute as meaning that?

Mr. Langston: Yes, Your Honor, to mean that.

Question: As meaning that. . . . it would cover a teacher telling about Darwin as well as teaching th[at] Darwin was right?

Mr. Langston: That is correct. If Mrs. Epperson would tell her students that, "Here is Darwin's Theory, that man ascended or descended from a lower form of being," then I think she would be liable for prosecution.

Question: What are we to take to be the authoritative interpretation of the statute by the Supreme Court of Arkansas?

Mr. Langston: I think the first sentence of the opinion.

Question: That is, that it is a valid exercise of the state's power to specify the curriculum in the public schools?

Mr. Langston: Yes, Your Honor. They have not decided the question. . . .

Question: [A]re we to take this to mean that [all they have] said is that this statute is valid as regards the curriculum in the public schools meaning primary schools or does this mean that it is valid as regards teaching in any university, college, public school or other institution?

Mr. Langston: I think any tax[-supported] school in Arkansas would be covered.

Question: So public school here covers colleges and graduate schools?

Mr. Langston: Yes.

Two things need to be said about this exchange and Langston's argument. First, the United States Supreme Court cannot interpret the meaning of a state law; it can only judge the law's constitutionality in light of the meaning given the state statute by the highest state court. Since the Arkansas Supreme Court expressly refused to give the statute any clear meaning, either (1) there is no meaning and thus no law that the United States Supreme Court can judge under the Constitution; or (2) the meaning must be supplied by another authoritative source of Arkansas state law, which in this case is the attorney general. Langston is supplying the law's meaning in the absence of any decision by the Arkansas Supreme Court.

This leads to the second point, which is that Langston is suggesting a meaning of the law that is the broadest possible one: the law prohibits just mentioning Darwin's theory, and it applies not only to first graders, but to graduate students in college, too, including (presumably) graduate students in biology. Not only is this the broadest possible meaning, it is also the meaning most likely to lead to the law's invalidation under the religion guarantees of the First Amendment. Langston, in effect, has handed Eugene Warren the case on a silver platter.

The argument now turns to the state's purposes in enacting the law.

Question: What is the state interest you are protecting through this statute?

Mr. Langston: We feel that the state has a right to set the curriculum in its schools. That is our main point, Your Honor, that states can prescribe their curriculum in schools and not have chaos [in the schools].

Another point that could be made . . . is . . . that this is a religious neutrality act. . . . It could keep the discussion of the Darwin [Theory] versus the Bible Story out of the teachings in the public schools and keep them outside that forum, in private forums, and that could go to the orderly management of the Arkansas schools.

Question: On that theory, would you think that the state would provide that within its mathematical courses . . . it [could be made] illegal to mention or teach geometry?

Mr. Langston: Of course there is going to have to be a line drawn somewhere.

Question: That is our problem, too.

Mr. Langston: I might say that I am glad that your problem is not mine.

Question: Apparently, the Supreme Court of Arkansas felt the same way.

Mr. Langston: That could be another rumor, Your Honor.

Question: Since your Supreme Court has disposed of the lower court's opinion in two sentences, would you object to us disposing of that in one sentence?

Mr. Langston: As I state in my brief, it is a neutrality act and keeps [teachers] from discussing the Darwin Theory and its opposing theories in the schools.

Langston surely knows that the "state power over school curriculum" argument won't work. If it did, a state could require the teaching of racial hatred without any fear of constitutional scrutiny. It is hard to imagine that Langston doesn't also know that the "neutrality" law argument won't work either. The law only prohibits teaching Darwin's theory. It's as if he has come up with the weakest possible arguments on purpose—ones that can be defeated easily. The Justices, however, let him down lightly, as if they understand exactly what is happening.

Question: [The law] doesn't say anything about an opposing theory, does it?
Mr. Langston: No, it doesn't.
Question: It simply forbids the teaching of the Darwin Theory, doesn't it? Isn't this rather similar to the statute? What if Arkansas would forbid the theory that the world is round?
Mr. Langston: I would . . . hope that the Courts and the people would think that that would be an unreasonable encroachment.
Question: I appreciate your problem here. I appreciate the way you have presented it to us. . . . I thought a few minutes ago you said that a reason for preventing the teaching of the Darwin Theory was so that it would not collide with what I think you referred to as the Bible story—the literal reading of the book of Genesis. Does the state concede that that is the purpose of this prohibition? If it does, you run right into the question of the First Amendment, don't you?

The problem being alluded to is that if the purpose of the statute was to prevent a "collision" between the Darwin theory and the Genesis story in order to protect the Genesis story from that collision, the purpose would be a religious one. Under the Supreme Court's developing establishment clause doctrine, the First Amendment would strictly prohibit a religious purpose, and a law born of such a purpose would be invalid.

It should be said that the religious purpose test has always had significant problems. One reason is that a law enacted with a bad purpose can simply be reenacted with a good one, and if the terms of the law are otherwise constitutional, there is nothing that a court can do about the second law. So what's the value of a purpose test if the underlying law is valid? The only obvious value is to avoid having to explain the unconstitutionality of the underlying law. Second, it is saying too much to say that any law with a religious purpose—a purpose to aid or assist religion—is per se invalid. If a teacher excuses a student on a religious holy day out of respect for the student's religion, is the teacher acting unconstitutionally because his or her purpose is religious? If churches are given tax exemptions partly because they are religious institutions, is the exemption unconstitutional because its purpose is religious? And if so, couldn't the exemption simply be reenacted for the purpose of rewarding the good works and charitable activities of churches, rather than because of their religious character and value, making the purpose inquiry seem even less valid?

But Langston accepts, as he should have in 1968, the rule against religious purpose, and takes the position that the Arkansas law has no religious purpose. In this he is unsuccessful.

Mr. Langston: Yes, sir. Your Honor, we don't take th[e] position [that the law has a religious purpose.] . . . Of course, whenever I say "religious purpose" I mean that [the law] could keep the Bible story versus the Darwin Theory out of the schools and in the private forums between science and—

Question: So your Bible story could be discussed in the schools?

Mr. Langston: I suppose.

Question: In other words, as my brother [Justice] Stewart . . . suggested, there is no general prohibition, is there, against discussing how man came into being and there is no general prohibition so that theories such as and including the Bible, the literal reading of Genesis, could be discussed in the schools, except for the Darwin Theory. Is that right?

Mr. Langston: Evidently.

Question: In other words, out of that whole area of the origin of man, Arkansas has excised only a segment, that segment being the Darwin Theory, is that correct?

Mr. Langston: That is correct.

The Chief Justice: Thank you.

And with that, the oral argument in the case was over, and with it Arkansas' case. Warren wisely elected to make no rebuttal. After all, there was really very little in Langston's argument that he would wish to rebut.

It didn't take the Supreme Court long to write an opinion and issue a decision in the *Epperson* case. The opinion was more than one sentence long. But it was unanimous, with two Justices also concurring in separate opinions explaining their views a bit differently, though not disagreeing in the result. And it was issued in a brief time frame reserved largely for cases whose outcomes are pretty obvious from the beginning.

Mr. Justice *Fortas* delivered the opinion of the Court.

The antecedents of today's decision are many and unmistakable. They are rooted in the foundation soil of our Nation. They are fundamental to freedom. Government in our democracy, state and national, must be neutral in matters of religious theory, doctrine, and practice. It may not be hostile to any religion or to the advocacy of nonreligion; and it may not aid, foster, or promote one religion or religious theory against another or even against the militant opposite. The First Amendment mandates governmental neutrality between religion and religion, and between religion and nonreligion.

There is and can be no doubt that the First Amendment does not permit the State to require that teaching and learning must be tailored to the principles or prohibitions of any religious sect or dogma. . . . While study of religions and of the Bible from a literary and historic viewpoint, presented objectively as part of a secular program of education, need not collide with the First Amendment's prohibition, the State may not adopt programs or practices in its public schools or colleges which "aid or oppose" any religion. This prohibition is absolute. It forbids alike the preference of a religious doctrine or the prohibition of theory which is deemed antagonistic to a particular dogma. As Mr. Justice Clark stated . . . , "the state has no legitimate interest in protecting any or all religions from views distasteful to them."

It is much too late to argue that the State may impose upon the teachers in its schools any conditions that it chooses, however restrictive they may be of constitutional guarantees. In the present case, there can be no doubt that Arkansas has sought to prevent its teachers from discussing the theory of evolution because it is contrary to the belief of some that the Book of Genesis must be the exclusive source of doctrine as to the origin of man. No suggestion has been made that Arkansas' law may be justified by considerations of state policy other than the religious views of some of its citizens. It is clear that fundamentalist sectarian conviction was and is the law's reason for existence. Its antecedent, Tennessee's "monkey law," candidly stated its purpose: to make it unlawful "to teach any theory that denies the story of the Divine Creation of man as taught in the Bible, and to teach instead that man has descended from a lower order of animals." Perhaps the sensational publicity attendant upon the Scopes trial induced Arkansas to adopt less explicit language. It eliminated Tennessee's reference to "the story of the Divine Creation of man" as taught in the Bible, but there is no doubt that the motivation for the law was the same: to suppress the teaching of a theory which, it was thought, "denied" the divine creation of man.

Arkansas' law cannot be defended as an act of religious neutrality. Arkansas did not seek to excise from the curricula of its schools and universities all discussion of the origin of man. The law's effort was confined to an attempt to blot out a particular theory because of its supposed conflict with the Biblical account, literally read. Plainly, the law is contrary to the mandate of the First, and in violation of the Fourteenth, Amendment to the Constitution.

The judgment of the Supreme Court of Arkansas is reversed.

In thinking about the *Epperson* case and whether we agree with it, a number of things must be considered. The problem in the case, as we have noticed already, lies not so much in the result reached—though even there questions can be raised—but instead in the reasoning supporting the result and the implications of that reasoning for the religion guarantees in general. We will start with the possible reasons for the result reached by the Supreme Court, and then we will turn to some additional questions from the other direction, including specifically the free exercise claims that might have been made, and might be made in future cases.

There are a number of bases upon which the Court's decision might rest. The first, and the one the Court relied on expressly, is the state's purpose in enacting the law. Arkansas attempted to "prevent its teachers from discussing the theory of evolution because it is contrary to the belief of some that the Book of Genesis must be the exclusive source of doctrine as to the origin of man." The purpose, the Court said, necessarily follows from this: to enact "the religious views of some of its citizens. It is clear that fundamentalist sectarian conviction was and is the law's reason for existence. [T]he motivation for the law was . . . to suppress the teaching of a theory which, it was thought, 'denied' the divine creation of man."

Let us assume that the purpose identified by the Court was, indeed, the purpose of the law. What does purpose achieve as a basis for striking the law down under the establishment clause of the First Amendment? It basically says that the motives and intentions of those enacting the law—in this case all of the citizens of Arkansas who voted by initiative—were bad. If the motives were as described, they were bad: we shouldn't, as voters or legislators, try to enact our religious preferences into law at the expense of all others, including the beliefs of those who are not religious. This is what the religion guarantees, and the establishment clause in particular, are all about. But if a law is declared unconstitutional on the basis, and only on the basis, that those enacting it had a bad purpose, what is to prevent those same people, or their successors, from enacting the same law again—but this time with lots of window dressing that suggests a good purpose?

What if, for example, Arkansas reenacted the same law after the Supreme Court's decision, applying it only to primary and secondary schools, and basing it exclusively on the purpose of preventing discord and emotional harm to students? It is, after all, the addition of Darwin to the existing course of study that triggers the discord and distress, and such distress is clearly a tenable problem with which the state might be concerned. Whatever we might think of this purpose, it seems clear that it is not the forbidden purpose of enacting a religious preference into law. Indeed, it seems clear that it is not a religious motive or purpose at all, but one based on maintaining a calm learning environment free from stress. In this sense it is kind of like Sunday closing laws, which the Supreme Court has upheld on the ground that the purpose of such laws is not to enact the Christian day of rest into law, but instead just to have a day when everyone can have quiet, enjoy family activities, and recover from a stressful world of work. The fact that the assigned day falls on the mainline Christian day of worship is convenient, but in terms of purpose is simply accidental.

But is it so obvious, as the Court suggests, that the purpose was bad, that the law was intended to enact one religious view into law? Ascertaining the purpose of a law, as opposed to its effect, is tricky business. For the inquiry to make sense we must get into the minds and intentions of the lawmakers in order to see what they had in mind for the law—not in terms of personal motive, perhaps, but at least what they hoped the law would accomplish. How do we get into the mind of each legislator who votes on a law, voting perhaps for as many different reasons as there are legislators. Some might have religious reasons; others might have reasons of order and emotional tranquility; others might seek to prevent teachers from exceeding their role by entering the religion debate through Darwin's theory; and others might vote because they will, in exchange, get support for their own favorite piece of legislation. And so on. These difficulties in ascertaining purpose are infinitely more complicated with a referendum where all registered voters can vote. It may be, as the Court seemed to assume, that the Arkansas law, enacted in the wake of the Scopes trial, presents a clear enough picture that these problems of ascertaining purpose can be overcome. But it won't be quite so easy with most kinds of laws, like tax deductions for churches, Sunday closing laws, zoning laws, and the like. And even where purpose is clear and prohibited because it is religious, all that might be gained from striking the law down is a new version reenacted with a cleaned-up statement of purpose.

There is a final problem with purpose analysis in religion cases. The Court's condemnation of the law in *Epperson* reflected its general doctrine that a law with a religious purpose is, for that reason, unconstitutional. But does that really ring true? It may be that a purpose to enact one religious belief into law is bad because the establishment clause was intended to prohibit a government-established or -preferred religion. Enacting the truth of the Genesis account would certainly seem to fit that description. But is a religious purpose to assist all religions—say, a tax exemption for the value of housing which ministers receive (which has been in the IRS code for years)—the same as one discriminating against or in favor of only one religion? How about a law intended to accommodate the religious beliefs of only one religion—to bend the rules applied to everyone in order to adapt to that religion, or to create an exception for only one religion or even a single religious leaning, such as Christian fundamentalism? Is that a religious purpose, and therefore an unacceptable one? The Court's doctrine would suggest that the answer is yes, but common sense (and, indeed, the Court's own decisions) would suggest otherwise. Does a law intended to assist all religions, like the tax exemption for ministers, rabbis, and the like, really violate the purposes of the establishment clause? Does it threaten to create a state religion? Does it threaten religious liberty? Should the establishment clause be interpreted to prohibit laws that prefer religion to nonreligion? The Court has said so, in *Epperson* and in *Everson,* but do we really agree with that, at least in terms of the evils to which the establishment guarantee was directed and the fact, which the Court has acknowledged over and over, that "we are a religious people"?

If a religious purpose to assist all religions is not necessarily bad, then how about a purpose to assist only one religion—to accommodate to that religion's beliefs and practices? Such a law would clearly qualify as one with a religious purpose—assuming that purpose can ever be found. And it would be one that discriminates in favor of one religion, like the Monkey law in *Epperson.* But the same can be said about the decision of a public school teacher to excuse a Jewish student on Hanukkah or a Christian student on Good Friday. Indeed, the same can be said of the state law that exempts Old Order Amish from school beyond the eighth grade. How are these laws any different from the Monkey law in enacting a religious view into law? It is true that these examples do apply to everyone in the name of the religious few, like the law in *Epperson.* But what about the Christmas holiday in school? And even if the other examples, like the Amish exemption, are different from the *Epperson* case, as they surely are, does the difference have anything to do with purpose? If not, the purpose inquiry may be very hard to justify as a test under the establishment clause of the First Amendment.

But if not purpose, what criteria might be used under the establishment clause? The alternative to purpose, of course, is effect: what does the law say and do in fact, as opposed to whether its purpose is good or bad? The effect analysis has much to offer, for it judges the constitutionality of laws in real life and in terms of how they actually operate. Laws with a bad purpose but that don't operate to establish religion should be permissible. A moment of silence requirement at the beginning of the school day, intended to encourage prayer but which actually encourages all forms of religion, might be an example. Likewise, laws with a good purpose but that operate to establish religion should be prohibited. The Monkey law in Arkansas may be analyzed as precisely such a law—a law whose purpose was to prevent discord in primary education but whose effect was clearly, as the Court put it, to "suppress the teaching of a theory which, it was thought, 'denied' the divine creation of man" and thus violated the beliefs of a single, preferred, religion.

This, it seems at first glance, is a perfectly apt description of how the Arkansas law operated in fact. And a law that suppresses a religious view would clearly seem to violate the establishment clause. So why didn't the Supreme Court simply rest its decision on effect rather than purpose? Maybe the effect analysis, too, is more fraught with difficulties than it at first appears. Much of what we discussed in relation to purpose analysis would apply also to effect analysis. For example, a law that assists or encourages all religions over nonreligion (say, a tax exemption for "churches," broadly defined) may not, on reflection, always or even ever be inconsistent with the purposes of the establishment clause, for it does not tend toward *a* government-favored religion. Likewise, a law that has the effect of assisting one religion over others might not always be unconstitutional for that reason. Christmas holidays, excuses from school for religious worship, and exemption from high school for the Old Order Amish are all, according to the Supreme Court, examples whose effect prefers one religion to others, but that the Court has deemed consistent with the establishment clause. The same is true of using tax funds to reimburse bus transportation for students attending religious schools. If these laws are all permissible, then how is the effect of the Monkey law in Arkansas distinguishable from them?

Can we even say that the Monkey law singles out one religion for preferred treatment? The law—at least the cleaned-up Arkansas version—didn't say anything about religion. It just said no to Darwin. Was the effect of the law to enact a preferred religious view? Not directly. It seems difficult to say that the absence of Darwin has the effect of preferring Christian fundamentalism, any more than the absence of astronomy in grade school has the effect of preferring a religion premised on the earth being flat. Is a law that permits schools to "celebrate" Halloween a law that enacts Wicca as a preferred religious view? Not necessarily. What about a law prohibiting the celebration of Halloween? Is that a law whose effect is to, in the Court's words in *Epperson,* "suppress the teaching of a theory which 'affirms' the divine" nature of witchcraft, magic, sorcery, and witches, thus preferring all other religions? Can effect analysis really yield clear answers in such cases?

Maybe the key is that the Monkey law has the effect of discriminating *against* a religion rather than in favor of one. Such an argument would have to be indirect in nature. That is, prohibiting Darwin's theory isn't prohibiting a religion or religious view, for Darwin's theory isn't religion in itself. So the argument would have to be that by prohibiting Darwin the law effectively prohibits or discriminates *against* any religion that accepts or rests upon evolution, such as Judaism, liberal Christianity, Hinduism, Islam, and the like. But the causal chain from "no Darwin" to "no Islam," for example, seems too extended and weak for constitutional analysis under the establishment guarantee. It would require the invalidation of a wide array of laws, including those dealing with informed consent in medical care, inheritance, abortion, compulsory education, and on and on.

So what is left of purpose and effect analysis? Perhaps the Court's decision could be justified by the combination of purpose and effect: both the purpose and effect of the law tend, weakly when viewed separately but strongly when viewed in combination, to support the conclusion that fundamentalist Christianity was being preferred by government, and/or other religions and nonreligion were being suppressed. But if both elements of the test are weak, does their combination logically yield anything more reliable?

Perhaps the Court instead might explain that the law had the prohibited effect *in its context*—that is, in the context of its enactment after the Scopes trial; its enforcement in the South, the Bible Belt; its actual enforcement by the state. This, it can be argued, is a very compelling argument in 1926, or 1930, or even 1940, when fundamentalist Christianity was not just the majority but was the truly dominant religion in Arkansas; when Darwin was an evil icon; when the bitter memory of the Scopes trial was fresh and a teacher's fear of being run out of town if she or he taught Darwin was real and immediate. But this reasoning would suggest that in time, as with the Sunday closing laws that were originally enacted for religious purposes but later upheld, the taint of original purpose and initial effect would be removed. Was 1968—after forty-two years of failure to enforce the law, when teachers disregarded it at will, and when Christian fundamentalism was strong but no longer dominant—still too early for the initial effect to wear off? Was the law now just a narrow-minded and unenforced relic? Would its actual enforcement, if that ever happened, present a better opportunity to decide the establishment clause question? Perhaps the problem with the law, circa 1968, might better be seen in terms of academic freedom and state discrimination based on ideas in violation of the free speech guarantee of the First Amendment, rather than a violation of the establishment guarantee. Wouldn't a free speech government censorship theory be more coherent and acceptable than an establishment clause rule that can't easily be understood and that is so riddled with exceptions (for Amish, for holidays, for minister housing) that it can't withstand scrutiny?

Two final matters should be touched on before ending our survey of the *Epperson* case. Everything in the Court's opinion and in the oral argument and briefs concerns the establishment clause problem. Nothing is said about the free exercise guarantee. The Court picked the establishment clause as the basis for its decision, but why did it do so? One reason might be that the state didn't make a free exercise argument. But if that argument would have been controlling of the constitutionality of the law, the failure of the state to make it should lead not to a premature and ultimately faulty decision striking down the law, but instead, as Justice Black implied in his questions and stated in his concurring opinion, it should lead to dismissing the *Epperson* case for want of jurisdiction and awaiting a case that raises the proper issue.

The reason the Court didn't mention the free exercise clause, then, must be that the Justices didn't believe that a free exercise claim could be made. But that is not entirely clear. The free exercise argument would presumably be that the teaching of Darwin's theory was deeply offensive to the religious views of many parents and children in the schools, that it undermined their religious beliefs and training, and that it caused emotional distress to the children. Thus, to accommodate their freedom to exercise their religion without interference or penalty (harm) at the hands of the government, the children and parents are entitled either to an exemption from the study of evolution or to a general rule excluding evolution from the curriculum. The implications of such an argument, if accepted, are vast—no Halloween costumes in school, no enforcement of zoning laws on churches, no teaching of "values" in school. But the Court would accept this very argument just three years later in the *Yoder* case, where the harm was undermining religious beliefs and trauma from exposure to disruptive ideas during adolescence.

One might reply to this argument by observing that the Amish only got an exemption; every student didn't have to pay the price of their religious belief. This is a good point, but the Sunday closing laws, the Christmas holiday, and a tax to support bus transportation to religious schools, to pick but three examples, all operate just like the Monkey law by making everyone pay the price for the accommodation to the religious preferences of the few.

Another reply might be that the undermining of religious belief and the emotional distress arguments may work for grade school and, even, high school, but certainly not for college-age and graduate students. This is surely correct. We are all obliged, in a society devoted to individual freedom of belief, religion, speech, and press, to have a thickened skin as adults. So the

Arkansas law would probably fail to pass any free exercise test as applied to university and graduate students. But this would be a very different result than the Court actually reached in *Epperson,* where the law was declared unconstitutional in all its applications. The free exercise claim would at least allow the law's enforcement at the primary and perhaps secondary levels, and require the Court to acknowledge such a limitation in its voiding of the law so that the State might later consider a narrower and possibly constitutional alternative—and so that narrower laws already in effect in other states would not be subject to being wrongly declared unconstitutional in lower courts.

In the alternative, one might conclude that, since *Yoder* had not yet been decided, the *Reynolds* rule that the free exercise guarantee applies only to belief and expression, and not to conduct (education and teaching), still held sway. Thus, a free exercise claim based on the *act* of teaching would not be recognized. But by the time of *Epperson,* the Court had already rejected the belief–conduct distinction by extending a *Yoder*-type exception to Sabbatarians who would otherwise be required to work on Saturday under South Carolina's unemployment compensation law. So the basic free exercise argument had been accepted, and it would be only three years later that virtually the same Court would decide the *Yoder* case.

It is possible, in the end, that reasons of practical politics played a role in the *Epperson* decision. Perhaps the *Epperson* case was complicated enough already, and, given the Scopes trial, it was politically imperative that the Monkey law be stricken from the books. A free exercise decision on behalf of the Christian fundamentalists, the dominant religious group in Arkansas in 1926, would seem misplaced, if not downright distasteful. These may be good enough reasons for the Court simply to ignore the free exercise question, and in the process make the Court's decision cleaner and clearer and more absolute. We will, of course, never know the real reason(s), any more than we can know a law's true purpose.

The final and perhaps most important subject to be discussed is the significance of the statement at the end of the Court's opinion that "Arkansas' law cannot be defended as an act of religious neutrality. Arkansas did not seek to excise from the curricula of its schools and universities all discussion of the origin of man." This description of the law is surely correct if one accepts the religious effect of the law. What is important about the Court's statement, however, is that it implies that if the law were "neutral," the constitutional questions would be different and the law might be constitutional.

What might a neutral law look like? Most people—more accurately, most fundamentalist Christians—who read the opinion concluded that a law prohibiting all discussion or teaching of the origin of man would be constitutional. Even better yet would be a law that permitted the teaching of evolution *only if* the creation account, first dubbed "creation science" and now called "intelligent design," were also taught, for such a law would get the Genesis story *into* the curriculum under the credible heading of "science." No Genesis, no evolution; or else no nothing. It could not be said, many people concluded, that such a law had a purpose or effect that was religious, or that it discriminated for or against a religion, or even that it discriminated for religion and against nonreligion. This was because creationism was now to be understood as "creation science" or "intelligent design"—the study of the creation view and the scientific evidence supporting it or undermining evolution. So it was "science" and not religion. Furthermore, such a law would clearly be neutral, preferring neither account but instead simply requiring equal time for each.

It should have come as no surprise that, in light of the statement in *Epperson,* many states adopted such general laws, including Louisiana. Perhaps it will also not be surprising that when it finally confronted Louisiana's law, the Supreme Court declared it unconstitutional on grounds of its purpose—this time over the dissent of Chief Justice Rehnquist and Justice Scalia.[8] There was, the Court said, no valid secular purpose for the law, so that even if the effect of the law might not violate the establishment clause, it was still unconstitutional. Indeed, the Court was explicit in saying that its opinion did not prohibit the teaching of creationism or scientific alternatives to evolution, but only so long as the purpose in doing so was not religious. And the free exercise clause remained in the shadows, unmentioned.

The establishment clause theory of *Epperson* had prevailed again in the Louisiana case. But in acknowledging the possible validity of a similar law enacted for a proper purpose; in revealing the shortcomings of purpose analysis itself; and in failing to be able to explain why there was any problem with the actual operation of the law, the Court's opinion in the Louisiana case laid the foundation for the ultimate collapse of traditional establishment clause analysis and with it the high and impregnable "wall of separation between church and state." In the stories to come we will see what new ideas have emerged to replace the *Reynolds* and *Everson* principle of strict separation.

For now, all we can say is that confusion appears to reign.

As to the conflict between Darwin and Genesis, there is yet no clear winner.

8. *Edwards v. Aguillard,* 482 U.S. 578 (1987).

STORY 5

School Prayer

Engel v. Vitale, 370 U.S. 421 (1962)

The Supreme Court's decision in the school prayer case was felt widely and deeply in American life. It hit home in public schools in every corner of the country, and it hit hard: no more school-sponsored prayers read at the beginning of the day. Immediately following the decision and for months thereafter, the Court received a torrent of mail, virtually all of it critical.

Following the decision in late June 1962, the Reverend Billy Graham said, "God pity our country when we can no longer appeal to God for Help." "The Supreme Court," declared James A. Pike, Episcopal bishop of San Francisco, "has just deconsecrated the nation." The Vatican, more inscrutably, said, "The possible implications are such as to give rise to certain preoccupations."

As it turns out, the Court's decision was less wrong than the critics claimed, and less right than the supporters imagined.

* * *

Michael Engel, age 7; Naomi, David, and Judy Lichtenstein, ages 10, 12, and 15; Cynthia Lerner, age 7; Jeanne, David, and Wendy Lyons, ages 9, 11, and 13; and Joseph and Daniel Roth, ages 10 and 13, were all students in the public schools of Nassau County, New York. Their schools were the Searingtown School in Albertson and the Herricks Junior and Senior High Schools in New Hyde Park. In each of the schools the day was begun with the Pledge of Allegiance and salute to the flag of the United States, after which the teacher led the students in recitation of a prayer:

> Almighty God, we acknowledge our dependence on Thee, and we beg Thy blessings upon us, our parents, our teachers and our country.

Reciting the prayer was voluntary (though there was some question about whether the parents had actually been informed of that fact). Parents could request that their children be excused from the room while it was read. Few if any such requests were made, however. As one objecting mother explained it, she and others who shared her concerns did not seek to have their children excused because "we didn't want to make pariahs of them."[1]

The prayer was drafted and unanimously approved by the New York Board of Regents. It took the form not of a mandate to local schools, but of a recommendation to them. On November 30, 1951, the regents issued a statement entitled "The Regents' Statement on Moral and Spiritual Training in Schools."

> Our State Constitution opens with these solemn words: "We, the People of the State of New York, grateful to Almighty God for our Freedom, in order to secure its blessings, do establish this Constitution."
>
> We are convinced that this fundamental belief and dependence of the Americans—always a religious people—is the best security against the dangers of these difficult days. In our opinion, the securing of the peace and safety of our country and our State against such dangers points to the essentiality of teaching our children, as set forth in the Declaration of Independence, that Almighty God is their creator, and that by Him they have been endowed with their inalienable rights to life, liberty and the pursuit of happiness.
>
> We believe that at the commencement of each school day the Act of Allegiance to the Flag might well be joined with this act of reverence to God: "Almighty God, we acknowledge our dependence upon Thee, and we beg thy blessings upon us, our parents, our teachers and our country."
>
> * * *
>
> We believe that thus the school will fulfill its high function of supplementing the training of the home, ever intensifying in the child that love for God, for parents, and for home which is the mark of true character, training, and a sure guarantee of a country's welfare.

The regents' action seems not to have been a product of religious fervor or discontent, but instead of the cold war and the dangers of communism and its atheistic underpinnings—and, in the minds of many, of anti-Semitism. Confronting students "with the basic truth of their existence" and

1. "5 L.I. Parents Who Started Suit Hailed Decision," *New York Times*, June 26, 1962, at 17.

inspiring them "by the example of their ancestors," the regents declared, "is the best way of insuring that this Government and our way of life shall not perish from the earth."

It was not until July 8, 1958, however, that the regents' prayer, as it had come to be called, was adopted and mandated for use by the Board of Education of Union Free School District No. 9, Town of North Hempstead, New Hyde Park, Long Island, New York. Its recitation following the Pledge of Allegiance and salute to the flag was thus begun in the Searingtown School in Albertson and the Herricks Junior and Senior High Schools in the fall of 1958.

Acting on behalf of their children, Steven Engel, Daniel Lichtenstein, Monroe Lerner, Lenore Lyons, and Lawrence Roth objected to the prayer. They were a religiously diverse group: Steven Engel and his son, Michael, were Jewish, as were Daniel Lichtenstein and his children Naomi, David, and Judy; Monroe Lerner and his daughter were members of the Society for Ethical Culture; Lenore Lyons and her children Jeanne, David, and Wendy, were members of the Unitarian Church; and Lawrence Roth and his sons Joseph and Daniel were nonbelievers. Their objections to the prayer voiced to the school and the school board were, it appears, futile. It turns out that the prayer dispute was just a part of a larger controversy over religion in the New Hyde Park schools as well as other school districts in New York.

In 1957, the New Hyde Park School Board had approved, over the objection of parents—principally Jewish—the display of an "interdenominational" version of the Ten Commandments in each classroom.[2] But the state education commissioner promptly overruled the board because, among other concerns, the display of the commandments "stir[red] up dissension detrimental to the well-being of the school"[3] and produced "divisiveness, ill feeling and unwholesome controversy" in the community.[4]

In November 1958, the board adopted a policy prohibiting the discussion of Hanukkah in public schools if it interferes with the Christmas season. "While the Feast of Hanukkah is a religious and historical fact," the Board's policy explained, "it has no supersedence over countless other religious and historical events and should not be celebrated during the Christmas season in the public schools."[5] Understandably, a group of Jewish leaders in the community earnestly protested the policy, suggesting that "[t]he Board's

2. "School Can't Display Ten Commandments," *New York Times,* June 13, 1957, at 102.

3. *Id.*

4. "Protestant Council Opposes Bill to Let Schools Display Ten Commandments," *New York Times,* Mar. 7, 1958, at 24.

5. "Jews Protesting L.I. School Policy," *New York Times,* Nov. 27, 1958, at 31.

policy contains overtones of uncalled-for hostility to the Jewish residents of New Hyde Park."[6]

It was out of this soup of sometimes ugly religious controversy, mixed with patriotism and anticommunism, that Steven Engel, Daniel Lichtenstein, Monroe Lerner, Lenore Lyons, and Lawrence Roth made the decision to bring a lawsuit challenging the constitutionality of the prayer on grounds that it constituted a law "respecting the establishment of religion, and prohibiting the free exercise thereof." They brought their lawsuit in New York state courts. They lost in the trial court, but the judge did strengthen the procedures for excusing students, and restricted any attendant discussion of the prayer or of any students who excused themselves. The parents then appealed, but they lost their appeals in both of New York's appellate courts. Their last chance was an appeal to the United States Supreme Court, and they took it. The Supreme Court accepted their appeal and set the case down for oral argument on April 3, 1962. In the Supreme Court, the case bore the name of *Engel,* one of the parents, versus *Vitale,* the president of the board of education at the time the prayer was adopted.

* * *

The *Engel* case presented the Supreme Court with an issue that had never before been addressed. The case was but the opening salvo in a series of legal challenges to other practices, such as moments of silence in school, prayer at the beginning of legislative sessions, religious symbols in school and in public displays during the holidays, the teaching of creation science, the posting of the Ten Commandments in courthouses, and Congress's addition in the mid-1950s—in a climate of anticommunism, patriotic fervor, and perceived assault on Christian traditions—of the phrase "under God" in the Pledge of Allegiance.

The oral argument was held near the end of the Court's Term. It was an eight-Justice Court that heard the case. Justice Charles Whittaker, appointed by President Eisenhower in 1957, had just resigned, and Justice Byron White, nominated to fill Whittaker's seat by President Kennedy, had not yet been confirmed. The Chief Justice was Earl Warren, appointed in 1953 by President Eisenhower. The Associate Justices were Hugo Black, Felix Frankfurter, and William O. Douglas, all appointed by President Roosevelt; Tom Clark, appointed by President Truman; and John M. Harlan, William J. Brennan Jr., and Potter Stewart, appointed by President Eisenhower.

The lawyer for Steven Engel and the other plaintiffs challenging the prayer

---

6. *Id.*

was William J. Butler of New York. The lawyers representing, respectively, the board of education and a group of parents and students who supported the prayer were Bertram B. Daiker of New York and Porter R. Chandler, also of New York.

Chief Justice Warren called the case and invited Butler to begin.

Mr. Butler: Mr. Chief Justice, members of the Court:

[F]undamentally, [the] issue here . . . is the Government's role in the religious education of our youth through the public school system of our Nation. To what extent . . . can the State participate in the religious training of our youth? To what extent can it insert in its compulsory institutions prayers or religious observances?

Question: Reading a prayer which is specifically required to be read?

Mr. Butler: Yes, Your Honor, exactly.

Question: I thought you also [alluded to] the reasons for it.

Mr. Butler: Yes, Your Honor. [The regents' statement, in its express reference to religious traditions, to God's guidance, and to moral values] provides the Court with the motive behind the saying of the prayer; why it was introduced in the school system; and exactly what the state authority recommended was adopted by the local school board.

There is no doubt that the regents' motive, or purpose, in adopting the prayer is religious, especially if the motive is to sponsor or inculcate religion. But motive and purpose are tricky things in law. Let's assume that the regents adopted a perfectly valid policy, like the reading of a statement of moral beliefs like kindness and honesty and respect, but did so because the regents believed the statement would be conducive to inculcating religious values and belief in God. Should such a statement of belief be deemed unconstitutional simply because of the improper motives of its authors or the improper religious purpose that spawned it? If so, couldn't the regents just reenact the prayer, keeping their mouths shut about their motives and explaining the policy in acceptable nonreligious terms, and then argue that the statement of belief is now constitutional? On the other hand, let's assume that the regents adopted the very prayer involved in the *Engel* case, but could honestly claim that they did so without religious motive and for purposes of creating what they deemed a better educational atmosphere. Should the lack of religious motive or purpose make a difference on the prayer's constitutionality?

In the ensuing arguments, we will see repeated and often confusing references to the motive and purpose of the regents and their bearing on the constitutional questions presented in the case. We will also see reference to alternative approaches: the text or content of the prayer; the effect of the prayer on the students required (absent an excuse) to read it aloud; the manner of the prayer's use in the classroom; and the role of the government in authoring and leading the prayer (the regents, the teacher in the classroom). Each of these criteria for constitutionality, singly or in combination, may yield quite different results in the case. For example, is a moment of silence for meditation or prayer at each student's choosing unconstitutional because its poorly disguised motive and purpose is to facilitate and indeed tacitly endorse the children's religious beliefs? Or is it constitutional because the content of the exercise is not, literally speaking, religious, or because the government is not authoring a prayer or even leading one in the classroom? Or might it be unconstitutional because, despite the lack of overtly religious content, the students will perceive the exercise as encouraging them to pray or to believe in a higher power—God?

Because the *Engel* case is one of first impression to the Court, the Justices are concerned not only with the outcome for the parties to the case, but even more with the reasons given for the result. Can the decision be constitutionally tied to the text and purposes of the establishment and free exercise clauses? Can the Court live with the consequences its decision will produce for future cases, like moments of silence in school, prayer at graduations, and even the phrase "In God We Trust" on the nation's currency? The Justices are searching for an acceptable set of reasons for their decision, and the narrowest possible grounds on which to rest it.

Question: And did I understand you to say that the school board said that it adopted the prayer for the reasons that the Board of Regents had set down?

Mr. Butler: Yes. . . . [A]fter July 8, 1958, in response to the order of the board of education in this particular school district, this prayer was recited daily in the public schools of this district. Each day, after the school bell opened the school day, the students would salute the flag of the United States. After the salute to the flag, this prayer is said. Now, we think that the manner in which it's said is also important in this case, because the saying of the prayer, number one, is said in unison with all members of the class participating. Also, it's led by a teacher in the particular classroom where the prayer is being said. And on some occasions the teacher nominates . . . a child or a student in that particular class, to lead the saying of this prayer.

Question: The whole premise of your argument is that this prayer is teaching, isn't it?

Mr. Butler: No, the premise of our argument is that it is teaching . . . of religion in a public institution.

Question: Yes. Well, have you concluded your argument to demonstrate that this is the teaching of religion?

Mr. Butler: Well, I can only go back, one, to the statement of the Board of Regents, which [said] that the main function of the inclusion of this prayer in the public school system was, "the essentiality of teaching religion in the public schools."

Question: Well, didn't I understand you to say before that even if, on this record, it can't be said that that statement was incorporated in this board's resolution, you would still be arguing that on its face we must read the prayer as teaching religion?

Mr. Butler: Yes, Mr. Justice Brennan, there is no dispute between me and my friends [opposing counsel] as to whether or not this is the purpose of saying this prayer. It's agreed upon that the reason why this prayer is said every day in the public schools is to inculcate into the children a love of God and a respect for the Almighty. And there's just no question as to whether or not this religious activity is designed to bring the children into a religious activity which in the long run, my friends say, will preserve the religious and even Christian heritage of our society.

Question: Is that a bad thing?

Mr. Butler: No, Your Honor. I want to make it absolutely clear before this Court that I come here not as an antagonist of religion; that my clients are deeply religious people; that we come here in the firm belief that the best safety of religion in the United States, and freedom of religion, is to keep religion out of our public life and not to confound, as Roger Williams said, the civil with the religious. My clients say prayer is good. But what we say here is, it's the beginning of the end of religious freedom when religious activity such as this is incorporated into the public school system of the United States.

Butler has rested his argument heavily on the regents' religious purpose, yet in response to Justice Brennan he also claims that even without a religious purpose the prayer would be invalid. Justice Brennan is trying to get Butler to explain how that can be. If purpose is not dispositive of the case, then why is the prayer bad? Butler says that it's bad because the prayer constitutes "teaching religion" by the public schools, something the establishment clause pretty clearly prohibits (at least if it is "a" religion being taught). But Butler doesn't explain why the prayer constitutes "teaching." Would reading a prayer in a religion course be "teaching" religion?

More basically, should the Constitution prohibit "teaching" or "endorsing" religion—religiosity in general, but not one form of it? We are, after all, "a religious people," as the Court had said in an earlier case, and religion is undeniably a great—perhaps the primary—source of our collective moral values. Some of those values, of course, are good, like love and honesty. Some are bad, like "smiting" nonbelievers or condemning homosexuality, perhaps. The regents' prayer simply picks some of the good ones—those also most directly relevant to learning and education—and grounds them in religiosity, not Catholicism, Christianity, Judaism, Islam, Buddhism, or any other specific religion. Why shouldn't the regents be able to do that, assuming that's all they actually were doing?

The Court continues the question about teaching and begins a long line of questioning focused on the precise constitutional wrong, if any, the school board committed.

Question: If you don't persuade me that this is a form of teaching, does that end the problem for me? Why do you submit that this all turns on whether this is teaching? Do we have to decide that this is teaching in order to decide this case?

Mr. Butler: No, we do not.

Question: I thought you answered that it did.

Mr. Butler: No, I said that's one of the aspects of this case, Mr. Justice Frankfurter. [The] teaching of religion isn't the only religious activity that is prohibited by the First Amendment. An act of compelling someone to believe in a religious belief, I think, is also outlawed by the Constitution. [As you have written,] Mr. Justice Frankfurter . . . , an act compelling profession of allegiance to religion, no matter how subtly or tenuously promoted, is bad, but an act promoting good citizenship and national allegiance is within the domain of governmental authority. [I]f, [as we argue,] this prayer . . . is an act compelling profession of allegiance to a god, then that's an illegal activity, also barred by the First Amendment.

Question: Supposing, instead of this resolution providing for a prayer, that the resolution had said there shall be a ten-minute period of Bible reading led by the teacher. Would that be unconstitutional?

Mr. Butler: Mr. Justice, of course that's not . . . my case. To answer that question legally, as a lawyer, I would have to know a great deal more about the circumstances surrounding the reading of the Bible. But let's assume that just—

Question: That's all right, just assume my question.

Mr. Butler: Just assume that just the Bible reading was said in the public school system, ten verses of the Bible? Your Honor didn't mention which version, the King James version or the Douay version.

Question: Well, the King James version, for my question.

Mr. Butler: Well, I would say . . . that the saying of the King James version of the Bible [would be] unconstitutional as an attempt by the State to insert in its compulsory institutions an act of religious prayer.

Question: Well, that's a very different question.

Mr. Butler: Yes, Your Honor, a quite different question than this case. This case, it's not the Bible; it's the State making up the prayer.

Question: Suppose instead of reading the version of any one of these Bibles, there's a provision for five minutes of silence, silent meditation?

Mr. Butler: Did you add the word "meditation," Mr. Justice?

Question: Of silence, for purposes of meditation.

Mr. Butler: I can't—I don't see any argument for its unconstitutionality.

Question: That wouldn't bother you?

Mr. Butler: Not as you state it, Your Honor. I will reserve my right to inquire into any additional facts.

Question: Well, I didn't give any.

(Laughter)

Question: How about reading passages from the Koran?

Mr. Butler: I would definitely, without any hesitation, Mr. Justice Douglas, say that was unconstitutional.

Question: Why?

Mr. Butler: Because I think any religious activity, any attempt by the State to impose any religious view or to engage in any kind of religious activity, if the purpose of the saying of the prayer is to compel a belief in a religion—of course, I distinguish between teaching religion and teaching about religion. . . .

Question: I merely asked you the question "Why?" because you draw such an apparently quick distinction between that and reading another religious book called the Bible.

Mr. Butler: Well, if the purpose of the reading of the Bible is to inculcate into the children a belief in a religion, I think this is an activity on the part of the State that's barred by the First Amendment.

Butler returns to the question of purpose when challenged on whether reading from the Bible is "teaching" religion in violation of the establishment clause. This is not surprising, as purpose is his strong card, given the regents' own explanation for the prayer and the school board's admission that it required the prayer for the same purpose as the regents adopted it. But it is also increasingly clear that purpose alone will not work to answer the case. Butler has said as much by stating that even without purpose, the prayer would be unconstitutional in his view, even though he has yet to clearly explain that conclusion. If the Bible were read in the course of a class on the study of religion, would that be unconstitutional? If not, is that because its purpose is different and valid, or because its context suggests that the reading is part of teaching *about* religion, but not teaching religion? Isn't this really a question of manner and effect of the prayer, in context, rather than purpose? Should it matter, as Butler implied at one point, that the "prayer" was written by the State?

Question: Suppose this prayer invokes some other god besides the one it apparently invokes?

Mr. Butler: It would still be unconstitutional, I think. . . . This Court [has] said that theistic religions are only one kind of religion. There are also nontheistic religions. There are concepts, religious concepts, that don't have God as their ultimate goal. Buddhism, American Culture Society, Taoism, Human Secularism, all of those religions were mentioned by this Court . . . when it said that belief does not have to be in a theistic religion.

Question: That would include Zen, Zoroaster, [Bhagavad Gita], any of the books that are identified with religious movements—the Book of Mormon?

Mr. Butler: Yes. The reason, Mr. Justice Douglas, is a religious reason. If the purpose is to use a state authority to promote one religion, regardless of what it is, of course it's unconstitutional.

Again, Butler keeps coming back to purpose, qualifying all of his conclusions by that measure. But as we have noted, purpose is difficult to prove, and with a large body of decision makers, like a legislature, it is both impossible (everyone has a different reason for their vote) and inconceivable (are all of the legislators put on the stand to testify as to their motive or purpose?) to prove. In any event, the problem in the case is the students' recitation of the prayer before beginning classes, regardless of the purpose of the exercise. One might, of course, say that the purpose in such a setting is obvious. But that's not necessarily so. One might claim, as the regents did, that reciting the prayer is morally uplifting and puts students in the proper mood for learning, irrespective of the religious content. And what about a moment of silence for "meditation or prayer"? The Court would much later decide that the addition of "or prayer" at a later date to "meditation" violates the establishment clause, even though a benign, albeit technically "religious," purpose could easily be hypothesized: making sure teachers and students don't misinterpret "meditation" to exclude and prohibit prayer.

The Justices keep pressing Butler for alternatives to his "purpose" explanation.

Question: I don't suppose the fact that it's in the school makes it a distinctive problem, does it? Would the fact that it would be in the halls of the legislature be the same? Any public institution supported by tax funds? We have not decided whether compulsory prayer in the halls of Congress is constitutional.

Mr. Butler: No, it has not been decided by this Court.

Question: Is that case on its way here?

(Laughter)

Question: It could be.

Mr. Butler: If it is, Your Honor, I'm glad I'm not bringing it.

(Laughter)

Getting back to your original question, I do make a distinction between saying a prayer or an invocation; or "God save this honorable Court" or "In God We Trust," or so many other illustrations of our national background that take place in our society. Here there are two distinct differences. One is, of course, that the public school system is compulsory, that every child is obligated to go to school. The second is, of course, teaching. The environment in which it's said is a teaching environment, and when it's participated in directly by state officials, I think that makes no doubt in my mind, and I hope in yours, that this is an activity prohibited by the First Amendment.

Question: Supposing this resolution, this board resolution, had said there shall be a period, right after the flag salute, of affirmation of beliefs, that those who believed in God could assert it and assert it according to their own denominational methods, and that those who were disbelievers, agnostics, atheists, could assert their disaffirmation: Would that be unconstitutional?

Mr. Butler: Would this be said aloud?

Question: Yes, but everybody according to his own beliefs.

Mr. Butler: Yes, I think the argument was made in *McCollum*[7] that all [the school's alternative to study hall program] was doing was letting each [stu-

7. The *McCollum v. Board of Education* case involved a released-time program in public schools by which students would be excused from ordinary classes, or study halls, to attend religious instruction in a classroom in the public school. The Court declared the program unconstitutional, distinguishing it from an earlier case, *Zorach v. Clausen,* which upheld a released-time program under which the religious students left the school to attend instruction at a religious site.

dent] go to their own religious instruction and assert their own beliefs. This Court held, in a very strong opinion, eight to one, Mr. Justice Harlan, that the use of the public school itself, the physical use of the public school, to aid all religions, to aid all sectarian religions, even though the nonbeliever didn't have to go, was an illegal use of state property under the First Amendment. . . .

Why is prayer at the beginning of a legislative session different? On their face, Butler's two reasons don't hold up. Attendance is equally compulsory, at least for the legislators who are expected to attend but, like the students, may choose not to be present. And the traditional justification for the legislative invocation is "teaching"—an appeal to the higher values and purposes being sought in the legislative chamber.

And why, in contrast, is a program in which religious students can go to a room for religious training rather than study hall unconstitutional, as it was deemed by the Court in the *McCollum* case? Can it be, as Butler says, that the problem is simply the use of public buildings for a purely voluntary and separate religious activity? If so, the Supreme Court Clerk's invocation at the beginning of each session of "God Save this Honorable Court" would be questionable. More basically, Butler's explanation would prohibit the use of public buildings—schools, city-owned conference centers, and the like—by any group engaged in religious activity, like the Boy Scouts or a church group. Does the Constitution really require, in the name of preventing government establishment of religion, such a degree of hostility to religion?

Mr. Butler (continuing, turning to the Free Exercise Clause): On the free exercise side, we submit to the Court: Isn't this really compulsion? Would the little child, would "Johnny," leave the classroom; or would the parent be expected to ask the school system to excuse his child, who may be singled out as a nonconformist? And I must adopt Mr. Justice Frankfurter's thesis . . . that the law of imitation applies. Little children want to be with other little children. Very few parents, if any, would want to excuse their children from this kind of activity, which, it must be remembered, is accepted in the large majority by the community in which it's said. The effect would be to cast upon this child's mind some indelible mark, and I think that it can be sustained that, in effect, the children are coerced into saying this prayer, because of these reasons.

Butler's argument is that the nonconforming children are penalized for their different religious beliefs, or their nonreligious beliefs, when they are required to leave the room and suffer embarrassment and ridicule. If they choose instead to remain and recite the prayer, they are forced to profess a belief that they do not hold. Either way, their individual freedom to exercise their own religion free from government compulsion to the contrary is denied. The argument is intuitively strong, but in the end it must confront some very substantial hurdles. First, the prayer is, in fact, voluntary, even though the price for nonparticipation is high, especially for small children. Second, does Butler's argument suggest as well that students objecting to material presented in a course—like Buddhism in a religion class, or religious music in choir—can also prevent the teaching of Buddhism or the singing of "Ave Maria" under the free exercise guarantee?

Mr. Butler (continuing): Now, I would like to, for a few moments, address myself to the arguments of my friends. My friends make three major arguments. Their first argument is that, [as] Mr. Justice Douglas [wrote in the *Zorach*[8] case,] we are a religious nation whose institutions presuppose a Supreme Being; and that the State may act to accommodate religion; that the State should not be antagonistic toward religion; and that the duty of the State, under certain circumstances, is to promote or to safeguard the religious heritage of our nation. We say, of course, that this [reasoning] does not apply. [Here we have] direct participation by the State in the religious activity complained of. And we also say that . . . although . . . the State can cooperate in certain areas with religion, [it] cannot condone a religious activity where the State itself composes its own prayer, and then it's instituted in a compulsory institution.

The second argument my friends make is. . . . that this Court should follow *Barnette v. Board of Education,*[9] [where] the Pledge of Allegiance [was not stricken but the objecting Jehovah's Witnesses had a right to be excused from reciting the Pledge.] In other words, [our friends] say that here the prayers should be said, as long as the children are excused from saying it. Of course, the distinguishing fact between that case and our case is, as Mr. Justice Frankfurter said, [that] one is the act of allegiance or political faith and the other is an act of religion. One is barred by the Constitution, we suggest; the other is not so barred.

8. *Zorach* involved releasing public school students for instruction at their churches, not in the public school, which the Court judged constitutional.

9. The *Barnette* decision held that the free speech and religious liberty of Jehovah's Witness children were violated by a requirement that they say the Pledge of Allegiance. The saying of the Pledge was not stricken in schools, but an exception for those objecting on the basis of their belief, including religious belief, was required.

The third argument that my friends make is that the petitioners in this case are in the minority; that they do not represent a cross-section of the community. They boldly argue that the majority should control in this particular instance, and that this is a case where the minority is imposing its views upon the majority. Of course, our answer to that is simple. We say that the very purpose of the Constitution is to protect the minority against the majority, to protect the weak against the strong in matters of keeping separate forever the functions of the civil and the religious.

Finally, they make the argument that we do not object only to prayer, but that we object to God in general in public institutions, an argument which I cannot accept, nor can I let go without answering before this Court. My clients, four out of five, are deeply religious people. They come here, not as antagonists to religion. They come here not to destroy religion, but in the hope that they can persuade this Court, in its long traditions—from the Virginia Bill of Religious Liberty, from Madison's Remonstrance, down through the times—that it's best not to confound the civil with the religious. . . .

And . . . as to the nonbeliever, of course, we take the basic position that the rights of the nonbeliever are as important in constitutional history as the rights of the believer. The State can no more prefer one religion as against another than it can compel one to believe or not to believe. This is our [position].

Two points should be noted. First, Butler seems inconsistent in saying that the prayer is unconstitutional because it was written by the regents and instituted in a compulsory setting, yet he does "not object to God in general in public institutions." Second, he argues that the religion guarantees protect the nonbeliever just as much as the believer. Perhaps this should be so, but it is hardly obvious from the history of the First Amendment or from the text and purposes of the religion guarantees. If a public school decides to excuse believers from attendance on their religious holidays, would this mean that those who do not believe in a religion but, say, "worship" the philosopher John Locke, should be excused for a day to celebrate his work and ideas?

Question: Mr. Butler, earlier in your argument you started to say that each one of the parties had a different grievance about this prayer, and then you proceeded to say that they had one thing in common. You told us what that one thing was. I don't know if you ever did tell us what their separate individualized grievances were. . . . I was interested in this point, because you have now concluded by saying that, of your five clients, at least four of them are deeply religious people. I assume they believe in God, do they?

Mr. Butler: Well no, that isn't what I mean at all, Mr. Justice Stewart. One of our clients is an Ethical Culturist. [Another is] an agnostic, who does not believe in God. And then there are two of the Jewish faith who, of course, believe in God. And one who's a Unitarian, who believes in God.

Question: What is there in this prayer—so far as the complaint shows and without getting into a theological discussion—what is there in this prayer that people of the Jewish faith find objectionable?

Mr. Butler: [T]hey object, for instance, to the manner in which it's said. Orthodox Jews, Mr. Justice Stewart, pray only in the synagogue. What's more, they pray only with yarmulkes on. And what's more, they pray, some of them, facing East. [And the prayer is] also in English, and the Jews only believe you should pray in Hebrew.

Question: And a good many of the Catholics run the Catholic services in Latin.

Mr. Butler: Yes, Your Honor.

Question: One other question: . . . as I understand it, you have no objection, or at least have not objected, to the saying of the Pledge of Allegiance to the Flag.

Mr. Butler: No, I have no objection to that, Your Honor. I agree with Mr. Justice Frankfurter that that's an affirmation of a political utterance and not a religious utterance.

Question: Well, it now includes in its language the expression, "One Nation under God."

Mr. Butler: "Under God," yes. But it's a political . . . affirmation. The whole tenor of the utterance is not religious, whereas the utterance in this case is solely religious.

Question: The preposition "under" presupposes and implies a dependence upon a Supreme Being by this entire Nation, does it not?

Mr. Butler: Yes, that's correct. A dependence upon a God, Mr. Justice Stewart.

Question: Yes, a Supreme Being identified by the word "God."

Mr. Butler: Yes.

Question: Now, what's the difference between that and this prayer?

Mr. Butler: One is an affirmation of an allegiance to a country and the other is an act of religious faith.

Question: I don't think you've answered that, because—

Mr. Butler: . . . I don't think that the salute to the flag is an attempt by the State to insert into its compulsory institutions an act of religion. I think it's merely an act of political faith in the country. I draw that distinction.

Question: What do you do about that phrase? That's what you haven't answered, at least to my—

Mr. Butler: Well, if this Court would be willing to place a construction upon the salute to the flag as you have just suggested, that the purpose is to inculcate into the children a belief in God, and if that is the purpose, then I would have to suggest that there's an argument for unconstitutionality. But I don't think that.

Question: Well, what do you suggest that phrase means? "Under God," "One Nation under God"?

Mr. Butler: Well, . . . I can't interpret the minds of Congress when they put it in there—I think it means a manifestation of a Christian belief.

Question: It's not necessarily Christian, is it?

Mr. Butler: Well, I think it is, Your Honor. That's the basic reason behind it. But that would be subject to interpretation.

The Pledge of Allegiance is more of a problem than Butler is willing to admit, but he clearly wants to get past it quickly so as not to confuse his clients' very different claim—a state-composed and -led prayer in school—from a ceremonial statement. The problem is that Butler's purpose analysis won't easily work with the Pledge. After relying on descriptive terms like patriotic, affirmation of allegiance to a country, not to a God, Butler is forced to retreat to the purpose behind "under God." The problem with purpose is that "under God" was not in the original Pledge. It was added in the mid-1950s, and for reasons that can only be described as fostering a general belief in God. The legislative debates and reports in Congress belie any other conclusion as to purpose. While Butler denies that the Pledge is unconstitutional, his own reasoning can lead to no other conclusion.

Question: Now, [you argue that] the saying [of the prayer] . . . and the manner and setting in which it is said constitutes the teaching of religion. I want to know if anywhere there is any kind of clear statement: Who of your petitioners is or are offended by *what* is said, not the fact that it is said.

Mr. Butler: I see, Your Honor. I would like to make this distinction, and I think Your Honor has pointed to something which is important here. We don't claim, Mr. Justice Frankfurter, that the prayer is unconstitutional. A prayer, in our opinion, cannot be unconstitutional. There's no legal significance, no legal interpretation. All we say is—

Question: Let me interrupt. The whole—not the whole, but the basic problem with reference to the reading of the Bible, the question that Mr. Justice Harlan asked you about, turns on the fact that one of the important, one of the major religious beliefs in this country rejects the King James version, and therefore to subject children to the reading of the King James version, the New English Testament, is subjecting them to religious utterances contrary to their faith, because they have a different authorized version, namely the Catholic Bible. So that there is an objection in the Bible cases to the contents of what is said, as well as the fact of it. I now ask you whether there is any such allegation in this petition. I'm not even saying that—

Mr. Butler: You're going to the sectarianism of the prayer.

Question: Not sectarian. I'm not choosing here between different religious beliefs. The point of the Catholic parents in the Bible controversy is that their . . . authoritative, ecclesiastically ordained, official—if I may use that adjective—Bible is the Douay version, not the King James version, however beautiful that may be, and therefore you make Catholic children listen to formulations that they reject.

Mr. Butler: Correct. That's also true in our case. The prayer itself, Mr. Justice Frankfurter, is a theistic prayer, and we have two of our petitioners of nontheistic religions, and this is an attempt to force down the throats of believers in nondeistic religions a theistic prayer, and in that sense the content of the prayer is objectionable.

Question: How many of your petitioners are nondeists?

Mr. Butler: Two.

Question: All right then, you can speak for those two; but Mr. Engel isn't in that position.

Mr. Butler: Well, he says that the manner in which it's said—

Question: The manner doesn't matter.

Mr. Butler: I'm sorry, Your Honor. I can't say that the prayer itself is unconstitutional.

Butler first tries to explain his argument in terms of the Bible's content—theistic. Then he shifts to the manner of its presentation. What about purpose, upon which Butler has relied so heavily? Is he saying now that purpose is not the, or not the only, test? Or is he saying that content and manner are not themselves bad, but they reveal purpose, like killing someone after buying a gun is evidence of premeditation, a state of mind? Buying the gun shortly before shooting someone doesn't directly prove premeditation, but it is powerful circumstantial evidence of it. The Justices press him, trying to probe the relationship among purpose, manner (effect or interpretation), and content, as it goes to the fundamental question of why the prayer is unconstitutional. Butler, in response, kind of lumps them all together in a thick broth.

Mr. Butler: It has to be taken in the context in which it's used by the State, the manner in which it's said and how it is said and the whole factual pattern.

Question: Well, Mr. Butler, I'm still puzzled how much of your argument rests basically on the notion that this is teaching religion. You said earlier, I think, that—you answered me first that much of it did, and then later you withdrew that.

Mr. Butler: Well, I say that our argument is equally important for two reasons: One is that the prayer is religious teaching in the school.

Question: Well now, in that respect, how do you differentiate "God save the United States and this honorable Court"?

Mr. Butler: Because that's not the teaching of religion. That's not an attempt by the State to use its power and its assistance and its great authority—

Question: Because it's not in the schoolroom?

Mr. Butler: —to inculcate into children a teaching of religious concepts.

Question: Well, do we come back, basically, that your argument does rest on the proposition that this prayer is the teaching?

Mr. Butler: That's one item. That's one half. The other half, of course, Mr. Justice Brennan, is that this is a religious practice, and that is equally barred.

Question: Under the Free Exercise Clause?

Mr. Butler: Under the establishment clause of the First Amendment. This is a ritual, a prayer set in a ritual. It's the practice of religion, we say, in State-owned institutions, led by leaders of the State.

Question: Because it's the schools.

Mr. Butler: Because, in this particular instance—because it's the school, yes, Mr. Justice.

Question: And what you're saying, Mr. Butler, if I understand your argument: If there were schools in which concededly every member of the school was a communicant of the Episcopal Protestant Church, and the Lord's Prayer as sanctioned by that church were required to be uttered at a morning assembly, a devout Episcopalian parent could object to having that prayer said . . . although it's precisely the prayer that is uttered in that petitioner's church every Sunday morning?

Mr. Butler: Yes, Your Honor, because it violates the establishment side of the First Amendment.

Question: All right, now you get down to a real legal point.

How does the fact that the prayer is spoken in the public school fit in? Is it that the prayer is written by the state? Is it that the children have to say it, rather than just listen? Is it that the public school setting, with impressionable children, necessarily transforms the prayer, whoever writes it (including a prayer from the Bible), and whether read aloud or just listened to? If so, shouldn't it make a difference if the prayer is spoken in high school, or college, rather than to immature primary and secondary school students? Butler has earlier said that it would make no difference.

Perhaps the problem is government sponsorship itself, through the prayer's authorship by an arm of government (the regents of the state of New York) and its delivery by a government official (public school teacher). If so, why would this be a problem? Would it be because government itself is forbidden from active engagement in religious belief and religion, whatever the effect of the government's action? Even if all of the students subscribe to the prayer? Such a rule, while answering this case, would raise many questions. Isn't the placement of "In God We Trust" on coins equally an instance of government engagement in religion? Or "under God" in the Pledge of Allegiance, a phrase added for avowedly religious reasons in the cold war era of the 1950s? And if government involvement through writing and reading or leading the prayer is the problem, would it be permissible for a school simply to select students to lead the class in a prayer of their own choosing? Could students be required to offer the benediction at high school graduations, as long as the prayer is their own? These, of course, are real and difficult problems that the Court has had to face in the wake of the *Engel* case. We will have more to say about that later. For now, the Court presses the point with Butler one last time, without much satisfaction.

Question: One last question, Mr. Butler: Suppose this prayer in the schoolroom were "God save the United States and this schoolroom"?

Mr. Butler: It's Your Honor's interpretation that that is a prayer?

Question: It's not my interpretation of anything. I'm trying to find out your argument. Suppose they followed up the salute to the flag, instead of with this prayer, with the children in unison saying, "God save the United States and this school."

Mr. Butler: I would have to say, if, as in this case, the purpose is to inculcate into the children a love for God and to have the teaching of religion in the schools, that . . . it would be unconstitutional under the First Amendment.

Question: Then we come back that this is teaching religion.

Mr. Butler: No, I do not, Your Honor. I come back, one, to teaching religion; and two, that this goes further than your hypothetical question, in that it is a religious practice. It's an act of reverence to the God. It's man holding his hands together in an act of prayer. It's a religious ritual, a religious activity, which is also barred by the First Amendment; and I can't abandon that argument, Mr. Justice Brennan.

Question: I'm going to ask you a question that requires some candor on your part, and I conceive that it's the duty of lawyers to have candor about their position: Is it your position that our public schools, by virtue of our Constitution, are frankly secular institutions?

Mr. Butler: Absolutely yes. I say that our public . . . school system, the public school system can never be used by the State for religious purposes. I think that that avenue was wisely barred, too, by men of great foresight, in an attempt to protect religious freedom in the long run of us all.

Thank you, Mr. Chief Justice.

At the very end, the Justices have tried to push Butler to a consistent position—or at least one that is acceptable to the Court, and narrow: a prayer written by government and required to be recited by non-objecting students outside of regular classwork and in a public school is unconstitutional. Why is government authorship bad? How are public schools different? What is the substantive meaning of non-establishment in this setting? Is it the nature of the government's overt involvement in religious belief, irrespective of its purpose or manner, that is forbidden? Is it that the government's action, in its setting, has the effect on the participants—schoolchildren, not adults—of endorsing a religious belief, or religion over nonreligion? Or is it the government's purpose—everything is fine about the prayer and its presentation as long as the government's purpose is not to inculcate a religious belief in the participants, schoolchildren or adults, in a classroom or in city hall?

In the end, Butler fails to point the way. Instead, he throws most everything into the mix *except state authorship and the teacher's leading the students in prayer,* while always coming back to the inscrutable question of purpose or even the evanescent inquiry into effect.

The Court now turns to the arguments supporting the prayer. The first lawyer to argue is Bertram Daiker of New York, representing the school board.

Mr. Chief Justice Warren: Mr. Daiker?

Mr. Daiker: Mr. Chief Justice, and may it please the Court:

I am representing the Board of Education which adopted the resolution instituting the Regents' prayer as a part of the daily opening exercise. Mr. Chandler is. . . . representing a group of taxpayers and interested parents within the school district having children now attending there, who likewise feel that the prayer is sound and the saying of it is not unconstitutional.

We have heard the petitioners say that their test case rests primarily on whether religious teaching is involved. Is this a religious teaching? And here is where my friend and I depart in our thinking. Since the earliest days of this country, going back to the Mayflower Compact, the men who put the country together have publicly and repeatedly recognized the existence of a Supreme Being, a God. When, therefore, we say here this prayer, which Mr. Justice Frankfurter characterized as an avowal of faith, an avowal which recognizes that there is some Supreme power, some Supreme Being, we are proceeding fully in accord with the tradition and heritage which has been handed down to us.

The outlines of Daiker's argument are clear. His argument is that like "In God We Trust" on coins, the celebration of Thanksgiving and Christmas, and the many other appeals to God's guidance in the Court and in legislative halls, the regents' prayer is not "a religious teaching" but instead is a deeply traditional appeal to a higher power, a Supreme Being in its broadest, indeed metaphorical, sense, and an avowal of belief in that and that alone. While it is religious in some sense, it is dominantly historical and traditional in the American culture and public life. The prayer, Daiker will argue, is not an exercise of religion, but an accommodation to God's *historical* reality.

Mr. Daiker (continuing): We know, of course, that in the Declaration of Independence we have four references to the Creator, to the Supreme Being who gave us our inalienable rights. Our colonies, one by one, as they adopted a constitution, recognized the existence of an almighty God, a Supreme Being. And as of today, with our fifty states, [forty-nine] out of the fifty so recognize this [in their own Constitutions]. We . . . find their language quite comparable, one after another starting out, "We the people of the State of Arkansas, grateful to Almighty God for his blessings and acknowledging our dependence upon him. . . ." These are the constitutions which protect the rights of the citizens of the states, and in an effort to arrive at a prayer which would continually recognize that Supreme Being as part of the opening exercises at our schools, the words were lifted, if you will, from these preambles and constitutions, and made a part of this prayer. So we go back again to saying, "Almighty God, we acknowledge our dependence upon thee," as a paraphrasing of what appears in most of our state constitutions.

Now, we're not unfamiliar with the *McCollum* [in-school released-time] case and the *Everson* [school bus transportation] case, and we realize the reliance in those cases on the words "separation of church and State." We recognize also that in those cases the Court used language which said: The State and religion need not be hostile to each other, it need not be alien and unfriendly, but that there is an area of accommodation which can be made between the State and religion. This Court has said many times we are essentially a religious people.

But we are not trying here in the Herricks School District to teach religion, as my friend has characterized it. [If] the prayer used in the Herricks School District were paraphrased to meet the exact wording of the prayer of this Court, "God bless the United States and the Herricks School District," would this make it a religion?

And now we get down to . . . semantic[s], whether or not the recognition of a Supreme Being on a public occasion amounts to a religion, to "an establishment of religion." We have had our presidents, one after another, so recognize. President Kennedy in his January message concluded with words asking for God's blessing on the United States of America. This is something which comes from within us, but which is ingrained in us from the time we are children, from the time we start to learn that what rights we have emanated from God—a God, a Supreme Being. We are of varying faiths. We have, I presume, varying faiths on this Supreme Court. And yet, you find a common denominator in the prayer with which the Court starts.

We note that at the conclusion of the administration of the oath, the Clerk here says, "So help me God." And my friends seriously argue this is a religion or an establishment of religion. We say no.

Daiker's argument is ingenious. He doesn't deny that the regents' prayer is a prayer. He doesn't deny that it "teaches." He doesn't deny that the prayer is a purposeful act of government. He instead argues that the prayer teaches only a faith in a Supreme Being, or higher power; that this is not teaching a religion, but instead a faith at its most general or cosmic level; and that, while "religious," it represents a form of universal appeal to the guidance of some higher power that reflects the history and culture of the nation. It is a statement of faith or even religiosity in its spiritual sense, not an inculcation or government endorsement of any particular form of belief or institution of religion. It states a principle of spirituality and mystery that is universal to all humans. And to the extent that it is described as teaching religion, it amounts to a teaching of religiosity or spirituality.

Daiker argues that the establishment clause does not prevent government from encouraging spirituality or religiosity. It prohibits the establishment of *a* religion or set of religious beliefs as found in the tenets of particular institutional faiths. The traditions and history of America, however, do not require the government to be mute and hostile on the subject of religiosity. Instead, history and tradition are full of examples of government accommodating to religion, as with the provision of bus fare for children to attend religious schools, as long as government does not act in a manner that prefers one religion or one form of religion.

Daiker's argument thus sweeps away all of the problems of purpose, effect, manner, and the like. His test, in effect, is whether the prayer or appeal fits the historic and traditional model of universal appeal to a form of faith in a Supreme Being or power. One need only look to the text of a statement and the context of its use to answer this question.

More fundamentally, Daiker's argument sweeps away a central premise supporting separation of church and state, which is that government should be separate from religion, not just from preference or assistance to one religion. The separation argument is that religion—spirituality in Daiker's terminology—must occupy a separate and private realm from government. The secular and democratic state must be based on reason and universal rules of participation, not on convictions born of religious faith and exclusion of those who do not share it. The state should not intrude on matters of religious belief. Religious institutions and beliefs should not intrude upon policies of the secular state. The preservation of these separate realms keeps government and religion in their places and, just as important, preserves space for individual religious freedom to be fostered and preserved. Government support for religion or religiosity (but not for nonreligion), in other words, is as problematic for the separationist as is government support for one religion over another religion.

The distinction between separationism and Daiker's accommodationist and nonpreferentialist view is a fundamental one, but the Justices do not press Daiker on it, choosing instead to focus their questions on narrower and more practical problems.

Question: Mr. Daiker, I wonder if it would be any different in your mind if, instead of our marshal saying, "God bless this honorable Court," if we were to require every litigant and every lawyer who comes into this Court, before he receives any recognition from this Court, to deliver the prayer that your children in the schools deliver.

Mr. Daiker: I think [that would] come very close to . . . requiring . . . a religious test for public office, which this Court [has] said, certainly, was unconstitutional, barred by specific provisions [of the Constitution other than the First Amendment]. I [also] think you are now approaching the word "compulsion," and that has been used this morning many times by my adversary in his argument. He talked about the compulsory prayer in the Herricks School District. From the moment the prayer was instituted there was no compulsion.

Question: Do you not have compulsory education?

Mr. Daiker: You have compulsory education, but we're now—

Question: Do you have compulsory attendance?

Mr. Daiker: Yes, sir. We have compulsion on both. But we're now talking about the compulsion that the Chief Justice was referring to, of a litigant or a member of the bar appearing in this Court and being required, in effect, to profess a belief in God as a condition to appearing here. [T]he principals had been directed that no child was to be required to join in this prayer if he felt it was against his religion or his parents' wishes.

Question: May I ask you: Your answer to the Chief Justice, that if there were compulsion you would find this offensive to the Constitution?

Mr. Daiker: Yes, sir.

Question: Am I right, does that imply that the unobjectionability of the contents of the required prayer doesn't settle the matter? The mere fact that the prayer—that it expresses what you argue—is a common presupposition of our national life, doesn't save it, save its constitutionality, if added thereto is a compulsion to express that common faith of the nation, as you argue. Right?

Mr. Daiker: I would so agree, Mr. Justice.

By so answering, Daiker has undermined his own argument—unless the justification for a compulsion criterion comes from a different constitutional source than the establishment clause. If the prayer is simply an appeal to spirituality and therefore not an establishment of religion, then compulsion shouldn't matter. It's a perfectly valid statement of spirituality and an accommodation to the cultural value of a belief in a higher power. It's like an oath committing the oath-taker to honesty, fairness, compassion, respect for diversity of religious beliefs.

Daiker backs down from the logical implications of his argument by agreeing that requiring a lawyer before the Court to profess such a belief would be unconstitutional. He must explain why this is so, despite what he has said about the establishment clause. Is it because speech legally compelled by government violates his freedom of conscience protected by the free speech guarantee and the free exercise clause? If so, it wouldn't matter whether the compelled statement is religious or political or philosophical. It would only matter that the statement is voluntary. Or is a profession of religious belief, even one of the most general and universal variety, different from a profession of political allegiance, like an oath to support the Constitution? If so, when and why?

Question: So we have to go beyond merely whether the content offends anything?

Mr. Daiker: Correct. Because . . . [t]he prayer here as such is not unconstitutional. But if it is administered with compulsion, then we have an unconstitutional practice, which the courts will strike down—but we suggest to this Court, not by barring it or abolishing it . . . , but merely permitting those who do not find an accommodation between this and their own religious beliefs to remain silent or be excused.

Question: So from your point of view . . . , the case really gets down to the narrow question, or at least the limited question: Whether the circumstances under which this prayer was administered—if you can administer a prayer—was recited by the teacher in unison with the classroom, whether those circumstances differentiate it from [compulsion]? That's what the case gets down to?

Mr. Daiker: Right, sir.

Daiker is lucky at this point. Justice Black shifts focus of the questioning to the purpose of the prayer, allowing Daiker, for the moment at least, to avoid defining what he means by compulsion and why the children's natural inclination to conform wouldn't add up to compulsion.

Question: May I ask you one question?

Mr. Daiker: Mr. Justice Black?

Question: When you began your discussion, you referred to Mr. Justice Frankfurter's reference to this prayer as an avowal of faith. I gathered then that you agreed that it was, and I assume from what you are saying now that you do agree to it. Is that right?

Mr. Daiker: Yes, sir.

Question: Yes. Now, may I ask you this question, Mr. Daiker: Will you tell us, please, in your words, why or what the reasons were for having this prayer, as shown by the Board of Regents or by the school board or both?

Mr. Daiker: Basically, the Board of Regents—and I am using some of their language—was interested in promoting the belief in traditions, the belief in the moral and spiritual values which make up part of our national heritage.

Question: But you shy away from the word "religion." Was it the purpose of the Board to promote religion?

Mr. Daiker: I don't believe so. I think the purpose of the—

Question: Why do you say ethical purposes and things of that kind, but shy away from religion, when the entire wording of the prayer is in the words of religion?

Mr. Daiker: Well, I don't want to have the Court understand my words as saying that the board of education was trying to teach religion in the schools.

Question: Well, I know you want to keep away from that.

(Laughter)

Question: But what I'm trying to find out is, how you analyze the language of the Board of Regents, the action of the Board of Regents, the action of your school board, and the delivering of this prayer every morning, without getting to the question of religion.

Mr. Daiker: I don't think you can stay away from religion. So long as you have a prayer, there is a religious facet to it.

Question: Well, was that the purpose of the Board of Regents in promoting that in the schools?

Mr. Daiker: I don't believe their purpose was to promote religion as such. But they did—and they so stated—seek to promote a continuation of what they felt to be the traditions of this country, in which God is inevitably mentioned, and in which inevitably every document and every pronouncement recognizes that what we have, we got from God. They had no more desire to teach religion in schools—

Question: Do I fairly summarize, do I fairly understand the line of your position in the course of the colloquy that we've had these few minutes, that you say it isn't teaching religion to take for granted that which underlies our whole national life . . . ? Is that your position?

Mr. Daiker: That is my position, sir.

Question: Well, Mr. Daiker, as I understand Mr. Butler, neither he nor his clients object to any such prayers anyplace except in the public schools, where the children are compelled to come, and where they will be indoctrinated with the prayer as a matter of training, and where they will be held up to contempt or ridicule if they or their parents should want them to be excused, and pointed out as being different from the others.

Mr. Daiker: I lost your question when you got to the end of that.

Question: It got pretty involved, I guess.

Mr. Daiker: It did.

Question: Take it as far as you remember.

(Laughter)

Mr. Daiker: When we get back to the word "a religious practice," we refer the Court, for instance, to the language of our own court of appeals, which . . . [said]: Whenever people gather together in a group and utter a prayer, a recognition of the Almighty, as has been consistently done since the founding of the country hundreds of years ago, we don't find constitutional objections. How, then, can we say that prayer is all right on any public occasion in a State-paid-for building, with state employees, except in the school?

Daiker has made a good and generally clear argument. He was fortunate that the Justice couldn't recall all of his last, factually complex question, for if he had restated the question, Daiker would have had to explain what he meant by "compulsion," why the facts presented by young schoolchildren needing to avoid embarrassment and ridicule didn't amount to compulsion, and what the exact constitutional source of a noncompulsion, or voluntariness, requirement is. But Daiker did face right up to the fact that the prayer was religious. He argued that the nettlesome purpose, place, time, author, and effect distinctions on which Butler relied couldn't be justified in constitutional principle or on the basis of the text or its history. Without saying so in such terms, his is a tradition, collective values and habits, and "chill out" approach. Butler's approach would eliminate everything, including the Pledge. Daiker's approach would permit everything as long as it appeals only to a general and universal "God," and as long as it is not coercive. Lines would of course have to be drawn, but they could be drawn narrowly and on a case-by-case basis—such as distinguishing elementary school (governed by the "rule of imitation") from the secondary or high schools, where excusing objecting students might be sufficient.

Chief Justice Warren next calls on Porter Chandler of New York, who represents a group of non-objecting parents who want the daily prayer to continue.

Mr. Chandler: May it please the Court: My clients include three Jewish parents, seven Protestant parents of five separate denominations, one person of no religious affiliation whatever, and five Catholics. When this case started they had 37 children in the public school. [O]n the last count my clients now have 41 children in the public schools.

(Laughter)

Why are my clients here at all? They are here in the name of the free exercise of religion, if you want to put it that way. They are here because they feel very strongly that it is a deprivation of their children's right to share in our national heritage, and that it is a compulsory rewriting of our history in the fashion of George Orwell's *1984* to do what these petitioners are now seeking to do, namely, to eliminate all reference to God from the whole fabric of our public life and of our public educational system.

Question: Is that a correct statement, from our public life?

Mr. Chandler: Our public educational system, which is an important part of our public life. Mr. Butler at the start of his argument used one phrase which I wish to criticize. He spoke about this being an attempt by the State to introduce religious practices into public schools. It is nothing of the sort. The attack here is from the other direction. It is an attempt to drive out of the public education system practices which are long-established, venerated, and practiced without objection throughout the country from the very beginning. The practice of prayer in the public schools of New York, to be specific, goes back to 1837. According to figures cited in our brief, the practice either of prayer of some sort or another or Bible reading or hymn singing, or any two or three of them, is prevalent throughout the public schools of at least half the states of the Union.

The historical argument Chandler is making is, frankly, a bit dicey, especially given the history of the establishment clause, Madison's Remonstrance in Virginia, Thomas Jefferson's frequent statements objecting to religious references in public statements and ceremonies—objections, however, that Jefferson did not act upon when serving as president. Yet the fact is that prayers have been regularly given in most public schools from the beginning of public education, though not without generating great controversy, especially since urbanization and immigrant groups came to the country in the late nineteenth century. That history leaves a murkier impression than Chandler might have us believe.[10]

Question: Mr. Chandler, is there in your brief a reference to this history of prayers in New York public schools? As I have already indicated, I'm a product of them.

Mr. Chandler: Yes, Your Honor.

Question: We did have flag salute, I remember vividly. But I think I am quite clear that in my day in my public schools there wasn't prayer. I'm not saying that there isn't elsewhere, but—

Mr. Chandler: There is some reference to it—I was speaking of schools in New York State. New York City, I know—here's what is done in New York City right now, Your Honor: As an opening exercise, a religious exercise, if you will, every day in every public school in New York City they sing the last stanza of "America," which is a prayer and is intended and sung as such.

Question: The last stanza?

Mr. Chandler: The last stanza:

---

10. For a wonderful account of prayers in schools and the controversies, political and legal, that they have spawned from the early nineteenth century forward, see Joan Delfattore, *The Fourth R: Conflicts over Religion in America's Public Schools* (2004).

Our fathers' God, to thee, author of liberty, to thee we sing.
Long may our land be bright with freedom's holy light.
Protect us by thy might, great God our king.

That is as religious an exercise and as much of a prayer as anything here involved, and that is the practice in all the public schools in New York City. Let me come to the question that Mr. Justice Stewart raised, about the flag salute. The flag salute in 1954 had the words "under God" added to it, and the question was asked whether that had a religious connotation or was a religious exercise. And I say unequivocally, yes, and I say it on the authority of the House report which recommended those words. And the Pledge of Allegiance is in almost every public school throughout the country, and this is why the words "under God" are recited by school children in that pledge. This is what the House Committee said:

> Our American Government is founded on the concept of the individuality and the dignity of the human being. Underlying this concept is the belief that the human person is important because he was created by God and endowed by him with certain inalienable rights which no civil authority may usurp. The inclusion of God in our pledge would further acknowledge the dependence of our people and our government upon the moral directions of the Creator.

It would, in the view of the parents whom I represent, be a warping of our national heritage forcibly to rewrite the curriculum of every public school to excise everything that slants in that direction. Yet, nothing less than that is what my friends are now asking.

Question: Mr. Chandler, may I ask: Just what is the basis of your clients' objection, that it deprives their children of the right to have religious instruction in the schools?

Mr. Chandler: I wouldn't go that far, Your Honor.

Question: Well, you emphasize to us that some are Protestants and some are Catholics, some are Jews, and so forth. You put it all in a religious context. And then you tell us that your people are denied that. Now, is it because of religion?

Mr. Chandler: This is my position: That it is part of our national heritage to have this kind of thing, including the principles of the Declaration of Independence; and that, if a school board, having in mind local sentiment and responsive to local needs, feels that it is appropriate to include that sort of thing in the curriculum, it is a—I won't say a destruction, but—an impairment, an infringement of our children's rights to share in what we regard as our national heritage, to have that excluded on the suit of petitioners who . . . claim that this prayer is not particularly objectionable, and who have shown no compulsion and no coercion against themselves.

Question: But your clients, religious though they are, do not contend that if petitioner was to prevail that this would deny them of any religious—

Mr. Chandler: I think it would be a step in the direction—

Question: Beg your pardon?

Mr. Chandler: I think it would be a step in the direction of denying us a share in the religious heritage of the country which we feel is part of a proper educational system. That's the best answer I can give.

Question: You reject, then—you reject the suggestion that the school system for minor children must be kept on a wholly secular basis? Or do you say that it is a secular basis in any valid sense if it also takes for granted the religious foundations of our nation?

Mr. Chandler: I would take the latter, Your Honor. I would agree with Your Honor on that definition of "secular." "Secular" in the sense of excising every mention of God from our national history and from our education is not the kind of secularism that I think the First Amendment contemplated. I would take Your Honor's second definition, and accept it.

Question: Of course, the issue in this case isn't quite: The name or the appellation of "God" must never be allowed to be made in the public schools.

Mr. Chandler: This case, Your Honor, is not that?

Question: It's not that.

Mr. Chandler: My impression is that it is. My impression is that that's the claim of my opponents, and I should be interested and relieved if they were to say otherwise.

Question: Well, I had the idea from listening to Mr. Butler that—although he didn't say this—that, for instance, if the word "God" appeared in some poem in English, that they would have no objection to that, that that wouldn't—

Mr. Chandler: Oh, yes, that is quite true.

Question: It wouldn't be the practice of religion. But he objects to this because it's pinpointed at religious training.

Mr. Chandler: Well, is it religious training, I would ask Mr. Butler, to recite the words of the Declaration of Independence, or to say that all men are created equal and that they're endowed by their Creator with inalienable rights?

Question: Well, I understood him to say that he would not object to that.

Mr. Chandler: He would, I take it, object to reading such things as the constitution of New Jersey, which contain a definite acknowledgment of dependence on God.

Question: Now, do I understand your position to be that the problem immediately before us, the recitation of this prayer in the circumstances in which it is made, in the school in which it is being carried on, raises precisely the same question as though, in the classes—whatever they're called, government, current affairs—the teacher thought it desirable to read the constitution of the state of New York, including this preamble?

Mr. Chandler: Not exactly the same. It's exactly the same as if this prayer read, "Almighty God, we are grateful to you for our liberties," which is what the constitution says. And if, by a change of grammar, that prayer were said at the beginning of school, we would have precisely this case.

Question: Very well. The words of the preamble to the New York constitution of 18–whatever it is—

Mr. Chandler: The constitution of 1896, and copied from constitutions as far back as 1826.

Question: Do you say that in a class on government or political science, or whatever the appropriate label would be, dealing with the New York constitution, that to read that, the whole constitution, for that purpose in those circumstances, would raise the same questions—or rather, the case immediately before us raises the same questions as my hypothetical case?

Mr. Chandler: Almost the same. Thank you, Your Honor.

(Whereupon, argument in the above-entitled matter was adjourned.)

Chandler presented a very powerful argument. How can the prayer be distinguished from singing the last stanza of "God Bless America" each morning before school? It can't, he said, and the reason is historical and traditional and cultural, not religious. Chandler also soft-peddled the question of coercion, a somewhat logically inconsistent limit in light of his argument that the prayer was not "religious" in the sense that the Constitution uses that term. And he held his ground on the last set of questions, arguing that the regents' prayer—an educational exercise that was part of the program of the public schools and that taught history and tradition and values—was really no different from reading the opening sentences of the Declaration of Independence in a history class.

Chandler didn't, however, fully reveal his true colors. His view is neither separationist nor based on "neutrality" under the establishment guarantee. It is instead a view premised on accommodating to religion by laws and actions that are religious in purpose, but not sectarian in preference. Government can, in other words, encourage religion or religiosity over nonreligion because of the social and cultural benefits religion and religiosity yield to society (or to education); it just can't prefer one religion or religious belief to others. Government is not wholly secular. It is nonsectarian. This is a coherent but dramatically different view than had prevailed in the Court's establishment clause jurisprudence.

Good arguments, however, aren't necessarily winning arguments, as the outcome of a case rests not on which lawyer is most eloquent but on the judgment of the Justices, steeped in the text and history and purposes of the Constitution. One can imagine a Justice applauding a great argument, but then stepping back from the case a bit and, on reflection, saying, "This just isn't the right thing for government to do under the establishment clause." Logic isn't everything when it comes to interpreting the Constitution.

But one would hope, at least, that the necessarily separationist explanation for why it "just isn't the right thing" might be articulated. The facilitation or encouragement of individual religiosity is not a proper part of the government's role, the strict separationist would claim, lest the government become too actively involved in favoring certain kinds of beliefs by citizens (religious), and discouraging other (perhaps philosophical or ideological) types of belief. How far is it to move from government approval of religious beliefs over others to the government resorting to religious rather than secular justifications for its laws?

Unfortunately, the Supreme Court was no more anxious to address such underlying issues in its opinion than it had been to explore them in oral argument. Gone was the dissenting voice heard in the *Everson* case.

* * *

The Supreme Court's opinion in the *Engel* case was handed down at the very end of the Court's Term, on June 25, 1962. Justices Frankfurter, who would soon retire, and White, who had just been appointed to the Court, did not participate. Justice Douglas concurred on separate grounds, and Justice Stewart dissented. The Court's opinion thus reflected the view of five of the seven participating Justices, a majority of the full nine-member Court. Given the sensitivity of the case, a full majority of five was no doubt considered necessary to deciding the case in 1962 rather than (as with *Roe v. Wade,* the controversial abortion decision) holding the case over to the next Term of Court, when the full complement of nine Justices could participate.

The opinion was written by Justice Black, the author of the earlier *Everson* case that first set forth the strict separation view of the establishment clause and erected the wall of separation between church and state.

Mr. Justice *Black* delivered the opinion of the Court.

It is a matter of history that [the] very practice of establishing governmentally composed prayers for religious services was one of the reasons which caused many of our early colonists to leave England and seek religious freedom in America.

By the time of the adoption of the Constitution, our history shows that there was a widespread awareness among many Americans of the dangers of a union of Church and State. These people knew, some of them from bitter personal experience, that one of the greatest dangers to the freedom of the individual to worship in his own way lay in the Government's placing its official stamp of approval upon one particular kind of prayer or one particular form of religious services. . . . The Constitution was intended to avert a part of this danger by leaving the government of this country in the hands of the people rather than in the hands of any monarch. But this safeguard was not enough. Our Founders were no more willing to let the content of their prayers and their privilege of praying whenever they pleased be influenced by the ballot box than they were to let these vital matters of personal conscience depend upon the succession of monarchs. The First Amendment . . . stand[s] as a guarantee that neither the power nor the prestige of the . . . Government [can] be used to control, support or influence the kinds of prayer the American people can say—that the people's religions must not be subjected to the pressures of government for change each time a new political administration is elected to office. *Under that Amendment's prohibition against governmental establishment of religion . . . , government in this country, be it state or federal, is without power to prescribe by law any particular form of prayer which is to be used as an official prayer in carrying on any program of governmentally sponsored religious activity.* [Emphasis added.]

The respondents' argument that the program does not require all pupils to recite the prayer but permits those who wish to do so to remain silent or be excused from the room, ignores the essential nature of the program's constitutional defects. Neither the fact that the prayer may be denominationally neutral nor the fact that its observance on the part of the students is voluntary can serve to free it from the limitations of the Establishment Clause, as it might from the Free Exercise. The Establishment Clause, unlike the Free Exercise Clause, does not depend upon any showing of direct governmental compulsion and is violated by the enactment of laws which establish an official religion whether those laws operate directly to coerce non-observing individuals or not. [T]he purposes underlying the Establishment Clause go much further than that. The Establishment Clause stands as an expression of principle on the part of the Founders of our Constitution that religion is too personal, too sacred, too holy, to permit its "unhallowed perversion" by a civil magistrate. Another purpose of the Establishment Clause rested upon an awareness of the historical fact that governmentally established religions and religious persecutions go hand in hand. The Founders knew that only a few years after the Book of Common Prayer became the only accepted form of religious services in the established Church of England, an Act of Uniformity was passed to compel all Englishmen to attend those services and to make it a criminal offense to conduct or attend religious gatherings of any other kind. . . . And they knew that similar persecutions had received the sanction of law in several of the colonies in this country soon after the establishment of official religions in those colonies. It has been argued that to apply the Constitution in such a way as to prohibit state laws respecting an establishment of religious services in public schools is to indicate a hostility toward religion or toward prayer. Nothing, of course, could be more wrong. [People left] the cross-currents of officially established state religions and religious persecution in Europe and [came] to this country filled with the hope that they could find a place in which they could pray when they pleased to the God of their faith in the language they chose. And there were men of this same faith in the power of prayer who led the fight for adoption of our Constitution and also for our Bill of Rights with the very guarantees of religious freedom that forbid the sort of governmental activity which New York has attempted here.

The judgment of the Court of Appeals of New York is reversed and the cause remanded for further proceedings not inconsistent with this opinion.

Reversed and remanded.

Mr. Justice *Stewart,* dissenting.

I do not believe that this Court, or the Congress, or the President has by the actions and practices I have mentioned [—including prayers and appeals to God in the Star Spangled Banner, the National Anthem by Act of Congress, the Pledge of Allegiance, the National Day of Prayer, appeals to God by every President—] established an "official religion" in violation of the Constitution. And I do not believe the State of New York has done so in this case. What each has done has been to recognize and to follow the deeply entrenched and highly cherished spiritual traditions of our Nation—traditions which come down to us from those who almost two hundred years ago avowed their "firm Reliance on the Protection of divine Providence" when they proclaimed the freedom and independence of this brave new world.

I dissent.

* * *

The lawyers in the *Engel* case had argued both establishment clause and free exercise principles, as both guarantees were deemed essential to resolving the case. We will begin our discussion of the *Engel* case with the issue the Supreme Court didn't mention at all—the free exercise clause. Understanding the meaning of free exercise will help us better understand the Court's interpretation of the establishment clause.

Justice Black's opinion spoke only in the language of the establishment clause. Why? In ignoring the free exercise clause, Justice Black necessarily implied that the prayer did not violate the religious liberty of nonbelievers or those whose beliefs required different forms of prayer or worship. On their face, neither of these free exercise claims is frivolous, but the Court answered them with silence. What does the opinion's silence tell us about the meaning of free exercise and the relationship between the free exercise and establishment clauses?

What is an "exercise" of "religion?" Does the free exercise of religion include not only the individual's freedom to engage in an affirmative act that is a part of his or her religious practice, but also the right not to be exposed to an expression or act that conflicts with her or his religion? The right to be free to engage in one's own religion, including practices such as praying, attending worship, and even being educated in one's church community, seems clear enough. But what about the right to be free of government-compelled profession of another faith, or forced exposure to another faith? And what about the right to be free of forced exposure to or participation in religiously neutral activities, such as driving a car for the Old Order Amish or learning evolution for the fundamentalist, because those nonreligious activities are offensive to or inconsistent with one's religion? Where does school prayer fit in?

Daiker's argument on behalf of the state and the school board was, essentially, threefold. First, forced profession of another faith violates the free exercise guarantee. If state schools require students to say a prayer or engage in a religious act as a statement of their own personal belief or obedience despite religious objection, the requirement is unconstitutional. Thus, requiring a student to read a prayer as part of a play, or as part of the study of history or literature or religion, would be permissible. And excusing a student from participation, as in *Engel,* would also be permissible. William Butler, representing Engel and the other challengers, agreed with this principle. Voluntariness would satisfy any free exercise claim by the objecting students. For Butler, the case was instead mainly about the establishment guarantee.

Second, compelled or coerced exposure to a statement of belief or a practice of another faith does not violate the free exercise clause even if the government's purpose is to teach, as long as the purpose is not to proselytize the religion or religious belief. The keys here are compulsion and purpose. Daiker argues for the schools that if there is no compulsion, including coercion in the circumstances (subtle compulsion), then exposure itself is not a violation of the student's free exercise rights. The objecting students can remain seated, silent, or leave the room. This is so even when the statement or practice is itself religious, such as a stated belief in God. But if the state's purpose is to teach the religious statement or act as a religious statement or act, rather than as a statement of historical interest or secular educational or patriotic value, for example, the state's action would be unconstitutional even if voluntary—not because of the free exercise rights of the children but, instead, because such a state purpose would violate the establishment clause. So a teacher-led, state-written prayer is constitutional so long as it is (1) voluntary and (2) serving a secular purpose, such as patriotism, expressing secular values, instilling respect and appreciation as an act of political allegiance, and the like.

Butler, representing the challengers, parted company with Daiker here. He took two distinct and independent positions. First, he said that if the state writes, sponsors, or leads a religious statement or activity, it does not matter what the state's purpose is or whether it is voluntary. The state's action violates the establishment clause, and free exercise of religion has nothing, really, to do with it. In this sense, the problem in *Engel* was that the state of New York wrote the prayer for official use, here in the schools. Butler escapes the full implications of this fairly absolute rule—for example, its application to "God Save This Honorable Court" at the beginning of each session of the Supreme Court itself, or prayer at the opening of legislative sessions—by claiming that those are really ceremonial, political, and historical statements that contain references to but are not statements of religious belief (at least when used in those contexts), and therefore they fall outside the rule, which applies only to statements or activities that are religious. The distinction, as we will later see, can be a tricky one if applied to a crèche in a city's holiday display. It seems to be a distinction resting on the inherent nature of the statement or act, or its meaning in context, but not on the government's purpose.

In the alternative, Butler argues that even if such intrinsically religious statements or acts are permissible in contexts removed from religion and coercion, they are impermissible if the government's purpose is to teach or persuade, for then the profession of agreement with the statement or act would include professed agreement with the religious part of the statement. This would, it appears, violate the establishment clause as well as the free exercise guarantee, in Butler's view. The schools in *Engel* were teaching the contents of the prayer to the students, and the religious parts could not be excised or somehow neutralized by the other parts. This would be true, also, of a statement like the Declaration of Independence or the constitution of a state that calls on God's guidance, or even a reading from the Bible, if it were used to teach or persuade listeners or readers of the truth of the statement. As for "God Save This Honorable Court," or "In God We Trust" on currency, Butler would argue that such occasions and uses are not intended to, nor do they, teach or persuade about the contents of the statement.

The third and in some ways most far-reaching question is whether one's free exercise of religion can ever be violated by mere exposure to statements or acts that are not themselves intrinsically religious but that offend or contradict one's religious beliefs. Such cases would not involve direct government prohibitions, like the outlawing of polygamy or serving wine to minors, or compelled action in violation of one's religion, like working on Saturday for Sabbatarians. There the individual is barred from engaging in acts required by his or her religion, or compelled to violate his or her religion. Instead, the question here is the individual's exposure to nonreligious acts or statements that offend her or his religious beliefs. Such cases would include, for example, learning about evolution as part of the generally applicable public school curriculum; witnessing or participating in the wearing of costumes at Halloween; wearing athletic attire in gym class; using currency; saluting the flag; or saying the Pledge of Allegiance. In terms of the free exercise of religion guarantee (as opposed to the distinct free speech guarantee), would, or should, the witnessing of or participation in the Pledge of Allegiance be a violation of an objecting person's free exercise rights, at least unless it is wholly voluntary? Should exposure to religiously offensive materials ever, absent coercion perhaps, be a violation of the individual's religious liberty? Must we, in a society based on the freedom of speech and the exchange of many, often offensive ideas in the pursuit of knowledge, wisdom, and political truth, brace ourselves for the unwelcome and deeply upsetting expressive acts, including religiously offensive ones?

Daiker argued for the schools, with some difficulty, that the New York prayer at the beginning of school could be seen in such terms—as a statement of belief and value that is not in fact intrinsically religious, despite its text. The students, in fact, seemed largely to see it that way too, with virtually no one objecting. It was a ritual, just like reading a poem with a religious reference out loud. It is important that children be trained to exist in a culture that is wide open and robust, in which offense to sensitivities is not a justification for prohibiting speech but instead an occasion for listening with tolerance and then arguing and expressing contrary views. The difficulty for the state in making this argument, of course, is that the prayer could not be said to be "secularized," like Sunday blue laws had been, according to the Supreme Court. Moreover, the speaker whose views we must brace ourselves for in *Engel* was the government. But the rules of tolerance and wide open and robust debate apply to private individuals stating their opinions, not government stating its.

So while Daiker made such an argument for the school board, he did not rely heavily on it, nor did he need to. And Butler didn't really talk about the third issue, religious objections to curricular material, either. That is an issue best left, perhaps, to another day when the Court would address evolution in the schools, or compulsory education laws that force students to be exposed to offensive ideas like history, sociology, and science.

* * *

Justice Black's opinion in the case was limited to only one piece of this larger puzzle. He rested the Court's decision only on the establishment clause, and limited its scope only to "compos[ing] official prayers for any group of American people to recite as part of a religious program carried on by government." The decision was not limited to schoolchildren and it applied whether the recitation was compelled or voluntary. Those factors would only be relevant to a free exercise claim, which the Court did not address. On the other hand, the decision applied only to *government-composed* official prayers for recitation as part of a government-conducted religious program. Thus, the decision did not address any of the issues related to Bible-reading or religious content not of the government's creation, like religious music or speeches and prayers by private speakers. It did not touch on the issues involved in compelled or voluntary exposure to, rather than recitation of, nonreligious (but religiously offensive) material, like evolution for Christian fundamentalists or modernism for the Old Order Amish, or compelled exposure to religious material like prayers at graduation. And it did not apply to any setting other than a government-conducted religious program. This would seem to exclude the opening of the Supreme Court sessions, legislative sessions, or graduation ceremonies (excluding baccalaureate and other religious ceremonies that are often a separate part of graduation). It did, however, include the prayer at the beginning of school, which must have qualified as a "religious program carried on by government" by viewing the prayer in isolation from the Pledge of Allegiance or other rituals made part of the beginning of school. This leaves a government-composed prayer at the beginning of a legislative session in some question, though the absence of recitation by those in attendance would leave it outside the scope of the Court's decision in any event.

The Court's opinion, in other words, left many questions to be decided in the future. A few of these are worth mentioning briefly in light of the other arguments the lawyers made but the Court did not resolve. The first issue is that of prayer at the beginning of legislative sessions. When the Court confronted this question in a case challenging the Nebraska legislature's practice of having a minister give a prayer at the opening of legislative sessions, the Court concluded that all prayer is not the same. In the case of a legislative prayer not written by the government and not recited, the Court decided that the occasion was not truly a religious one and the "prayer" was a ceremonial, historical practice that placed the religious content of the ceremony in a secular context, thus not raising an establishment or free exercise issue.

But it was not so easy to remain within the narrow scope of *Engel* when, a few years after *Engel* was decided, the Court was forced to decide the constitutionality of required reading of Bible verses and recitation of the Lord's Prayer to non-objecting public school students. Unable to limit its decision to state-composed religious material and unwilling to sustain the practices on voluntariness grounds, the Court struck down the practices on the basis of purpose: the only purpose for the government's requiring voluntary Bible-reading and prayer was to inculcate and reinforce religious beliefs. No matter how ecumenical or voluntary the program serving such a purpose, it is unconstitutional because government is purposefully conducting a religious program in violation of the establishment clause. This was the fixed rule of *Engel* expanded beyond government-composed prayer and then transplanted to purpose, with all of the difficulties that purpose analysis presents. But it was enough to dispose of the Bible-reading problem left hanging in *Engel.*

Purpose once again became the main instrument when the Court addressed moments of silence. On their face, moments of silence for meditation, in whatever form (i.e., reflection about life, prayer, baseball, girlfriends), are constitutionally unobjectionable, for they are not intrinsically religious in content and simply allow each individual to choose for himself or herself how to use the moment, whether for religious or nonreligious thoughts. They are, in fact, quite consistent with the free exercise of religion. In an Alabama case decided in 1985, however, the Court revealed the opening fissures of disagreement among the Justices on basic principles of the establishment and free exercise clauses and, indeed, the reasoning of *Engel* itself. Alabama had enacted a moment of silence law, providing specifically for a moment for "meditation." While meditation would clearly include prayer, the legislature subsequently decided to make extra sure of this, so it amended its law to add, after "meditation," the two words "or prayer." On the basis of *Engel* it would be hard to get one's constitutional hands on the amendment, for it simply made explicit what was implicit in meditation; indeed, had the legislature originally enacted a law providing a moment of silence for "mediation or prayer," the law would likely have been constitutional.

The problem was the "or prayer" amendment that added nothing but "prayer" and thus was alleged to be religious. The Court agreed with this characterization, though not without various views of why that result should be reached—and not without strong dissent. The basic reason the amendment was unconstitutional, the Court said, was that the legislature's purpose was bad because the amendment, and thus the legislature's purpose, was quite clearly and explicitly religious. The bill was a response by the legislature to religious political forces and had no purpose, and indeed no consequence, other than stating an official religious view. This was surely correct, but resting the decision on this ground revealed the weakness of bald purpose analysis, for the legislature could reenact the amendment in a heartbeat and without any reference to religion, but instead simply to avoid the possibility that some teacher would prohibit students from silently praying during the moment in the name of the Constitution. Such an amendment would, it seems, be perfectly constitutional.

The Court's opinion began to foretell the fracturing of consensus on the Court, for there was really no governing rationale that any five Justices fully agreed to (though five agreed with the purpose analysis, some reluctantly), and Justice O'Connor first suggested an altogether new way to judge establishment clause violations.

The state, she said, has made a law "respecting an establishment of religion" when its action—here the enactment of the amendment—"conveys a message of State endorsement and promotion of prayer" to those who witness it. This test would be formalized in ways that we will discuss in greater detail in a later story. For present purposes, Justice O'Connor's "endorsement" idea is notable because of the radical reformulation it effects in the *Engel* test. Constitutional violations do not so much depend on what the state does (composing prayer, conducting religious exercises), or why (purpose), or how it does it (voluntarily, in a secular setting, by teaching), but instead on how outsiders who witness the state's action interpret it: how students and parents interpret the prayer at the beginning of school; how groups react to the teaching of evolution; or how legislative prayer is interpreted. Do they understand the state's action to be an endorsement of the religious act or statement, or an endorsement of a religion or religion in general? If so, it violates the establishment clause.

The endorsement standard is in some ways a narrower rule because it is less certain: not all state-composed prayers will fall, only those perceived as a government endorsement of a religion or religion in general. Purpose is not determinative, since laws with a religious purpose, but which are not seen as endorsing religion (like student bus transportation to religious schools, perhaps), would be permissible. Yet the endorsement idea also can yield a vastly broadened rule, depending on people's perception. Thus legislative prayer may easily been seen as a state endorsement of religion, just as the president of the United States saying "May God Protect Us" could also be. And finally, just how does a court go about deciding how people witnessing a government action interpreted the "message" of that action? A court can't just take the word of those who complain, for they may be a small minority and their antennae may be overly sensitive, and thus neither ordinary nor reasonable.

With two final cases, the fracturing of consensus on the Court became obvious and apparent to all. The first involved prayers at public high school graduations. The Court split, as it now commonly does on religion cases, 5-4, striking down a clergy-led, nonsectarian prayer. Among the five Justices in the majority, there were three separate opinions based on three different rationales.

One Justice viewed the practice as coercive, forcing students through peer pressure to stand and bow their heads and listen even though they were free not to do so. Implicit in the coercion view is that the government may support or assist religion as long as it does not coerce those witnessing the government's act to participate in religion or a religious exercise. The establishment clause wall separating church and state is a very low one with many doors.

Two Justices thought *Engel* and the Bible-reading decision could dispose of the case, for the prayer was a religious ceremony promoting religion over nonreligion, conducted by government. Purpose and effect (coercion) were not determinative. State support of or engagement in religion was strictly prohibited. This, of course, is the separationist view, and the wall of separation between church and state is very high indeed and knows few (student bus transportation to religious schools under a generally applicable safety program) if any exceptions.

Finally, two Justices in the majority judged the prayer, in its setting, to represent a government endorsement of religion. This is Justice O'Connor's idea, which permits a wide range of religion-conscious government action as long as it stops short of creating the impression of government endorsement of religion or a religion.

The four dissenters were largely of one mind. Justice Kennedy's idea of coercion through peer pressure, they argued, was a concept at odds with a free society in which people must have a thick skin and brace themselves for unwelcome ideas. *Engel* doesn't answer the case because, in context, the ceremonial use of prayer was a secularized ritual only; and the very idea of endorsement, resting as it does on the interpretation of those witnessing an event, is unmanageable and incapable of limitation. The graduation prayer should therefore be judged constitutional because it did not prefer one religion to another, and in preferring religion to nonreligion it did nothing that violated the establishment guarantee, which only applies to government preferences for, or establishments of, *a* religion. The dissenting view, in short, was nonpreferentialist: government can neither prefer one religion to others, nor discriminate against one religion and not others. It can't use a Christian prayer and not a Jewish one. It can't grant a tax exemption to all churches except Buddhist Temples. Government can, however, prefer religion to nonreligion as a means of promoting religion and religiosity, as by exempting churches and religious buildings from property taxes or zoning laws. But it cannot discriminate against religion and in favor of nonreligion; if government requires compulsory schooling and provides public schools, it cannot prohibit private religious schools from satisfying the state education requirements, too.

There is a certain anarchy to such a divided Court, but there is also a certain coherence to the range of views on the establishment clause, from strict separation, to neutrality, to more accommodating tests of endorsement and coercion, to highly accommodating tests of nonpreferentiality and nondiscrimination among religions.

But in other cases the appearance of coherence completely breaks down, as in the final case—two cases, really—which involved Christmas holiday displays. In deciding that a county-sponsored Nativity scene was unconstitutional, but a city-sponsored display of a menorah accompanied by a sign saluting liberty and a Christmas tree was permissible, the Court split apart in every direction, like a flywheel breaking up. Different combinations of Justices decided the two 5-4 cases. The establishment guarantee seemed to have descended into incoherent squabbling over details. And so, for the moment at least, it had.

There are additional questions that have yet to be answered but that are now working their way through the courts. These include the phrase "under God" in the Pledge of Allegiance (which a federal appellate court struck down on the force of the Bible-reading case), the moment of silence purpose analysis, and the endorsement concept. Take your pick. In applying the Supreme Court's fractured opinions, one must use at least two and often three separate rationales.

On the other side of the establishment clause and free exercise tables are cases in lower courts that *require* government to sponsor and support religious activities. The cases involve the constitutionality of a federal statute that provides that any zoning restriction that hinders a religious building—say a requirement for parking spaces, or for setback on an addition to a church, or limiting changes to a church in the interest of historic preservation—is presumptively unconstitutional. The law, like the *Yoder* case, compels a different rule for religious places in the interest of protecting and promoting religion and religious freedom. Is it therefore unconstitutional under the establishment guarantee because it endorses religion, because it lends support to religion, because its purpose is to promote and assist religion? If not, why isn't an appeal to a universal "god" through a prayer at the beginning of school equally permissible?

* * *

Those who are not religious may not like the prayer. Many taxpayers whose taxes pay for student aid to ministers-in-training would object mightily. Those who own buildings used for nonreligious purposes (commerce, education, the display of art) won't be happy either. Nor will the neighbors of the churches, or the historic preservationists. But in the case of zoning exemptions for churches, the United States Congress concluded by a very wide and bipartisan margin that it is perfectly fine—indeed, quite important in the scheme of things—to encourage and support religion because of the many ways in which religion contributes to the happiness and stability of a secular state.

This is enough to make one wonder whether an ecumenical prayer at the beginning of school, like the one New York drafted in *Engel,* is such a bad thing, after all.

Almighty God, we acknowledge our dependence upon Thee, and we beg Thy blessings upon us, our parents, our teachers and our Country.

STAGE III The New Awakening

Over the course of roughly forty years, from the *Everson* case in 1947 until the late 1980s, the stable and coherent strict separationist view of the religion guarantees broke down completely, leaving space for the emergence of new and quite different ideas of religious liberty under the First Amendment, and leaving the impression, by 1990, that the Supreme Court was utterly divided and confused. *Engel* had, in 1962, closed the schoolhouse doors to state-sponsored prayer in the name of non-establishment of religion. The *Yoder* case, just ten years later in 1972, reopened them, this time to an even broader exemption from compulsory education in the name of religious freedom. In 1968, the Court in the *Epperson* case said that objecting students could be compelled to learn about evolution in public schools. Yet in 1972, the Court in *Yoder* said that objecting students must be exempted from compulsory education—not just excused from classes, but exempted altogether—because "modern" secular subjects like history, art, science, and psychology offended their religious beliefs. Beginning with *Everson* in 1947, the Court stood firmly behind an establishment clause, separationist rule that tax dollars could not be channeled to religious schools and institutions. But by the 1980s the Court had allowed tax exemptions for churches and government funding of construction at religious colleges under the establishment guarantee. More remarkable, by the early 1990s the Court had held that public school facilities—rooms, auditoriums, and so on—*had to be made available* on equal terms to religious groups for religious activities and worship, in the name of the free exercise guarantee. The range of separate views on many of these cases was as broad as the membership of the Court—nine Justices, nine views.

Beneath the surface of the fractured and divided opinions, and the chaos produced by the disagreements, however, a new set of constitutional principles and rules was slowly emerging and gathering force. The new principles in some ways reflected the old strict separation view: free exercise claims were to be tightly limited, as with *Reynolds,* and the establishment clause was to once again become the dominant player in the decision of cases, as the *Everson* Court had said. But here the similarities ended, for as we will see, the meaning of free exercise of religion was to be radically changed, from a guarantee of liberty to a guarantee of nondiscrimination against religion, and the meaning of an establishment of religion was to be even more dramatically altered from a rule strictly separating religion and government to a rule that permits and even requires government support for religion and religious institutions. It is the story of this transformation in thinking under the First Amendment and the reasons supporting it that I call "the new awakening," a change in the Court and, as important, in the society at large.

In this final part of the book, we will turn first to the *Smith* case, involving religious use of illegal drugs. There we will see the abandonment of *Yoder* and the free exercise experiment and, with it, the redefinition of religious liberty protected directly by the free exercise guarantee. We will then consider the *Rosenberger* case, which involves public university funding for proselytizing by student religious groups. In *Rosenberger* we will see the abandonment of the separationist rules (that the establishment guarantee prohibits government from funding religion or preferring religion to nonreligion) and the replacement of those rules with another that simply prohibits discrimination against religion and among religions and religious practices. Free exercise and non-establishment are essentially unified in a rule of nondiscrimination against religion, a rule that for the first time, in the name of free speech, permits (and may impose a duty on) government to support religion, including a duty to provide funding. Finally, with the *Davey* case, we will survey the potential implications of such a conception of religious liberty in the context of school voucher plans, scholarships, and direct funding of religious activity.

The striking bottom line of the Court's new conception of religious liberty can be expressed in the following way. The *Reynolds* polygamy case today would present no free exercise of religion issue at all, and the belief/conduct distinction the Court erected to limit the free exercise clause would be largely irrelevant. Likewise, the *Everson* school bus transportation case would present no establishment clause problem at all, even if the reimbursement program were undertaken for the sole purpose of assisting religious students and religious schools. The new free exercise and non-establishment guarantees, in short, aren't even on the same radar screen as the strict separation views of *Reynolds* and *Everson*. The results would be the same today as then, but that is all that can be said.

STORY 6

Peyote: God versus Caesar, Revisited

Employment Division v. Smith, 494 U.S. 872 (1990)

Alfred Smith lost his job because he used peyote in a religious ceremony.

Smith was a sixty-three-year-old alcohol and drug treatment counselor for the Douglas County Council on Alcohol and Drug Abuse Prevention and Treatment (ADAPT) in Oregon. He was also a Klamath Indian and a member of the Native American Church, a church that began in the early twentieth century in response to persecution of Native Americans for use and worship of peyote. The church was first named the Church of the First Born, begun in Oklahoma in 1909, then the First Born Church of Christ; finally, after World War II, it was legally organized on a national level as the Native American Church. The Church combined elements of Christianity with traditional Native American beliefs in a God. Most important, it held firmly to the practice of using peyote, a hallucinogenic substance in the peyote cactus.

Smith had an alcohol problem as a young man, but he had not consumed it since 1957. He had been an alcohol and drug counselor since 1971, working for ADAPT since August 1982. As a member of the Native American Church, Smith participated in its ceremonies and, while it was not required that he do so, he ingested peyote. Peyote is a Schedule I [most dangerous] drug prohibited under the Federal Controlled Substances Act. It was also illegal under Oregon law. The federal law has long recognized an exception for religious use of peyote in the Native American Church. Oregon's law had no such exception.

In September 1983, Smith was warned by his supervisor at ADAPT that use of illegal drugs, including peyote, was unacceptable for ADAPT counselors. He was instructed to stop using it in the religious ceremonies. Shortly thereafter, Galen A. Black, another ADAPT counselor, was discharged because of his use of peyote in the Church's religious ceremony. Following Black's discharge, an announcement was distributed to ADAPT counselors, stating that use of illegal drugs was inconsistent with their responsibilities as counselors and role models for those they counsel.

Smith did not attend another Church ceremony until Saturday, March 3, 1984. The day before, Smith's supervisor had spoken with him about the upcoming ceremony, advising him not to use peyote. Smith responded that he intended to ingest peyote because it was an important part of the religious ceremony and experience. Upon his return to work on the following Monday, he confirmed that he had ingested peyote at the ceremony, and he was discharged from his job that same day.

Alfred Smith explained his actions by stating, "I did nothing wrong. How could they tell me I was attending a drug party when the ceremony was one of the most sacred Native American ceremonies that has survived for thousands of years?" Galen Black stated, "My job required me to learn culturally-specific treatments" for drug and alcohol abuse, and the Church's beliefs and ceremonies were intended to serve that very purpose.

The sacramental use of peyote has, indeed, continued for thousands of years in the Native American culture. Peyotism, as well as the theology of the Native American Church, "combines certain Christian teachings with the belief that peyote embodies the Holy Spirit and that those who partake of peyote enter into direct contact with God."[1] Peyotism was well established in the United States in the late nineteenth century, used by many different Native American tribes "following surprisingly similar ritual and theology" in such diverse places as California, Wisconsin, Montana, and Saskatchewan. Peyotism today is largely, though not exclusively, practiced through the Native American Church. The Church's membership is said to range from thirty thousand to two hundred fifty thousand members. The Church keeps no membership records, so the exact practicing membership is unknowable, but the Church is well established throughout the western United States and Canada.

The "meeting," or ceremony, in which peyote is used is quite formalized and occurs at relatively infrequent intervals ranging from once a month to

---

1. The following quotations and information about peyotism and the Native American Church are drawn, inter alia, from a concise summary of the subject in an opinion of the California Supreme Court, quoted in the Oregon Supreme Court's opinion in the Black case. *People v. Woody,* 61 Cal.2d 716, 720–21, 40 Cal. Rptr. 69, 394 P.2d 813 (1964), quoted in *Black v. Employment Division,* 301 Or. 221, 225–27, 721 P.2d 451, 453–54 (S. Ct. Ore. 1986).

twice a year. It is the central ceremony of the Native American Church, wherein peyote is both a sacramental symbol, like communion, and also "itself an object of worship; prayers are directed to it much as prayers are devoted to the Holy Ghost. . . . [T]o use peyote for nonreligious purposes is sacrilegious. Members of the Church regard peyote also as a 'teacher' because it induces a feeling of brotherhood with other members; indeed, it enables the participant to experience the Deity."

The ceremony in which Galen Black and Alfred Smith ingested peyote is described in detail by Omer Stewart, a widely respected scholar of Native American religion.[2]

> [T]he ritual . . . generally begins about nine o'clock on a Saturday night. Today the participants are both men and women, although men are usually the leaders. They come dressed in their best clothes, having clean shirts and dresses. Many men wear a silk handkerchief around the neck folded in a particular way and held together with a silver bola in the form of some peyote symbol—a button, a peyote bird, a cross. Some may wear red bead necklaces or other Indian jewelry, and some will have decorated cases which hold ceremonial feather fans handsomely beaded and tasseled with buckskin, to be used for incensing themselves with cedar smoke, and small gourd rattles similarly decorated. Some will wear blankets and shawls, . . . the preferred dress. Some, especially women, will wear moccasins.
>
> Even if the ceremony is held in a house, the peyotists sit on the floor in a circle, the roadman [spiritual leader of the ceremony] facing east, the chief drummer to his right and the cedarman to his left. The ceremony begins when the roadman takes from a special case his ceremonial paraphernalia consisting of a staff, usually carved or ornamented with beads and dyed horsehair (it will be placed in front of him in a Half Moon ceremony, stood upright in a Cross Fire ceremony); a decorated rattle; a special fan, probably of eagle feathers; and an eagle bone or reed whistle. He also produces a large peyote button thought to be the Chief Peyote, which he places on the moon altar. He also brings forth a sack of peyote buttons and usually a container of peyote tea to be consumed during the night, and, in the case of a Half Moon ceremony, two sacks of Bull Durham tobacco and papers of cornhusks for the prayer cigarettes.
>
> The Cedarman throws a quantity of cedar on the fire, producing a dense aromatic smoke, and all the ritual objects, including the drum, are passed through this smoke in order to purify them. In the case of the Half Moon rite, the sacks of tobacco and papers are then circulated clockwise, and when all have prepared a cigarette, the roadman prays aloud and smokes his cigarette in concert with the

2. App. A, Brief Amicus Curiae of Association on American Indian Affairs et. al, *Employment Division v. Smith,* 494 U.S. 872 (1990). See Omer Stewart, *Peyote Religion: A History* (1987).

others, who pray silently, all directing their smoke toward the fire and altar where rests the Chief Peyote. The sacks of peyote and tea are then passed clockwise around the circle, and each partakes either of tea or four buttons. The prayer and cigarettes finished and the first four peyote buttons eaten, the roadman, holding the staff and fan in one hand and vigorously shaking the rattle with the other, accompanied by the quick beat of the chief drummer, sings the ceremonial Opening Song, "*Na he he he an yo witsi nai yo,*" syllables which go back to the Lipan Apache, to the songs of the first U.S. peyotists. He sings the hymn four times. He sings three more songs four times, and then the staff, fan, and rattle are passed clockwise to the next participant and the drum to that person's next neighbor. The person receiving the staff, fan and rattle then sings four songs four times, and passes it on to the next participant, and so the staff, rattle, fan, and drum go around the circle, each participant singing four songs four times. Before midnight, the singing continues in this way only interrupted a few times when the peyote is circulated again. At midnight, the roadman sings another ceremonially determined song, the Midnight Water Call. Then the fireman brings a pail of water, which the cedarman passes through cedar smoke and blesses while smoking a prayer cigarette. After pouring a little on the ground "for Mother Earth," the water is passed around the circle to all participants. Today, instead of a common dipper as was used in the past, paper cups are often used. Sometimes during the Midnight Ceremony, the roadman . . . goes outside and blows the whistle to the four directions; this, however, is one of the more variable elements of the ceremony and may be dispensed with or changed. At the end of the Midnight Ceremony, there is a recess lasting ten to thirty minutes when everyone goes outside to relieve himself or to stretch. It is a quiet time with little talking.

When the meeting resumes, the singing begins again and continues. One-half to two-thirds of a peyote meeting is occupied in singing. Peyote may also be circulated. At this time the participants may take from their cases their own ceremonial rattles and fans for use during singing. Also, individuals may request a prayer cigarette from the roadman, and the singing will stop while all listen to the prayer. These prayers are sometimes testimonials, sometimes supplications for help and guidance. This is also the time for a special curing ceremony, if such has been planned. As the first rays of sunrise appear, the roadman sings another special song, the Dawn Song. He may also blow his whistle again to the four directions. This is followed by the entrance of the peyote woman, usually the wife of the host, who brings in water which is again blessed and circulated. She also brings the ceremonial breakfast of corn, meat, and fruit, which is circulated, with each person taking a bit of each food. Following the ceremonial breakfast, the roadman may give a little talk. If this has been a Cross Fire service, the roadman may read a text from the Bible and interpret its meaning to the congregation. In full daylight the roadman sings the last of the ceremonially determined songs, the Quitting Song. Then he and the others carefully put away the ceremonial paraphernalia, wrapping the fans, rattles, and any other ceremonial ob-

> jects in silk handkerchiefs and depositing them in their special boxes and cases. It is then that the meeting is over and all go outside to "welcome the sun."
>
> Now the congregation begins to visit with one another, and the women begin preparation for breakfast. This will be the best meal that the host, assisted by his friends, can offer. There will be a good deal of talk concerning the feelings and experiences of the previous night. In the afternoon the peyotists will begin to leave for home, which for some could be a considerable distance. It is not unusual for peyotists to travel more than a hundred miles to attend a meeting. Thus ends a typical ritual. . . .
>
> It should be pointed out that among peyotists their religion is more than a ritual to attend from time to time, generally about once a month. It is a part of everyday life. Peyote singing is enjoyed at home. Most peyote homes will have a peyote rattle hanging on the wall. It is easy to take it down, fashion a drum from a piece of inner tube stretched over a coffee can, and do some singing. Children use rattles and drums in play and try to imitate the peyote singing of their elders. Adults more formally practice hymns at night.

Following their discharge from ADAPT, both Alfred Smith and Galen Black sought unemployment benefits. They were at first successful, but an appeals board reversed the initial decision and denied them benefits because they were discharged for misconduct. Smith and Black then took their cases to the courts. The Oregon Court of Appeals reversed the agency and ordered that Smith and Black should receive the benefits because the use of peyote was part of a religious practice. The Oregon Supreme Court later agreed, saying that to deny Smith and Black benefits would deny them their right freely to exercise their religion under the First Amendment of the United States Constitution. The State then appealed the two cases to the United States Supreme Court, which, after first requesting clarification of certain matters by the Oregon Supreme Court, combined the cases and granted review in early 1989.

Oral argument in the *Smith* case was held on Monday, November 6, 1989, at 11:00. The attorney representing the state of Oregon was David B. Frohnmayer, Oregon Attorney General. Smith and Black were represented by Craig J. Dorsay of Portland, Oregon.

The Supreme Court Justices who heard the cases were a philosophically disparate group. The Chief Justice was William Rehnquist, a conservative appointed by President Nixon. The most senior Justices were all "liberal," which means in this context that they were more willing to depart from the strict text and history of the Constitution when those sources provided little guidance. They were firmly in the "separationist" camp. These Justices were William Brennan, appointed by President Eisenhower; Thurgood Marshall, by President Johnson; and Harry Blackmun, by President Nixon. The next four

Justices were hard to capture in liberal–conservative terms, and in varying degrees their votes in specific cases were not easily predictable in ideological terms. These Justices were Byron White, a fiercely independent Justice appointed by President Kennedy; John Paul Stevens, an often unpredictable Justice appointed by President Ford; Sandra Day O'Connor, a Reagan appointee who would soon become the decisive swing vote on the Court after the three liberal justices would retire in the 1990s; and Anthony Kennedy, also a swing vote in important cases, appointed by President Reagan. The final Justice, Reagan appointee Antonin Scalia, was a distinguished scholar and academic before becoming a judge, a brilliant and intellectually feisty man, and a true conservative who felt that the Supreme Court's power to act creatively when interpreting the Constitution was, at best, minimal. This was a Supreme Court in transition, though in the religion setting the transition was about to end.

The Chief Justice opened the proceedings.

Chief Justice Rehnquist: We'll hear argument next in Number 88–1213, *Employment Division of Oregon v. Alfred Smith.* Mr. Frohnmayer, you may proceed.

Mr. Frohnmayer: Thank you, Mr. Chief Justice, and may it please the Court: The [question] before this Court . . . is this. Does the Free Exercise Clause require every state to exempt the religious peyote use by the Native American Church, or perhaps even beyond that, other substance use by other religions, from the reach of generally applicable criminal laws regulating the use of controlled substances by all citizens? . . . We are obviously acutely aware, as in all Free Exercise cases, of the sensitive interests that are at stake. On one hand we recognize that this is a genuine church with doctrinal beliefs in peyote use that are real. The church's members are unquestionably sincere, and the adherents genuinely believe that the existence of their religion is threatened if they are not free to use this substance.

Question: Is it also true that the federal government and some 23 states exempt peyote use from their drug enforcement schemes?

Mr. Frohnmayer: There is an exemption in the Drug Enforcement Administration's regulations for bona fide use by the Native American Church. The figure of 23, Justice O'Connor, we believe, is wholly inaccurate. [T]he number by our count is closer to 12 or 13.

Question: But the federal exemption and the exemption in the 12 states you are talking about appl[y] only to use by a member of the Native American Church?

Mr. Frohnmayer: Justice Scalia, no, the exemptions are somewhat scattered in terms of how they are phrased. For example, in Arizona it is simply a defense through a prosecution rather than an exemption from Schedule I, and it refers to bona fide use of peyote [in the] practice of a religious belief.

Question: Any religious belief?

Mr. Frohnmayer: That is right. Others—in fact, I would—I think it is safe to say the majority of the exemptions single out the Native American Church, so—

Question: How about the federal?

Mr. Frohnmayer: The federal exemption is limited to the Native American Church.

Question: So, if you are sort of the Martin Luther . . . of the Native American Church, you are just out of luck. You can't start a branch religion using peyote . . . [i]n the states that limit the exemption to the Native American Church.

Mr. Frohnmayer: That is one of the deeply troubling aspects we find in the Oregon Supreme Court's decision, because there is another church, an offshoot of this church, called the Peyote Way Church of God, which also has many Native American members and which has strictly controlled religious rites which a lower federal court has denied the same exemption enjoyed by the Native American Church.

The questioning here, of course, involves the argument by Smith and Black that their religious use of peyote should be treated differently than all other religious uses of peyote, a special treatment accorded their religious exercise and religion that is reflected, as well, in the federal drug laws, which exempt peyote use only by the Native American Church. Such a narrow exemption would amount to discrimination in favor of a small group of churches, thus violating the establishment clause, unless the limited exemption of one church only is required by the free exercise clause. This somewhat unsatisfying accommodation of the two guarantees is a reflection of the tension between non-establishment and free exercise as they have come to be understood in the Court's decisions. The accommodation—selective benefits to a church are prohibited unless required by the free exercise guarantee—is essentially an ad hoc rule for each specific case and thus doesn't fit neatly within a general constitutional principle that can be tied to the history and text of the First Amendment and applied generally.

It is the tension and its ad hoc accommodation that is bothering many of the Justices, who would like a clearer and more general rule, such as the rule that free exercise rights can never override a generally applicable law regulating or prohibiting conduct, a rule similar in many ways to the rule established in the *Reynolds* Mormon polygamy case decided 111 years earlier (and rejected in the *Yoder* case decided seventeen years earlier). Justice Scalia, the questioner, and Frohnmayer are of one mind on the question and would prefer the *Reynolds*-like rule that general laws regulating conduct extinguish any free exercise claim that might otherwise exist.

But such a rule, as we will see, requires that some pretty bitter pills be swallowed: the Amish would have to return to school; Sabbatarians would have to work on Saturday; churches using wine for communion would have to get a liquor license and not serve underage communicants. And what would come of acts of legislative grace, such as laws exempting churches from certain zoning restrictions about height of buildings, on-site parking requirements, and the like; or excuses from school for religious holidays; or tax deductibility of tithes and donations to churches; or, more to the point in the *Smith* case, exemptions from the federal drug laws for religious use of peyote by the Native American Church? Would such laws fall because they are not generally applicable regulations of conduct and thus violate the establishment clause?

Or would the establishment and free exercise clause tension remain, with its accommodation taken from courts and given over to the political—legislative and executive—branches, thus placing the destiny of churches in the hands of the majoritarian democratic process? Under such a rule, religious acts and religious institutions could be singled out for special advantage if the legislature or president or governor so chooses, but otherwise no exemption in the name of free exercise of religion would be available under the First Amendment. Such a rule would amount to a pretty radical restructuring of the established understanding of "establishment" and "free exercise," and an equally radical cutting back of the power and responsibility of courts in interpreting and enforcing the First Amendment.

Question: Am I correct in thinking that one need not be a Native American to be admitted to the Native American Church, or to participate in its rituals?

Mr. Frohnmayer: Justice Rehnquist, I—I would be somewhat hesitant to answer that question, because that is more properly directed, I believe, to the communicants of the church. It is safe to say that the record is somewhat obscure on this point. We know that Respondent Black was not a Native American. . . . We believe it is a fair reading of the record that he believed that he was a member of the Native American Church. . . . Let me turn . . . to the fact that peyote is unquestionably a dangerous and powerful hallucinogen. Government's interest in controlling peyote and similar hallucinogens is real, it is compelling, and it is evident by universal and pervasive regulation. There are other religions using peyote, and there are other religions using other drugs which also clamor for First Amendment constitutional exemptions—

Question: Is there any documentation in the record or in reported opinions of the danger that peyote is diverted from religious use and, say, sold on the street in the normal drug distribution channels?

Mr. Frohnmayer: Justice Kennedy, we know that it is found in normal drug distribution channels, although not in great amounts.

Question: Is it used for the derivative mescaline, which in turn is used commercially? Or can you get mescaline from some other source?

Mr. Frohnmayer: Mescaline, as we understand it, can be produced synthetically, as well as, of course, being found as the psychoactive ingredient in peyote itself. In fact, the only thing that distinguishes peyote from mescaline is the presence of alkaloids in a natural way in the peyote button, which does create additional effects on the particular user.

The Oregon [law, which contains no exemption and applies the same prohibition to all uses of peyote, religious or not, serves] three compelling and intersecting state interests. The first is the state's interest in regulating all peyote and hallucinogenic drug use in order to further the health and safety interests of its citizens. The second is the state's interest in a regulatory scheme as a whole, so that law enforcement does not face a patchwork of exemptions of other drugs on a drug-by-drug, religion-by-religion, believer-by-believer basis. And the third and compelling interest is that the state constitution's heightened requirement of neutrality in our jurisdiction requires it to avoid giving the preference of one church over another.

Let me then examine these concerns in order. Peyote, by all accounts, is a powerful and unpredictable hallucinogen. . . . It stimulates respiratory changes, reflexes and pulse rates, which are physiologically measurable. The spectrum of effects experienced are similar, and in most respects identical, to those of LSD, psilocybin, and mescaline, accompanied by vivid visual and auditory hallucinations, altered perceptions of time, space and body—emotional reactions that range from joy and exhilaration to extreme anxiety and even terror.

There is no way to predict, even for the experienced user, how the user will react on a given occasion. There are effects on the central nervous system and behavior which cause inability to distinguish reality and nonreality. And it does induce psychotic reactions in a small number of users.

Question: How long do these things last?

Mr. Frohnmayer: It is said, Justice Blackmun, and I am now trying to recall from memory precisely, that the effect may last as long as 12 hours. To quote from the [testimony of a clinical drug abuse specialist] in Smith's case . . . , it is a powerful and potent agent which does sometimes have long-lasting negative effects on its user, with no predictability as to when that can happen. It is "very risky."

The record is consistent with what is known generally about this substance, and why every jurisdiction in the country regulates it intensely. It is almost universally a Schedule I drug, which means that it has a high potential for abuse. There is no currently accepted medical use, and there is lack of accepted safety for use even under medical supervision. These dangers are great enough that Oregon has chosen, with respect to any user, to have a blanket regulation without exemption.

In the face of these considerations, the Oregon Supreme Court has concluded, however, that the federal Constitution commands a judicially crafted exemption for sincere adult users of a single church. And this poses for us a dilemma. On the one hand, if the exemption is crafted so narrowly that it applies to one group on a de minimis basis, then that means that our state and federal constitutions have preferred one religion over another, and hopelessly compromised the constitutional requirements of neutrality.

Question: Can we say the same thing about the *Yoder* case?

Mr. Frohnmayer: No, we think not. Because there, in *Yoder,* the church was not singled out by name and by identity and by denomination, and there were no others similarly situated who were clamoring for that particular exemption.

Question: Well, suppose the Wisconsin legislature had singled out the Amish church. Just because this Court singles that out it is all right, but the legislature can't?

Mr. Frohnmayer: We think the problem is compounded when a legislature singles it out, because the judicial exemption is free of broader interpretation, whereas, if the legislature in its plenary judgment has singled out a specific church, we believe it has, in many respects, potentially run afoul of the Establishment Clause unless it treats other religions clamoring for equal treatment on similar grounds in similar ways.

Question: Are you arguing that the 23—or it isn't 23 under your figures?—but whatever the number of states is that grant exemptions, those exemptions all violate the Establishment Clause?

Mr. Frohnmayer: No, we are not. We did not come to this Court to argue that giving an exemption in some form or another is an impermissible state act in the exercise of its plenary authority. Our argument is simply that the Free Exercise Clause does not command every state in this union, as apparently our Oregon Supreme Court would command, to craft an exemption singling out a specific church. Some of those state exemptions, as we pointed out, Justice Stevens, do speak neutrally with respect to bona fide religious practices.

Question: But some don't. And those that don't you would say are invalid under the Establishment Clause?

Mr. Frohnmayer: I think we would need to know more. And what more we would need to know is whether, if a court were faced with a claim by another religion, those jurisdictions would open their doors to other claims, if properly advanced by other religions.

With all due respect, Frohnmayer is trying to have his cake and eat it, too. His effort simply doesn't work. On the one hand he says that an exemption for Native American religious use of peyote would be unconstitutional because it would prefer a single religion and thus violate the establishment clause. On the other hand he claims, for obvious strategic reasons, that the federal law doing just that, and the laws of at least twelve states are not unconstitutional. How can that be? His answer is that each law would have to be judged on a case-by-case basis to determine whether its specific exemption would be consistent with the exemption required by the free exercise clause, as in *Yoder,* and thus similar to what a court would order under the First Amendment. Yet his argument begins by asserting that the Oregon Supreme Court's decision carving out an exemption for use of peyote in religious rituals of the Native American Church—in effect amending the Oregon law to reflect the judicial interpretation of free exercise—was wrong and inconsistent with the establishment guarantee because it singled out one religion. This is precisely what the Supreme Court did in *Yoder.* Frohnmayer is caught in a circle that can't be closed, a loop based on an internal inconsistency. And he gets caught there.

But there are two logical ways out of the circle. The first is to argue that legislatively created exemptions favoring one or a few religions are different under the First Amendment from judicially crafted exemptions—and that the legislative preferences are *better* than the judicial ones, more favored by the First Amendment. Legislatures, therefore, can do what courts cannot: they can prefer religion and even some religions, or decide instead not to do so, without violating either the establishment clause or the free exercise clause.

But why should legislatures, rather than courts, have such special roles under the First Amendment? Wasn't the First Amendment, and the guarantee of religious liberty and non-establishment, placed in the Constitution for the specific purpose of limiting what legislatures could do? Doesn't the First Amendment say that "Congress [and now also the state legislatures] shall *make no law* respecting an establishment of religion or prohibiting the free exercise thereof. . . ."? Indeed, wasn't the very purpose of the Bill of Rights to correct an imperfection in the Constitution by placing specific limits on certain government powers in the interest of the individual's freedom and liberty, and not to give the definition of that freedom and liberty over to the legislative and executive branches of federal and state governments? Most historians and legal scholars, in 1989, would answer that these were, indeed, the purposes of the religion guarantees in the First Amendment, and therefore these should be reflected in any interpretation of the meaning of the terms of the amendment, such as "establishment" and "free exercise" of religion. Indeed, most would say, in light of this, that a rule giving power over to the Congress and the state legislative branches would effectively stand the First Amendment on its head.

The second way out of Frohnmayer's circle is to argue that the establishment clause does not limit states as greatly as it limits Congress, and that it allows specific exemptions—but only at the hands of the state legislatures, not the courts. Interestingly, scholars have taken such a view of the history of the establishment clause.[3] It was clearly intended, they say, that the establishment clause would be specifically and exclusively directed at Congress and the creation of a national religion. States, in contrast, were to be free to

3. See Akhil Reed Amar, "The Bill of Rights as a Constitution," 100 *Yale Law Journal* 1131, 1157–58 (1991) ("[T]o apply the [Establishment] clause against a state government is precisely to eliminate its right to choose whether to establish a religion—a right explicitly confirmed by the establishment clause itself! . . . The Fourteenth Amendment might best be read as incorporating free exercise, but not establishment, principles against state governments"); Akhil Reed Amar, *The Bill of Rights* (1998), 32–42; Steven D. Smith, *Foreordained Failure: The Quest for a Constitutional Principle of Religious Freedom* (1995), 49–50; Steven D. Smith, "Separation as a Tradition," 18 *Journal of Law & Politics* 215, 263 (2002) ("It may be, for example, that the Supreme Court was mistaken in *Everson* both in asserting that the Fourteenth Amendment was intended to incorporate the Establishment Clause against the states and also in asserting that the Establishment Clause was intended to adopt a position of "no aid separationism"); Chris Bartolomucci, "Rethinking the Incorporation of the Establishment Clause: A Federalist View," 105 *Harvard Law Review* 1700, note (1992); Daniel O. Conkle, "Toward a General Theory of the Establishment Clause," 82 *Northwestern University Law Review* 1113, 1142 (1988) ("The language of the Fourteenth Amendment, coupled with the federalistic motivation for the establishment clause, make it exceedingly difficult to argue that the framers and ratifiers of the Fourteenth Amendment intended to incorporate the establishment clause for application against the states"); Charles Fried, "Foreword: Revolutions?," 109 *Harvard Law Review* 13, 52–53 (1995) ("There is little doubt that the Establishment Clause (quite apart from its opening words 'Congress shall make no law') was specifically intended to preserve a freedom of action to the states while denying it to the national government"); Mary Ann Glendon and Raul F. Yanes, "Structural Free Exercise," 90 *Michigan Law Review* 477, 481–82 (1991) ("As a matter of judicial craftsmanship, it is striking in retrospect to observe how little intellectual curiosity the members of the Court demonstrated in the challenge presented by the task of adapting, for application to the states, language that had long served to protect the states against the federal government").

establish their own religions, as long as they did so in a way that preserved individuals' freedom to exercise their own religions. In fact, many states had established churches, required tithes and taxes for a preferred church, and the like well into the nineteenth century.

This view would mean that the due process and liberty guarantees of the Fourteenth Amendment, which was ratified after the Civil War, had the effect only of "incorporating" the free exercise guarantee and thus making it apply to states as well as Congress. The establishment guarantee, however, was from the beginning a protection of state authority from encroachment by Congress (i.e., by preventing the national government from supplanting the state-established religion with a single, national one), and therefore it is not an *individual* liberty made applicable after the Civil War to the states. This is a view recently suggested by Justice Clarence Thomas, who of course was not on the Court at the time of the *Smith* decision.

These are, obviously, very important and serious questions about the Constitution's meaning that Frohnmayer's argument in *Smith* raises, ones he cannot be allowed to escape.

Question: You just don't want to have to face up to those problems. You want to be able to—not to have any exemption at all.

Mr. Frohnmayer: That is correct. And this is not a theoretical issue for the State of Oregon, because we have pending in our appellate courts a case which in many ways is on all fours with this, in which sincere religious communicants who believe that their use of marijuana is religiously inspired, have asked for exemption from Oregon's drug laws. And that's part of the problem.

Frohnmayer must also explain why that is a problem in light of *Yoder,* which he justifies as an open-ended exemption that courts could expand to similarly situated religious uses by other religions and thus, in effect, a "neutral" (general) exemption not aimed at a single church.

Question: Well, that is also another problem in deciding what the states can do without offending the establishment clause. There is a problem in just allowing all religions to use peyote, but not allowing all religions to use marijuana, or any other hallucinogenic drug, I would assume. Isn't that a problem, too?

Mr. Frohnmayer: Justice Scalia, that is one of the major reasons we have brought this case to this Court. [This case] . . . is in fact the thin end of the wedge in which analytical distinctions are extremely difficult to draw, and in which claims certainly will be made, as they have been made in lower courts with increasing frequency, for other drugs and other—

Question: I take it, then, that your flat rule position would permit a state to outlaw totally the use of alcohol, including wine, in religious ceremonies?

Mr. Frohnmayer: That's a different question.

Question: Why is that different?

Mr. Frohnmayer: The issue of sacramental wine is different because, at least at the present, it is not a Schedule I substance. The—

Question: Well, but the state certainly could prohibit the use—the consumption of alcohol within its borders, or at least the sale or use of alcohol.

Mr. Frohnmayer: But there—there might be a religious accommodation argument of an entirely different order than is presented here.

Question: You mean, just a better-known religion?

Mr. Frohnmayer: No. It has nothing to do with—it is religion-indifferent. Even during prohibition there was a statutory exemption for the use of sacramental—

Question: Yes, but what I am asking is supposing a state did not give that statutory exemption.

Mr. Frohnmayer: There, an argument for accommodation [i.e., an exemption for religious use] is stronger, stronger in at least two respects. First is that there—that to the extent that this Court examines the potential danger of the ingestion of sacramental wine in small quantities, it might—might well question whether the state's overall interest in regulation of a very dangerous substance—

Question: So if this were a Schedule IV substance it would be a different case?

Mr. Frohnmayer: It could be a different case.

Question: I see.

Mr. Frohnmayer: The second is clearly that the use of peyote in the ceremonies is at least in part for its very hallucinogenic properties. That is to say, the religious experience, at least for some communicants, comes from the achievement of the heightened hallucinogenic effect, where this is also not true of the ingestion of sacramental wine in small quantities.

Question: You don't think there is any special spiritual feeling in taking communion?

Ouch! Frohnmayer's argument is obviously leaking badly at this point. He wants the state to be able to have a general rule while still allowing states to carve out an exemption (but not in any form) if they so choose, and to require a state in the name of the First Amendment to make an exemption, but only in limited cases where a court, otherwise dispossessed of most of its former power to enforce the religion guarantees, would so order. No exemption need be made for peyote; a state could, however, voluntarily make an exemption, but it would not be constitutionally required. An exemption, though, would be required for sacramental use of wine in the name of free exercise of religion.

Frohnmayer, of course, doesn't want to take on the sacramental use of wine in communion any more than he earlier wanted to argue that the federal law exempting religious use of peyote by the Native American Church was invalid. But in trying to steer a path among such shoals, Frohnmayer has sacrificed all logic and consistency in his argument. Logic and consistency are essential to the Constitution's meaning, for the Constitution is more than a partisan political document whose meaning can be changed willy-nilly on any given day and for any political reason. At least that is a central premise of the Supreme Court's claim that the judicial branch—a nonpolitical branch of government whose decisions must be consistent and based on principle, and whose power is so limited—has a special obligation to interpret the meaning of the Constitution and bind the political branches by its interpretation.

Mr. Frohnmayer: Well, the feeling is different than the induction of an actual altered state of consciousness. What I am saying is that those two factors at least distinguish, and would presumably cause this Court or any other to say that the argument for accommodation is much stronger in the case of those religious sacraments than in the case where it is unquestionably a very dangerous substance for everyone else, acknowledged and conceded to be, and where it is taken for the purposes of inducing the very state that causes the danger, at least with respect to everyone else.

Question: You would say that it would be at least a close case as to whether a state could prohibit this and not prohibit the use of alcohol in worship services to the point of inebriation.

Mr. Frohnmayer: I think that would be a very—that would be a much closer case, Justice Scalia.

Question: But a quite different case.

Mr. Frohnmayer: Yes, indeed it would. [I]t is ironic that while Respondents concede that the use of a Schedule I drug is dangerous as to everyone else, it is safe as to them. And the burden, we believe, lies properly on Respondents to show convincingly why the dangers of the drug use, or substance use, are less as to them. If there is to be a judicially crafted exemption, we are entitled to know who uses, with what frequency, in what amounts, for what purposes, and in what concrete ways do those uses reduce the risk. That is the nature of the state's undoubted compelling interest.

The record provides us no security. The sources cited in our reply brief are almost universally the same sources cited by Respondents . . . with respect to the nature of the practices. They show considerable variation in the ritual, in the dosage, in the membership, and yet no real information as to how the underlying danger of the substance or harm is in fact avoided.

Question: We don't know how much peyote is used in these ceremonies, I gather we don't know that it is just a, you know, a sniff or whatever?

Mr. Frohnmayer: Again, bearing in mind the admonition that it is not government's role to explore the centrality of religious practices of a belief, the record would fairly reveal that a hallucinogenic dose of four is common, and that ingestion of between eight and 30 of the peyote buttons is common. Beyond that, the anthropological literature and the other literature cited by both parties [are] somewhat variable. But it does seem clear that there is no uniformly prescribed amount, nor any real control over the number of peyote buttons that may be ingested by communicants at the particular religious ceremony.

And there is a final and critical point here related to our health and safety interest. That is that denominational practices, and indeed individual believers, even in long-standing religions, can and do change. They change the nature of their religious beliefs, they change the nature of their doctrine, and that is the very essence of freedom of religion and belief. So a constitutional exemption that is bound in time and place is very risky. If we exempt a practice, even if we are presently satisfied by its safety, control passes forever into private hands.

But then we must ask, before we let that control pass in the form of a constitutional exemption, denomination specific or not, now and in the future, what are the contours of that exemption and how will it be conferred. Because if the denominational or church controls weaken or change, there [is] still enshrined in the Bill of Rights a permanent exemption for the practices of that religion.

Question: You do concede, I take it, that the enforcement of the Oregon criminal laws would in effect destroy the Native American Church and its ritual in your state.

Mr. Frohnmayer: We don't concede that, Justice Kennedy, for a very practical reason. The Oregon criminal prohibition . . . has been on the books for more than a decade. There is no suggestion in our state that that religion has been destroyed by inappropriate police intrusion into the tepee ceremony. In most—

Question: What do you mean by inappropriate police intrusion? You are asserting that they have the right to intrude.

Mr. Frohnmayer: We are—

Question: If they haven't been destroyed, it is just that you have had inefficient enforcement.

Mr. Frohnmayer: We have had priorities in police enforcement that are understandable in terms of what is at stake. This, this—

Question: Are you saying you are not going to enforce the criminal law if we sustain it?

Mr. Frohnmayer: No, we are not saying that. We are saying that . . . there may be, in the specific context of the specific use by a person accused of a specific crime, special state constitutional restrictions on the state which have not yet been explored. We do not know the contours of those exemptions. But moreover, to answer your question generally—

Question: But if . . . if the contour is just to forgive or exempt the use of peyote by members of the Native American Church, you would then be back here arguing that that violates the Establishment Clause.

Mr. Frohnmayer: If the defense were that the specific church and that church only [were] entitled to the exemption, that would very probably be the case, Justice O'Connor.

I would like to reserve the balance of my time if I may.

Chief Justice Rehnquist: Thank you, General Frohnmayer.

Well! Frohnmayer had gotten himself caught in a web of internal inconsistencies, and, to the end, he never managed to escape it. His reluctance to argue that the federal exemption is unconstitutional is perfectly understandable, as that would make his argument infinitely more difficult to sell, even if it would be based on consistent principle. And his reluctance to argue that exemptions should be left entirely to the political process, whether for peyote or wine or uniform days of rest, was also understandable, for such a position would deal the courts out of most religious liberty cases and thus leave the meaning of the Constitution in the hands of legislatures and presidents and governors, a result which, since the famous case of *Marbury v. Madison*[4] in 1803, would be at odds with the very idea and source of judicial authority. "It is emphatically the duty of the judicial branch," Chief Justice John Marshall said in *Marbury,* "to say what the law is."

But Frohnmayer had to make one of these two arguments in order to be convincing. He didn't do so because he didn't believe the Supreme Court would accept either of them. Their consequences would be too extreme and distasteful. Instead, he argued that a form of ad hoc balancing between the importance of the state's interest and the strength of the religious claim

---

4. 1 Cranch (5 U.S.) 137 (1803).

would do. The federal government could exempt the Native American Church's use of peyote; states couldn't. But even if there were no exemption in Oregon, the law enforcement authorities might quite properly grant ad hoc exemptions as a matter of discretion. Peyote could be prohibited because it is hallucinogenic and dangerous. Wine in communion couldn't be prohibited because . . . because why? Because it doesn't alter one's state of mind? Because it isn't dangerous? Because Christians can be trusted to exercise discretion in the amount consumed?

Making such judgments is not very "judicial." The judgments are susceptible to inconsistency and to personal philosophical or political preferences of judges. And it would require substantial judicial intrusion into such questions as the meaning of religion, the validity of specific religious practices, and the relation of such practices to the religion's basic tenets.

In the end, as we will see, Frohnmayer's judgment was perhaps politically astute, but it was nevertheless wrong. The opposing counsel immediately bores in hard.

Chief Justice Rehnquist: Mr. Dorsay, we'll hear from you.

Mr. Dorsay: Mr. Chief Justice, and may it please the Court. I am compelled as an initial matter to address the subject raised by Justice Stevens relating to the use of alcohol, which I think raises one of the primary problems with this case as it comes before the Court. I think, if you looked at this situation and Indian people were in charge of the United States right now, or in charge of government, and you look at the devastating impact that alcohol has had on Indian people and Indian tribes through the history of the United States, you might find that alcohol was the Schedule I substance and peyote was not listed at all. And we are getting here to the heart of an ethnocentric view, I think, of what constitutes religion in the United States. And I think that needs to be looked at very hard before determining what is a dangerous substance and what is not.

Question: Well, it could—couldn't it be that the exception that the Oregon court was referring to might have been an exception for the use of peyote in insignificant quantities that could not produce any hallucinogenic or other adverse physical effect? And if that's the case, then your pointing to the traditional use of wine at religion services would not make any difference. I don't assume that the states would be compelled to allow excessive use of alcohol, drunken parties, on grounds of religion. I don't think that that is the—do you disagree with what the Attorney General said, that the whole purpose of the ingestion of the peyote is its hallucinogenic effect.

Mr. Dorsay: No, I do not disagree with that. What I disagree with is the fact that that ingestion is harmful. There is no documented evidence that the use of the peyote in these carefully circumscribed ceremonials has any harm to the individual, to society at large, or to the state's law enforcement efforts.

A couple of observations should be made at this early point in Dorsay's argument. First, he is arguing that the free exercise clause protects the use of peyote in the religious ceremony, and that to the extent this would result in an exemption from the drug laws for the Native American Church, that exemption would not constitute an unconstitutional preference for religion in violation of the establishment clause. The liberty guaranteed the individual by the free exercise clause subordinates the structural purposes (separation of church and state) served by the establishment clause. Dorsay's argument in this respect is precisely like the Court's reasoning in the *Yoder* case.

In another critical respect Dorsay's argument is also like *Yoder.* He claims that the government's interest in regulating illegal drugs can only override the free exercise right of Smith and Black if it can be proved that the harms giving rise to the drug laws occur *in their specific situation,* and that failure to apply the drug laws to them would undermine the objectives of the drug laws.

Dorsay therefore does not have to claim that the drug laws are unconstitutional. He can focus on the use of peyote in the religious ceremony only, claiming that the laudable goals of the drug laws are not served if they are applied to persons using peyote in the specific religious ceremony. This is why he begins with the suggestion that the very definition of "harm" from drugs is ethnocentric—wine is more dangerous for Native Americans, he says—and is ultimately, therefore, a relative question. He must be careful in making this specific point, however, for if he is understood to say that the general harm from peyote in any of its uses is simply a function of ethnocentric prejudice, he will lose. Peyote is indisputably a powerful, hallucinogenic drug. Its use is not like smoking pot around a campfire.

Dorsay's job, then, is to make a case about the particular ceremony, the particular uses of peyote in the ceremony, the particular people who participate in the ceremony. He needs to convince the Court, as the Amish did in *Yoder,* that the religion is established and longstanding, that the ceremony and the peyote use as part of it are deeply religious and traditional to the Church, that the participants in the ceremony are law-abiding people, that peyote use is controlled in a way that prevents harm and encourages a religious experience of great significance to the Church and its members, and that the Church's use of peyote does not yield socially undesirable behavior or attitudes. Therefore the purposes of the State's drug laws are not served by their application to peyote use in the ceremony of the Native American Church.

Question: How did [peyote] get to be a Schedule I controlled substance?

Mr. Dorsay: Well, I think it has—

Question: I mean, somebody thinks it is harmful.

Mr. Dorsay: Yes. It obviously . . . the drug mescaline has a high potential for abuse. That is what Schedule I says. The synthetic derivative has obviously been misused in society at large. There is, however, no evidence that peyote, as used by the Native American Church, has been misused in the sense that is has been misused in society.

Question: How would such evidence be acquired? Would you want the state to send agents into church services to observe them carefully and—

Mr. Dorsay: Well, we have a long history with this church of hundreds of years, and there has been no documented evidence. We have one or two anecdotal instances. I think, also, if you are going to look at the legislative judgment that peyote is a dangerous substance, you also have to look at the legislative judgment that peyote can be exempted. There is some kind of legislative fact-finding when Congress and other states have acted to exempt the use of peyote. They have based this in large part, for instance, on testimony before Congress that there ha[s] been no evidence that there have been harmful use[s].The state has failed to meet its burden under the First Amendment to justify what we believe would be the total destruction of this religion. . . . There is a sincere religious belief, it is a bona fide religion; that is conceded by the state. . . . The compelling state interest is the regulation of drug abuse generally, but we do not have any evidence *in this case* that peyote has been abused or that it contributes to the drug abuse problem. In fact, all of the evidence is to the contrary. We have the findings, for instance, of the federal agency charged with enforcement of the drug laws in this country, which . . . concluded that the religious use of peyote by the Native American Church does not cause a law enforcement problem in this country. And therefore there is no harm that is—

Question: Tell me, what does that mean?

Mr. Dorsay: Well, what it means is, for instance, that the entire supply of peyote is now used in bona fide religious ceremonies of the Native American Church. They found, for instance, that the marijuana problem in the United States, and the availability of marijuana and the use of marijuana was a much larger problem. And all of the courts that have addressed it have found that no accommodation can be made for marijuana.

Question: Well, I think a very good case could be made on the basis of what you say, that there is no risk of [peyote's] use spreading beyond the Native American Church.

Mr. Dorsay: That is correct.

Question: And that that Church has been responsible in its use. But why can't the state say we don't want Native American Church members to use it either? We think this is dangerous. It is harmful to people. We don't want children to be brought into this Church and taught to use this thing, it is harmful to them. It is a Schedule I substance; we have made that determination.

Mr. Dorsay: Because the First Amendment, I believe, requires something more than a mere legislative statement that we believe it may be harmful. States can come up with all kinds of reasons to outlaw all kinds of conduct. . . . [The] driving of Amish buggies without the reflector warning system is certainly a dangerous act. But if you allow the mere legislative proscription without an actual inquiry into whether harm has in fact occurred, then you are—

Question: Excuse me, what do you mean "in fact occurred"? You would not accept scientific evidence that the use of peyote is physically harmful?

Mr. Dorsay: I would not accept that.

Question: In general. You would require the showing in the particular context of [a] religious service?

Mr. Dorsay: Not in the context of [any] religious service. [With] respect to this Church, however, there is reliable scientific evidence that the use of peyote in the ceremony of the Native American Church contributes to rehabilitation of people who have problems with drug and alcohol abuse.

So the evidence is mixed. There is no evidence that anyone, and we need to keep repeating this, over 300 years or more, has ever suffered harm. There is one or two anecdotal—

Dorsay must be careful here. He doesn't want to say that there is no evidence of peyote's harmfulness in general, but instead that there is no evidence of harm (and some of actual benefit) in its specific use in the religious ceremony of the Native American Church, and that Church alone. He does not want to make the argument for peyote's use by other religions or in other contexts, so he focuses his argument, laser-like, on this case only. And he draws on the same themes as the Court did in *Yoder*—just as learning in the Amish way after eighth grade is critical to obtaining the living and thinking skills for a life in the Amish community, and such learning is also valuable in the larger world for those children who choose that course, so also is peyote a valuable part of the Native American religion and culture and spiritual values, and its use in the circumstances of the Native American Church actually helps treat alcohol and drug abuse. Dorsay believes that if he can make the same case the Court made in its *Yoder* opinion, the only way he can lose his case is if the Court overrules *Yoder.* He's wrong in this, but not very wrong.

But Dorsay doesn't get hit with questions about *Yoder* at this point; instead, he gets hit from the other side by a question about *Reynolds* and polygamy, surely a subject that he would prefer to avoid.

Question: But, Mr. Dorsay, under that analysis, is there any—can we possibly defend the state laws that prohibit bigamy? What is the evidence that bigamy is harmful?

Mr. Dorsay: Well, I think the evidence that bigamy was harmful in the 1800s perhaps may be different than exists today.

Question: What was the evidence then? It was against a lot of people's religious and moral beliefs, but did anybody ever prove it was harmful?

Mr. Dorsay: Well, I would say that the analysis conducted by the Court back in the 1800s was perhaps different, and maybe that statute would not be upheld in the present day. But—

Question: I think that is the logic of your position, that that statute probably falls, too.

Mr. Dorsay: I think it is not substantially justified. In that case the State, or the United States, was obviously alleging that bigamy was harmful to society in the United States. There is some evidence, for instance, that the beliefs of the Mormon Church were believed to be so outrageous that there were riots, massacres, and other things that occurred as the Mormon Church moved west from Indiana to Utah, and posed a substantial and actual threat to public order at that time.

Question: The riots probably were the result of the fact that they were a persecuted group.

Mr. Dorsay: Yes, that is correct.

To his credit, Dorsay has bitten the *Reynolds* bullet. The polygamy laws, he admits, probably wouldn't stand up today as against a claim by a member of the Mormon Church who practices polygamy out of religious conviction. This was an admission much to be avoided, for it could cost Dorsay votes on the Court if the Justices believe they effectively have to overrule *Reynolds* in order to agree with him. Dorsay's only retort—and it is a good one, but one that the Court won't want to hear—is that *Yoder* already effectively overruled *Reynolds,* and his case, involving peyote, is but a mirror image of *Yoder* and goes no further.

Question: Well, Mr. Dorsay, do you say that the State of Oregon can't rely at all on the fact that the peyote is shown as a Schedule I drug? That the facts behind that have to be proved all over again?

Mr. Dorsay: No, I am not ask—saying that. I would say that the legislative proscription informs the constitutional analysis, but it is certainly not a conclusion that this Court is bound by. We have just as reliable evidence by the legislature in terms of granting the exemption, we cannot presume that the legislature would be so outrageous—

Question: Well, wouldn't you think that the same exemption would be required for other . . . other sincere claims that the use of peyote is part of their religion?

Mr. Dorsay: Well, I have two points of response to that. Yes, I do believe it would be required under normal constitutional analysis, for other peyote churches, such as the Peyote Way Church of God, which have the same exact conditions that the Native American Church does. And there are a number of conditions that go to that that show that this church, or the use of peyote, is unique. However,—

Question: How about marijuana use by a church that uses that as part of its religious sacrament?

Mr. Dorsay: Well, see, I think we can get into a lot of examples, and I don't want to go down that road too far because we don't—

Question: I'll bet you don't.

(Laughter)

Mr. Dorsay:—have the facts here.

(Laughter)

Mr. Dorsay: But the fact is [that] a number of courts have looked at marijuana, and they have concluded that marijuana contributes substantially to the law enforcement problem. That has been the distinguishing factor in a number of cases. This drug does not contribute to the law enforcement problem. This substance is used by—as used in its sacramental purposes by the Church, does not cause those problems.

Question: Only because the law is not enforced. I mean, you know—if it occurs on the reservation and the law enforcement authorities say it can occur, I am not comforted by the fact that it doesn't cause a law enforcement problem. I don't know what that means.

Mr. Dorsay: Well, what it means is it doesn't contribute to the use of other drugs. It doesn't undermine the federal government or the nation's law enforcement efforts for other drugs. It doesn't get into the distribution system. It is not one of the drugs that is looked to by other people as a recreational substance.

Question: But why can't the state consider it itself as the law enforcement problem?

Mr. Dorsay: Peyote itself?

Question: The very use, even in religious services. Just as the state may consider the very use of marijuana, regardless of whether it pollutes commerce or anything else, as being itself a problem. We don't want it used. Why can't—

Mr. Dorsay: The state can look at it as the problem itself, but . . . it is my position, strongly, that they have to justify that position by showing some actual harm. Otherwise there would really be no free exercise right, because the state could outlaw any kind of conduct and say—

Here Dorsay must, and does, weigh in strongly on the argument that the free exercise guarantee requires the state's interests in prohibiting peyote to be judged in terms of the harm of the very particular use in this very specific case, and not on the general interest in prohibiting drug use, with its accompanying crime, health problems and risks, and the like. If the interest is cast at the general level, Dorsay will lose, as the statute's universal application is precisely consistent with and fitted to the overarching government policy against drug use—just as the interest in universal education in *Yoder* was precisely fitted to Wisconsin's requirement that everyone attend school through age 15. Dorsay's argument is that virtually every law, if judged at such an abstract and general level, would satisfy the strictest of constitutional scrutiny: tax laws, speed laws, liquor laws, marriage laws, laws governing sexual conduct. Such an approach would make the free exercise guarantee a nullity.

It is when otherwise sensible and even absolutely necessary general laws restrict religious exercise that the free exercise guarantee makes sense, inasmuch as it protects the individual believer from application of those laws to his or her particular religious practice and belief, unless the law can be shown to accomplish its general public purpose only if the religious activity is swept within its prohibition. Like free speech—which prohibits government from banning all speech on sidewalks in the interest of public order and safe passage even though such a prohibition would be a general law serving important public needs—free exercise of religion would also require government, in the interest of individual liberty, to show how such a ban of peaceful, non-obstructing religious speech serves the interests in safe passage and convenience and is essential to the accomplishment of the government's general interest.

Question: [The State can prohibit the use of peyote] so long as it does it generally, I think—why isn't that right?

Mr. Dorsay: Well, the problem is, [does] this law and [its] "neutral" prescription affect a particular religion only? And . . . this Court said in *Yoder* [that] neutral laws may in . . . application have an affect on other, on particular—

The point of the argument is getting a little muddled here. The Justice is asking why a law's general application shouldn't be enough for constitutional purposes, even if it incidentally bears down on a religious practice. Dorsay is saying that the point of the free exercise guarantee is that religious practice should not be unnecessarily impeded by law, and it doesn't matter whether it is a general law or not, because general laws are the ones that most often restrict religious acts or beliefs.

But at a different level the Justice is starting a line of inquiry into whether and why a constitutional exemption for religion from general laws is needed, and whether a rule permitting exceptions could be limited. Dorsay is being carried into the parade of horribles—the difficult hypotheticals—that he has said he wants to avoid. But he can't really avoid them. Indeed, what transpires in the following discussion is the very kind of searching analysis that the Court failed to address in the oral argument in the *Yoder* case. In effect, Dorsay's burden is to convince the Court about his own case and also convince the Court that it was correct in the *Yoder* case decided seventeen years before.

Question: Well, I suppose you could say a law against human sacrifice would, you know, would affect only the Aztecs. But I don't know that you have to make—you have to make exceptions. If it is a generally applicable law that the state—

Mr. Dorsay: Well, for instance, a better example I thought, the state is, for instance, cited to a case outlawing the use of dangerous snakes. Now, that is a legitimate belief. But, for instance, what happens if the state says we want to outlaw all use of snakes by religions. And you have a religion that believes that garter snakes, the common garden snake, is a deity. Would that general proscription hold up where you have an overbroad legislative proscription, and it is not necessary, though, in this particular instance of this—the garter snake in that case? And we would hold, and this Court has held, that the proscription must be narrowly drawn to only protect the interest that is harmed, not the general interest that is not harmed.

Question: [What if the law says poisonous] snakes? Nobody shall handle poisonous snakes.

Mr. Dorsay: Well, that would certainly be a large step in the right direction. If there are some snakes that have—are, for instance, are poisonous, but you can show, one, that they never bite people, two, that the effect is not really dangerous, that poison is not dangerous, then even in that case I would say you should not outlaw the use of that snake, because in fact it is not causing any harm to people.

Question: And the burden is on the state to show that.

Mr. Dorsay: Yes. All of the cases—

Question: So if there were a cult that used rattlesnakes, the state would have to show that in the use of those rattlesnakes somebody has been killed or hurt.

Mr. Dorsay: Well, I don't think there is any dispute about the harm that rattlesnakes can cause.

Question: I don't think there is any dispute about the harm that peyote can cause. You haven't disputed that, the general dangerousness of it, have you?

Mr. Dorsay: The misuse of peyote, no. We do not believe the circumscribed ceremonial use of this peyote constitutes misuse under any circumstances. The other—

Question: The Attorney General mentioned the incidence of 18 to 30 buttons being consumed. Would that be a dangerous use, or a use that the state could proscribe?

Mr. Dorsay: See, this is one of the problems with the record in this case. The normal, generally accepted use is four buttons, as it goes around—the use of peyote goes around twice during the ceremony. People can choose to take one to four more the second time it goes around. We do not know, the use varies in some instances, the circumstances—

Question: Well, I am not sure if it is a general problem with the record or a general problem with the exemption you seek to have us adopt.

Mr. Dorsay: If it could be shown that the ingestion of a large number, 30 or more peyote buttons, caused harm, I would say that perhaps the state could limit the use of peyote in the ceremony to a smaller amount that would not cause those problems.

Question: How often are these ceremonies held?

Mr. Dorsay: They vary among people.

Question: Like every day?

Mr. Dorsay: No. My client participates in them once or twice a year. Some people participate in them—the chiefs, road chiefs who conduct the ceremonies, do them once a week in different settings. I think the normal use is in the order of once a month or so.

Question: Is peyote habit forming?

Mr. Dorsay: No. It has not been shown to be habit forming or addictive in any respect.

I wanted to briefly address the other Establishment Clause issue, and that is the second reason for just upholding the Native American Church is that it's a federal exemption that is governed by the United States trust responsibility to Indian tribes. That's why the Native American Church has been singled out in the legislative history and in the American Indian Religious Freedom Act.

[Moreover,] the Oregon Supreme Court only exempted the Native American Church because that was the only Church before it. It was not there to look at a broad exemption for all churches. . . . [The] Court [has] said we realize it is difficult to balance between different religious beliefs, but the First Amendment requires it. If you have a long history, if you have organized tenets of a church, it makes the inquiry easier, but that does not get rid of that burden on this Court or other courts, if those organized beliefs aren't there. In this case they are here, there is—this church supports the state's drug enforcement effort in every respect. The tenets of the church believe any misuse of this drug, any misuse of other drugs or alcohol is sacrilegious. And so there is no disparity between the beliefs of this church, we believe, and the . . . the interests of the state in this case.

Question: I suppose any individual outside this church could have a sincere religious belief also that two buttons a month is required by my religious beliefs, and that can't be forbidden.

Mr. Dorsay: Well, the problem is, this is only ingested in a ceremony which is led by a road chief, in which no one leaves—

Question: I know, what if he says I have a ceremony in my house twice a month.

Mr. Dorsay: Well, see, that has been the distinction with other religions. In some of the marijuana religions, for instance, they believe we should be able to use it in any conditions under any circumstances. That, of course, implicates the state's law enforcement interest.

Question: I thought the record here showed that some members of the church do use it to cure illness, apart from these mass ceremonies where they use it, but some use it at home—

Mr. Dorsay: It is used in the ceremony, but it is also used for medical treatment as part of the ceremony.

Thank you.

Chief Justice Rehnquist: Thank you, Mr. Dorsay. . . . Thank you, General Frohnmayer. The case is submitted.

The issues of the meaning of free exercise and the relation of the free exercise clause to the establishment clause were clearly joined in the oral argument. The parties took diametrically opposite positions. The state argued that free exercise of religion didn't protect religious conduct, as opposed to belief, and that in any event a law of general application was, in itself, sufficient to extinguish any free exercise claim arising from its application to a religious practice. At its extreme, this would mean that the free exercise guarantee means little more than the establishment clause: government may not discriminate in favor of or against a religion or some religions, for to do so would be to favor and thus establish a religion, but as long as government acts equally toward all religions and does not prefer nonreligion to religion, the establishment clause is satisfied. But Frohnmayer didn't hold tightly to this line. Instead, he undermined his clear rule by arguing that certain exceptions *could* be made, and yet others might be constitutionally required, as the Court had done in *Yoder.*

Dorsay, in contrast, argued that the free exercise clause is a guarantee of substantive individual liberty, not just a guarantee of equality. A requirement of equality and no more would permit government to limit religious freedom as long as it limited everyone's equally. But for individual freedom or liberty, it doesn't matter whether a restriction comes from a discriminatory law or a general law; either way, an individual's liberty is restricted and the Constitution should extend protection just as it does for freedom of speech, or the right to a trial by jury, or the right to privacy. Religious liberty, moreover, should include the right to practice religion by act as well as by belief. Finally, the establishment clause is a distinct guarantee with distinct purposes related to separation of church and state. It prohibits preferences for religion in general or for any religion. But a preference, or an exception, that is necessary to preserve the individual's religious freedom can never violate the establishment clause, as religious freedom is the ultimate objective of the rule against establishments of religion, too.

The difference in position between the parties was constitutionally profound. Few cases present such stark and polar opposite views of the meaning of a central guarantee in the Constitution. Courts, and the Supreme Court in particular, prefer to proceed in smaller steps, avoiding absolutist choices and grounding incremental decisions firmly in fact and common sense judgment as well as in principle. The *Smith* case was therefore very much an exception to the rule. It could, of course, be decided on a more limited ground than the lawyers had argued, one that rested on a compromised and balanced view of the case and the issue it raised. This is what the Court had done over the course of its roughly forty-year experience following *Reynolds* and *Everson* in such cases as *Yoder* and *Epperson* and *Engel.* But the Justices were no longer so inclined—or at least a majority of them weren't. The increasingly deep divisions on the Court had begun to congeal around a new and very different view of the meaning of the free exercise and establishment clauses, and a newly emergent majority on the Court took advantage of the opportunity that the *Smith* case presented.

On April 17, 1990, the Court issued its opinion. The opinion shook the legal and religious world. It spawned immediate reaction in Congress, which passed laws to reverse the Court's decision forthwith (though to no avail, since the Court has the last say on the meaning of the Constitution). The opinion adopted the state's argument, but it went further and to a principled (many would say extreme) resting point: the individual's free exercise of religion can never be violated by a law of general applicability. The free exercise clause can never *require* an exemption from a general law for a religious practice. Belief and expression are protected, but largely under the free speech guarantee. Exemptions for religious practices, like use of peyote, can be granted, but only by the political branches of government. The establishment clause prevents unconstitutional discrimination in the granting of exemptions, but against the background of a rule that legislative and executive, but not judicial, accommodations for a religion or religions, and preferences for religion over nonreligion, are permissible and do not constitute establishments of religion.

The opinion was written by Justice Scalia and joined by Chief Justice Rehnquist and Justices White, Stevens, and Kennedy. Justice O'Connor concurred in a separate opinion. Only three Justices—Brennan, Marshall, and Blackmun—dissented.

Justice *Scalia* delivered the opinion of the Court.

The free exercise of religion means, first and foremost, the right to believe and profess whatever religious doctrine one desires. Thus, the First Amendment obviously excludes all "governmental regulation of religious *beliefs* as such." The government may not compel affirmation of religious belief, punish the expression of religious doctrines it believes to be false, impose special disabilities on the basis of religious views or religious status, or lend its power to one or the other side in controversies over religious authority or dogma.

But the "exercise of religion" often involves not only belief and profession but the performance of (or abstention from) physical acts: assembling with others for a worship service, participating in sacramental use of bread and wine, proselytizing, abstaining from certain foods or certain modes of transportation. It would be true, we think (though no case of ours has involved the point), that a State would be "prohibiting the free exercise [of religion]" if it sought to ban such acts or abstentions *only when they are engaged in for religious reasons* (emphasis added), or only because of the religious belief that they display.

Respondents in the present case, however, contend that their religious motivation for using peyote places them beyond the reach of a criminal law that is not specifically directed at their religious practice, and that is concededly constitutional as applied to those who use the drug for other reasons. They assert, in other words, that "prohibiting the free exercise [of religion]" includes requiring any individual to observe a generally applicable law that requires (or forbids) the performance of an act that his religious belief forbids (or requires). As a textual matter, we do not think the words must be given that meaning. It is no more necessary to regard the collection of a general tax, for example, as "prohibiting the free exercise [of religion]" by those citizens who believe support of organized government to be sinful, than it is to regard the same tax as "abridging the freedom . . . of the press" of those publishing companies that must pay the tax as a condition of staying in business. It is a permissible reading of the text, in the one case as in the other, to say that if prohibiting the exercise of religion (or burdening the activity of printing) is not the object of the tax but merely the incidental effect of a generally applicable and otherwise valid provision, the First Amendment has not been offended.

As described succinctly by Justice Frankfurter: "Conscientious scruples have not, in the course of the long struggle for religious toleration, relieved the individual from obedience to a general law not aimed at the promotion or restriction of religious beliefs. The mere possession of religious convictions which contradict the relevant concerns of a political society does not relieve the citizen from the discharge of political responsibilities." We first had occasion to assert that principle in *Reynolds v. United States,* where we rejected the claim that criminal laws against polygamy could not be constitutionally applied to those whose religion commanded the practice. "Laws," we said, "are made for the government of actions, and while they cannot interfere with mere religious belief and opinions, they may with practices. . . . Can a man excuse his practices to the contrary because of his religious belief? To permit this would be to make the professed doctrines of religious belief superior to the law of the land, and in effect to permit every citizen to become a law unto himself."[5]

The rule respondents favor would open the prospect of constitutionally required religious exemptions from civic obligations of almost every conceivable kind—ranging from compulsory military service, to the payment of taxes, to health and safety regulation such as manslaughter and child neglect laws, com-

---

5. The opinion attempted to distinguish *Yoder* as follows:

"The only decisions in which we have held that the First Amendment bars application of a neutral, generally applicable law to religiously motivated action have involved not the Free Exercise Clause alone, but the Free Exercise Clause in conjunction with other constitutional protections, such as . . . the right of parents . . . to direct the education of their children, [in] *Wisconsin v. Yoder.* The present case does not present such a hybrid situation, but a free exercise claim unconnected with any communicative activity or parental right."

pulsory vaccination laws, drug laws, and traffic laws, to social welfare legislation such as minimum wage laws, child labor laws, animal cruelty laws, environmental protection laws, and laws providing for equality of opportunity for the races. The First Amendment's protection of religious liberty does not require this.

Values that are protected against government interference through enshrinement in the Bill of Rights are not thereby banished from the political process. Just as a society that believes in the [freedom] accorded to the press by the First Amendment is likely to enact laws that affirmatively foster the dissemination of the printed word, so also a society that believes in the [freedom] accorded to religious belief can be expected to be solicitous of that value in its legislation as well. It is therefore not surprising that a number of States have made an exception to their drug laws for sacramental peyote use. But to say that a nondiscriminatory religious-practice exemption is permitted, or even that it is desirable, is not to say that it is constitutionally required, and that the appropriate occasions for its creation can be discerned by the courts. It may fairly be said that leaving accommodation to the political process will place at a relative disadvantage those religious practices that are not widely engaged in; but that unavoidable consequence of democratic government must be preferred to a system in which each conscience is a law unto itself or in which judges weigh the social importance of all laws against the centrality of all religious beliefs.

Because respondents' ingestion of peyote was prohibited under Oregon law, and because that prohibition is constitutional, Oregon may, consistent with the Free Exercise Clause, deny respondents unemployment compensation when their dismissal results from use of the drug. The decision of the Oregon Supreme Court is accordingly reversed.

It is so ordered.

With this, the Supreme Court executed something close to an about-face from the wall of separation between church and state. When rules of general applicability are at issue, free exercise involves only belief and expression, not conduct. Only purposeful and discriminatory prohibitions of a religious practice (i.e., conduct) raise free exercise concerns. The establishment clause, effectively, means the same thing. It does not prohibit laws promoting religion over nonreligion, and it does not prohibit religious-conscious and discriminatory laws favoring religion or some religions if those laws are intended to accommodate to the beliefs and practices and well-being of the religion.

For purposes of our understanding of the *Smith* case and its implications, two issues merit our attention. First, is a rule against discrimination sufficient to protect freedom of religion? Second, is separation of church and state, allocating questions of faith to the church and questions of reason to the state, the best way to safeguard religious freedom in a religiously pluralistic and democratic society? These are the two profound and foundational questions raised by the *Smith* decision. I will not offer answers to them here, but will instead raise and explore the questions they present.

The *Smith* decision states that free exercise of religion is protected only by a rule of nondiscrimination: a law of general application that affects religious and nonreligious persons alike will never violate a person's freedom to exercise religion. The liberty of religious freedom, in other words, is protected by a rule of equality of treatment. Does equality adequately protect the individual's liberty?

On the one hand, it might be argued, as Justice Scalia does, that such a rule is sufficient, at least in a religious country. As long as there are many religious people, and many religions, then a rule that guarantees all religions the same protection as other religions and as other nonreligious persons similarly situated affords a generous amount of protection. If the Catholics get a break, so must the Presbyterians, Buddhists, Jews, Muslims, and so on. If nonbelievers get a break, so must believers. If a philosophical objection to war warrants conscientious objection status, so must a religious objection to war; and if a Christian religious objection is recognized, so must a Muslim, Jewish, Buddhist, Taoist, or Deist objection. Add to this the ability of government to extend special exemptions or benefits for religion only—as long as they do not discriminate *among* religions—and the place of religion in the governmental order of things will be substantially assured—perhaps even more substantially and broadly assured than under the alternative approach of *Reynolds, Everson,* and *Yoder,* which required expensive and arduous judicial proceedings to perfect a free exercise claim.

An additional argument in favor of an equality-based approach to free exercise is that it largely (indeed perhaps entirely) avoids the need for courts to examine the bona fides of a religion or the sincerity and centrality of a religious belief. This is a substantial advantage, for the Court's approach in *Yoder* was in many respects troubling, given the Court's emphasis on the law-abiding character of the Amish and its romanticizing about the peaceful and productive Amish way of life. The Court itself had come close to doing what the dissent in *Smith* claimed the majority had done: employing a test that facilitated religious freedom only for the established and culturally elite or politically domesticated or powerful religions.

On the other hand, a rule of equality has at least two troubling aspects. The first is that it treats an individual's liberty as consisting of no more than what others are permitted by government to do. I have freedom to speak, but only if others have that freedom, too. Under such a rule, if government extinguishes all freedoms of speech, there is no constitutional problem because everyone has lost equally. This way of putting it, with free speech, has a hollow and unsatisfying ring to it, because freedoms and liberties are protected whether anyone else happens to use or enjoy them or not. My right to privacy protects me against government intruding on my private affairs, even if everyone else allows or invites government intrusion. I have a right to a jury trial even if no one else wants or has one. So also, the argument would go, with religious freedom. What kind of freedom is it if the government can just pass a law (as unlikely as it would be) that *no one* shall have religious freedom; that all churches are abolished and closed henceforth? The Court's answer in *Smith* is that such a law would be an unconstitutional, purposeful discrimination against religion. Fair enough. But is that a sufficient answer? Government needn't abolish churches so explicitly. What if churches were made subject to all general zoning rules and thus eliminated from residential areas, restricted instead to downtown or outlying areas where there is adequate space for parking and high buildings are permitted? Or subject to income tax on their donations?

The second troubling aspect of the *Smith* case's rule of equality is that it permits laws that accommodate to religion or to religious practices, as long as the political branches initiate the laws. At first glance this seems benign. Discrimination in favor of religion is different than discrimination against it. But what of new or different religions that petition for, but are denied, an exemption or a special favor? And what of the fact that most laws that discriminate in favor of someone necessarily discriminate against the excluded person or group? If a law exempting churches from the liquor laws for the sacramental use of wine were enacted, churches and religions that don't rely on wine are effectively discriminated against—even though in theory they could change their sacraments and then take advantage of the law. The same, of course, is true of the use of peyote, which if permitted would likely benefit only one church; or of exemption from compulsory education, which would similarly benefit only one or a few religions. And on the other hand, wouldn't state funding of public schools but not religious schools smack of a denial of equality and a purposeful discrimination against religion outlawed by *Smith* under the free exercise clause? Wouldn't the state, as Justice Scalia said, then be seeking "to ban . . . acts . . . only when they are engaged in for religious purposes?" As it turns out, a guarantee of equality for the protection of religious liberty isn't even an effective assurance of equal treatment.

Finally, what do the text of the First Amendment and the historical evidence of its intended meaning suggest about *Smith*'s new and largely equality-based view of the free exercise guarantee? On this question the ambiguities of the Court's terse language become evident. There is ample reason, both textually and historically, to conclude that the framers of the First

Amendment meant "free exercise" to consist mainly of a *liberty* for the individual believer. The historical evidence also suggests that "free exercise" was meant to include conduct as well as beliefs, though only limited forms of conduct, like church attendance, that were hardly disruptive. One might, in light of this, challenge the *Smith* decision as inconsistent with the proper understanding of the free exercise guarantee because an equality guarantee is substantively distinct from an individual liberty whose existence does not turn on the amount of liberty that other people enjoy. Indeed, this was the essence of the hue and cry that followed the *Smith* decision and that animated Congress's effort to enact a statute in the vain hope of reversing *Smith.* Religious liberty, it was said, is at great risk: prisoners and students will be denied their religious freedom; churches will have to abide by restrictions imposed on all other businesses; the Amish will have to return to public schools; churches will lose their property tax exemptions, and so on.

Yet none of this has happened. Property tax exemptions are secure if built into law. The Amish can leave school at age 16. Prisoners and students can practice their religion as long as the religious practices are consistent with educational or penological needs, which was always the rule. More to the point, one need not read *Smith* to deny a liberty to freely exercise religion, and thus one need not justify it as a departure from the text or the original intent of the framers. Justice Scalia's opinion in *Smith,* under this view, simply addresses the constitutional rule by which a liberty can best be protected, concluding that a requirement of general applicability and equal treatment is the most effective means of safeguarding liberty. Government cannot place any burden or disability on religion that it is unwilling to impose on every religion and on everyone else. Government can extend special benefits to religion, but only if it does so equally. Liberty is strongly protected by such rules, and the intrusion of the courts into the meaning of religion and the centrality of religious beliefs is significantly limited. *Smith,* in short, is a choice of means, not ends, and the text and historical evidence surrounding the drafting and ratification of the First Amendment say little, if anything, about means.

The second issue raised by *Smith* involves the dismantling of the separation of church and state by the fact that the establishment guarantee, too, is essentially seen to consist of a rule prohibiting discrimination *against* religion or some religions. Discrimination in favor of religion or some religions in the form of an accommodation is allowed. In accommodating to religion, government need not seek to achieve secular ends, but it can pursue sectarian and religious purposes. Religion's freedom and well-being are placed squarely in the political arena, something the separationists sought mightily to avoid.

The separationists believe that government choices and policies should be driven by reason and logic and the relation between secular means and secular ends. Matters of religious faith, being unprovable and indisputable, should be left to another, separate realm, the realm of religion and religious institutions and belief. To the extent possible, arguments of faith should not inform law in the secular state, and law should likewise not intrude into matters of faith. In the long run, the separationists believe, secular government in a pluralistic democratic state devoted to religious freedom cannot exist by any other rule. The injection of faith into law and the opportunity for religions to compete in the government sector, embodying their firmly held beliefs in law and applying them to others, will inevitably undermine democratic government.

This is a deeply entrenched view, long held in this country. It stems from the experience with the Crown in England; the patterns in many countries of government-assisted persecution of religious minorities. It resonates in the Virginia Bill for Religious Freedom and Madison's Remonstrance, and Madison's and Jefferson's views. It was eloquently expressed by Justice Black in *Everson,* even as he failed to abide by it. In a real sense, separation of church and state is a faith: we believe in it and react when it is challenged, as it was in *Smith.*

But what evidence is there for the proposition that only with the separation of faith from reason, church from secular state, can a democracy survive in a religiously pluralistic society? Precious little, perhaps. America may be the only pluralistic democracy that practices a strict form of separation of church and state. France has a preferred—indeed established—church, but also allows other religions to thrive. Israel is a religious democracy that hardly practices separation of church and state. In Germany, the state endorses and supports religion, yet allows religious liberty. The same is true in Japan and South Africa, and indeed in many states in the United States until the mid-1800s. It is also hard to claim, in the United States, that separation of church and state has prevented government-sponsored and -assisted persecution of, or discrimination against, religious sects or beliefs. Religion may be freer here than in most countries, but it is not entirely free of discrimination. Witness the Mormons, the Amish, the Native American Church, the Sabbatarians, and, most recently, the Muslims.

So religious liberty may not depend on separation of church and state. A government that instead accommodates to religion, that endorses religion over nonreligion, that prays or calls upon God at the beginning of legislative sessions or at the opening of sessions of its Supreme Court, can still be a government that strongly protects religious diversity and religious freedom. If religion in its many manifestations is, as Justice Scalia implies in *Smith,* the universal quest of mankind, then a rule prohibiting discrimination against any particular belief, coupled with the legislature's capacity to bend a bit in the interest of supporting religions in general, may well be enough of a rule in an open and free democratic society.

That, at least, is the leap of faith that Justice Scalia took in the *Smith* case.

STORY 7

Non-establishment as Nondiscrimination

Rosenberger v. University of Virginia, 515 U.S. 819 (1995)

In the fall of 1988, Ronald Rosenberger was an entering student at the University of Virginia. He was also a deeply committed, born-again Christian. In his early days at the university he saw what he judged to be a pervasive attitude of "political correctness," to which he increasingly took offense. Particularly grating were the student newspapers at the university, which "often mocked" Christians.[1] He was not alone in his view.

Ronald Rosenberger decided to correct the situation. He did so not by challenging the newspapers' right to voice anti-Christian and politically correct views, but instead by starting his own paper, this one overtly Christian and, in that sense and others, politically incorrect. In 1990, Rosenberger and a group of like-minded students founded *Wide Awake,* a twenty-four-page magazine published nine times a year whose avowed purpose was to challenge Christians "to live, in word and deed, according to the faith they proclaim, and to encourage students to consider what a personal relationship with Jesus Christ means."[2] The magazine's masthead quoted from Paul's Letter to the Romans: "The hour has come for you to awake from your slumber, because our salvation is nearer now than when we first believed."[3] The con-

1. "Church–State Issues Key in Court Case, University's Funding of Magazine Is Debated," *Dallas Morning News,* Mar. 4, 1995, at 1G.

2. Winnifred Sullivan, "The Difference Religion Makes," 113 *Christian Century* 292 (March 13, 1996).

3. *Id.*

tent of the magazine was thoroughgoingly religious, consisting of "articles about contemporary student life interpreted from a 'Christian perspective,'" and teaching and encouraging students to adopt Christian beliefs. It was an evangelical publication with a proselytizing mission. As Ronald Rosenberger explained, he "decided to start *Wide Awake* to let students know 'Christianity has relevance and meaning' and to encourage them to have a personal relationship with God."[4]

In the 1990–91 academic year, Wide Awake Productions, the group of students who founded *Wide Awake,* applied to the university's student council for a $5,800 grant to support publication of *Wide Awake.* The funds would be used only to defray printing costs and would be paid directly to the printer by the university. The student council was the body charged with allocating more than $300,000 raised from a $14-per-student activities fee to roughly 120 student groups who applied for and received funding that year. *Wide Awake*'s request for funding was denied on the ground that it was a "religious organization whose purpose is to practice a devotion to an acknowledged ultimate reality or deity." Under university guidelines, such groups could not receive funding from student activities fees because such funding would violate the separation of church and state mandated by the establishment clause. *Wide Awake* appealed this decision to a university committee overseeing student activities, but in a letter signed by the dean of students the denial of funding was affirmed. The university's decision was final.

Wide Awake and three of its members, including Ronald Rosenberger, its editor-in-chief, then brought a lawsuit claiming, among other things, that the university's decision violated their freedom of speech. They lost in the district court and the United States Court of Appeals. Both courts held that the establishment clause provided a sufficient—indeed, constitutionally compelling—justification for the university's refusal to fund the expressly religious activities of a student group. State funding of the proselytizing activities of a religious organization would violate the strict separation of church and state.

With the assistance of the Michael P. McDonald Center for Individual Rights, and the support of a wide array of religious organizations, Ronald Rosenberger, his colleagues, and *Wide Awake* sought review in the United States Supreme Court. Review was granted and the Court set the case down for oral argument. It was obvious that the case could yield a landmark decision with profound implications for the meaning of the religion guarantees. Would the *Smith* decision's rule of equality under the free exercise guar-

4. "Christian Soldier Wins Skirmish," *Times-Picayune* (New Orleans, La.), July 1, 1995, at D8.

antee mean that religion has an affirmative right to receive government funding under a general program of state support? Given the stakes, amicus curiae (supporting briefs) were filed by many religious, civil rights, and education organizations, on both sides of the issues presented.

Oral argument in the *Rosenberger* case was held at 10:00 A.M. on March 1, 1995. The Court was now fully in transition. The earlier liberal and largely separationist Justices (Brennan, Marshall, and Blackmun) were all gone. Their replacements formed a Court composed of two clear blocs, and three Justices were in the middle ground. The conservative bloc, as it is commonly called, consisted of Chief Justice Rehnquist and Justices Scalia and Thomas. In the middle ground to varying degrees were Justices O'Connor, Kennedy, and (occasionally) Breyer, a Clinton appointee. In the liberal group were Justices Souter, Ginsburg, and Stevens, the first two appointed by Presidents Bush and Clinton, and Justice Stevens by President Ford. It should be added, however, that the very definition of conservative and liberal had shifted since the days of the Warren and Burger Courts. The whole Court, and the whole country, had shifted to the right. There were no more Justices like Earl Warren, Hugo Black, Thurgood Marshall, William Brennan, and Harry Blackmun. This meant, in turn, that there was no clear and consistent voice of strict separation on the Supreme Court. The Court's religion jurisprudence was a mess: untidy, ad hoc, inconsistent, and confusing. Only the true conservative bloc had a clear and coherent view of the religion guarantees—a radically new one that had first emerged in full colors in the *Smith* case.

The lawyers in the *Rosenberger* case thus had a difficult challenge. They saw not two competing views of establishment and free exercise, but an untidy spectrum, ranging from separation (build a wall between religion and government), to neutrality (no wall, but keep religion and government at arm's length, especially with funding), to accommodation (help religion, but only a little), to nonsectarianism (anything goes as long as it doesn't prefer one sect or religion to another). Any decision in the case would by necessity have to represent a compromise among two or three of these views, for there were not five Justices holding any single view. Structuring an argument in the *Rosenberger* case thus must rest on tricky and often treacherous terrain.

The lawyers "privileged" to confront such a divided Court were two highly respected academics, Michael McConnell and John Jeffries. McConnell, who represented Ronald Rosenberger, was perhaps the leading and most prolific scholar of the religion guarantees. His views were very much influencing, perhaps even leading, the emergence of the clear and coherent conservative view held by the Chief Justice and Justices Scalia and Thomas, and, to a lesser extent, Justice Kennedy. At the time of oral argument, McConnell taught at the University of Chicago Law School. Today he is a judge on the United States Court of Appeals.

John Jeffries argued on behalf of the University of Virginia. He was a law professor and later the dean at the University of Virginia College of Law; he was also a widely respected scholar of constitutional law. Jeffries had been involved in the *Rosenberger* case from the beginning, winning the case for the university in the district court and the court of appeals.

Both lawyers were knowledgeable about the Court and the various views held by the Justices. Both knew that no matter how clear the principle they started out with appeared to be, it would likely be in shambles by the end, tossed and turned in the roiling waters produced by the Court's own uncertainty.

Chief Justice Rehnquist: We'll hear argument now in Number 94–329, *Ronald W. Rosenberger v. The Rector and Visitors of the University of Virginia.* Mr. McConnell.

Mr. McConnell: Mr. Chief Justice, and may it please the Court: It is common ground in this case that if a group of students satisfied all of the objective eligibility requirements to form a student newspaper—or in the terms of the university guidelines, a student news, information, opinion, entertainment, or academic communications media group—that they could not be excluded from funding under the guidelines simply because they espouse a controversial or otherwise political, ideological, or philosophical position of a secular sort.

Thus, if my clients this morning were the SDS [Students for Democratic Society], if they were vegetarians, if they were members of the Federalist Society, or black separatists, or whatever, there would be no need to be here this morning.

Question: What if they were Republicans?

Question: That's just the question I was going to ask. (Laughter)

Question: Well, then I'll ask Democrats, just to make it—(Laughter)

Mr. McConnell: Your Honor, even if they were Republicans or Democrats, they would not be excluded, because under the university's guidelines, an otherwise eligible organization is not excluded merely because it espouses political viewpoints within its activities, no matter how unpopular those may be.

Your Honor, this case is different because my clients are not the SDS or the Republicans, they are—their orientation is religious.

McConnell's argument is that Rosenberger's and *Wide Awake*'s religious expression is speech and should be treated that way under the First Amendment speech guarantee. Rosenberger's speech should not be excluded from university financial support just because its subject is religion, not politics (or classes, or parties, or volleyball). Religious speech, in other words, should be treated equally with nonreligious speech. Such equal treatment—even if that means equal government financial support—does not violate the establishment clause because equal treatment isn't an establishment of religion or a religious view, any more than requiring the government to treat communist ideas the same as socialist ones constitutes as government "establishment" of communism.

The point is a crucial one. McConnell is arguing that the case should be treated as a free speech case, not as a free exercise and establishment clause case. His focus on this theory gets derailed for the moment, however, as the Justices try to clarify precisely how the Virginia student funding system works, and specifically how political parties and groups are treated. Religious groups are in many, but not all, respects treated like political parties and organizations, which are excluded from the university program. However, the university's program excludes political parties *but not political speech* by any other student groups. In contrast, it excludes religious speech by student religious groups, whether or not associated with a particular religious view.

This is the essence of the discrimination argument McConnell is making: the government, through the university, is discriminating against some speech (i.e., religious speech) on the basis of its content and point of view. If so, the university's program would certainly be unconstitutional unless—as we will see—the university excludes the religious speech because to fund it would violate the establishment guarantee. McConnell's argument, however, isn't affected by the establishment guarantee, because he views the discrimination as garden-variety government censorship of speech because of its ideas. What the free speech clause requires (supporting the religious speech) the establishment guarantee can't prohibit. Or so McConnell affirms.

Why that is so is a very interesting and fundamental question. Why should religious speech be treated just like any other speech? Isn't religious speech different? Doesn't the First Amendment treat it differently, protecting it as an exercise of religion, not as free speech, and mentioning religion first, and free speech second? What is religious speech? What is religion? Should religious speech that proselytizes—preaches the Word—be seen as a distinct category of religious speech?

For the moment, these questions get lost in the technical questioning about the university's student activities funding program.

Question: You have to help me a little more on this question. I thought—I don't have it in front of me. I thought there was a provision that did exclude political groups such as Republicans and Democrats. Am I wrong on that?

Mr. McConnell: Your Honor, there are two relevant exclusions for political groups. One of those is for political organizations, and it might very well be that an organization set up affiliated with the Republican or Democratic Party could be excluded at the University of Virginia on that ground. Of course, that is not applicable here. My clients are not affiliated with any national or other religious organization.

Question: Would not the rule that you are arguing for entitle such a political group also to get funding?

Mr. McConnell: Your Honor, the guidelines expressly provide . . . that these restrictions on funding political activities are not intended to preclude [the] funding of any otherwise eligible student organization which espouses particular positions or ideological viewpoints, including those that may be unpopular, or that are not generally accepted.

As I understand this rule, Your Honor, the point is that if there's an organization that is simply engaging in electioneering, or lobbying, which are much narrower categories than the espousal of a viewpoint, that such groups can be excluded, but groups cannot be excluded because they are expressing even controversial political viewpoints in a student newspaper.

Question: As I understand it, Mr. McConnell, there are two bases for exclusion of religious publications. One is if the organization practices religion—I mean, if it's a prayer group, or something like that—and then there's a separate one if the publication exhibits religious belief?

Mr. McConnell: That's right, Your Honor, and there's been no—

Question: And the latter does not apply to the political exclusion. If you exhibit the belief of a Republican, your publication is not necessarily excluded, although if you are a Republican, Young Republicans or something like that, you would be excluded.

Mr. McConnell: That's exactly correct.

Question: Whereas for religions, if you are either a religious group or you exhibit religious belief, you're out.

Mr. McConnell: That's correct, and there's been no claim in this case that my clients are a religious organization.

Question: Mr. McConnell, the religious provision to which Justice Scalia refers is [for] an activity which primarily promotes or manifests a belief in and about a deity or an ultimate reality. That's the provision you say is the equivalent of exhibiting.

Mr. McConnell: Exactly.

Question: Yes, I see, and the political one is an organization primarily involved, and so forth and so on. I don't see the dramatic difference between the two provisions that you rely on. You acknowledge that the Young Republicans would still be excluded, that that exception would not let the Young Republicans run a newspaper that espouses Republican views. They would be excluded as a Republican political organization, no?

Mr. McConnell: Your Honor, whether the—the Young Republicans would presumably be a political organization, but that is not—my clients have not been excluded because they are a religious organization. They are not a religious organization.

Question: I understand. I'm just asking about the Young Republicans. You acknowledge the Young Republicans would not be able to publish a magazine of Republican viewpoints.

Mr. McConnell: Under the guidelines, that's exactly correct.

Question: But any other organization, if it's not a Republican organization, would be?

Mr. McConnell: That's right, and the very same students could get together and put out a newspaper. In fact, the *Virginia Advocate*, which is a funded organization, looks very much like the sort of newspaper the Young Republicans would publish, and that is funded.

Question: Let me make sure I understand you. You agree that a Republican publication would be prohibited by the guidelines. Do you also agree that it may constitutionally be prohibited by the guidelines?

Mr. McConnell: Your Honor, the line that we believe that this Court's cases establish, and that the First Amendment imposes, is a line that prohibits viewpoint discrimination. If the university is excluding all political organizations whatever their orientation or persuasion, our position is that that is not unconstitutional. Let me just point—

Question: Well, do you agree that it would not be unconstitutional to deny funding to a publication that says "vote Republican in the next election"?

Mr. McConnell: Your Honor, if that rule were in fact applied to all newspapers, that prohibited all endorsements of political candidates, we would not claim that that is unconstitutional. Of course, that is not the guideline. In fact, student newspapers regularly endorse candidates for office, and let me point out here that this case is extraordinarily—

Question: Those other newspapers are not affiliated with an identified partisan organization, I suppose, or at least in theory they're not.

Mr. McConnell: Just as my clients are not identified with any religious denomination or other organization. Let me point out—

Question: Suppose—just on this one point, suppose the religious newspaper engaged in soliciting members, proselytizing, coupons to fill out and return that are contained in the newspaper, does that change the case, or make it a more difficult case?

Mr. McConnell: I don't know, Your Honor. I assume that part of any student activity is usually recruiting other members, and I wouldn't think that *Wide Awake* would be any more precluded from inviting others to join in *Wide Awake's* activity than any other student group, and of course—

Question: That cannot be equated with the political restrictions against campaigning.

Mr. McConnell: Well, again I don't think that the *Virginia Advocate* is precluded from trying to persuade students to join the *Virginia Advocate*, or to join in its causes, and—

Question: Yes, but the *Virginia Advocate* is not a church.

Mr. McConnell: Wide Awake is also not a church, Your Honor.

Question: No, but I mean, going back to Justice Kennedy's question. If they were circulating coupons, sign up for membership in the First Presbyterian Church, that sort of thing. It's one thing to recruit members of one's organization, as such, and it's another thing to recruit adherence to God, to religious tenets.

Mr. McConnell: Your Honor, if you look at *Wide Awake* magazine—

Question: You admit the distinction, don't you?

Mr. McConnell: Your Honor, I'm not at all sure that a distinction of that sort would be administrable. I don't know how you can tell the difference. One is not converted to membership in God. There is a worldview which is theistic in nature. One is either convinced of the truth of that worldview, or one is not.

Just as there is a Marxist worldview, there is a libertarian worldview, there are a number of worldviews, and one is either convinced of the truth of those worldviews or not, and those world views have application to numerous issues, such as the questions that are addressed in this magazine.

The question being probed goes to the distinction the university draws between an affiliated organization, political or religious, and individuals expressing a view. McConnell wants this to be the distinction the establishment clause draws. While it may prohibit government support going to religious institutions—say, a church—it would permit (indeed require) such support being made available to independent religious activities of individuals.

The questions from the Justices, however, explore a different distinction, one between "electioneering" in politics or "proselytizing" in religion on the one hand, and discussion about politics or religion on the other. Could the government provide money to people who preach on street corners, or even in a church? Could the government fund the salaries of those who "preach" in Alcoholics Anonymous pursuant to a general substance abuse program? McConnell's distinction between an organization (political or religious) and an individual is a formalism of no value to the Justices' questions, which go strictly to the substance of the speech, not the identity of the speaker.

In drawing a line based on the identity of the religious speaker, not the content of the religious speech, is McConnell taking the position that religion is no different from any philosophy or ideology? Is religion special, and is that why the Constitution singles it out expressly? What is a religion?

Question: Well, Mr. McConnell, may I ask you a question that I think fits into this same line of inquiry? You argue for an overarching principle of neutrality, and you say if we will look at the program and see if it's neutral, that should be the test, and do you think that means that Government must never single out religion in legislating, or do you think that the constitutionality of a program under the Establishment Clause depends on its effects, its overall effects with respect to religion?

This is a very important question. Can't a program that is formally neutral with respect to religion have effects that make it violative of the establishment clause? If the government gave grants to churches because of their value in aiding the poor, might that not violate the establishment clause, even though the government also gave grants to nonreligious social organizations that do the same thing? If the government gives funds to public libraries, must it give funds to religious libraries? McConnell says yes. The Justice's question implies that "yes" is not an obvious answer, given the establishment clause, which the Court has held prohibits the giving of tax funds to religious schools—even though public schools are supported, and the religious schools are permitted to exist on the condition that they provide the same educational content and value to their students as the public schools do.

Equality, in other words, hasn't historically been the only question pertinent to constitutionality. One must also ask whether treating religions equally nonetheless constitutes an establishment of religion if the government and religion become too intertwined, which may mean, for example, providing taxpayer funds to religion or conveying a message of government preference for, or endorsement of, religion or one religion. Just as treating religion equally might violate the establishment clause, as the Court quite expressly stated in *Everson,* so also treating religion differently might not, as the Court decided in *Yoder.* It's complicated!

Mr. McConnell: Well, Your Honor, I can imagine situations in which the Government might be operating according to formally neutral criteria that have such disproportionate effects that one suspects that there's a religious gerrymander going on.

Question: Would some of our school funding cases fall in that category, where the Court spoke in terms of well, if we support this, 95 percent of the schools that will benefit are religious schools, and so forth?

Mr. McConnell: Yes, Your Honor, and in each of the parochial school cases the Court went out of its way to point out that the [ostensibly neutral] category . . . private schools is a category that in fact contained overwhelmingly religious schools, and more than that, overwhelmingly religious schools of one particular religious denomination.

And I think that those cases can be understood as the Court's reaction to—not to aid which is general in nature to viewpoints of all sorts, but rather to aid which the legislature knew, everyone knew, this Court knew, was being enacted in response to the needs of a particular—to religion in general, but especially to one particular religious denomination.

Question: Well, so if the student publication in question were really a mechanism of getting more members for the Presbyterian Church, for example, then you think it's appropriate to look at the effects of the publication?

Mr. McConnell: Well, Your Honor, no. I think that it's appropriate to look at the effects of the Government's action. That is, if the Government is drawing categories that have disproportionate effect, thus leaving us room to suspect that there's a religious gerrymander [purposeful preference] going on, we should look at effects in that sense, but [we should] not [be] concerned [that] the students benefiting from free facilities at the university might try to gain members, or recruit people to the Presbyterian Church, or whatever.

All that matter[s] [is that] all student groups [be] given an equality of free speech rights, and that is our position here.

Question: Mr. McConnell, may I ask you a question directed specifically to religious activities and the state of our precedent? Is there any decision so far that has authorized a direct cash contribution from the State . . . in support of a religious activity?

Mr. McConnell: Your Honor, I think that the closest case to that is the *Witters* case in which direct cash payments were made for vocational education at the Inland Empire School for Bible—

Question: Not for a purpose directed by the State, that is, vocational education, but for a pursuit that the religious group—that the group engaged in an avowedly religious activity has charted for itself. I don't—I'm not aware of such a case.

Mr. McConnell: Well, Your Honor, in this case, the University of Virginia is not channeling money to religious groups. It is trying to support the activity of students writing and editing and distributing newspapers.

This is a stretch. First, the "newspaper"—*Wide Awake*—was overtly proselytizing. Rosenberger probably would be offended by someone calling it a newspaper. Second, even if it is in a formal sense a newspaper, the reason for it, and virtually all of its content (even the advertisements), was pervasively religious. To say that the university is supporting student journalism by funding *Wide Awake* is to say that a university that sponsors prayer does so because of the aerobic physical exercise involved in bowing and kneeling.

Question: Well, I just—Mr. McConnell, I just wanted to know if there was any precedent. You gave me the case where the State was supporting vocational education, and you said, that's the closest case to this one.

Mr. McConnell: And Your Honor, I'd like to urge you [to accept] that that is in fact a very close parallel, because there the State was supporting vocational education, and here, the State is supporting student journalism, and in both cases the State is completely, or should be, completely indifferent as to whether the individuals who benefit or participate in those programs themselves decide to . . . use those benefits in a way that participates in a religious activity, because the establishment—

Question: There's a distinction in this case, because the claim is that the very nature of the publication itself is an espousal of religion. It is, in your phrase, a religious activity, so there's nothing left to chance here.

Mr. McConnell: But, Your Honor, the very activity in [the earlier case about providing a room in the school for a religious group] was a religious activity, too. [The students were] engaged in learning about . . . studying a religion, in a deeply, pervasively religious way.

The point is that the establishment—

Question: Well, is it your point that so long as the criterion for giving out the aid is at a sufficiently high level of generality that it does not identify religious purpose as its object, e.g., funds for education, funds for publications, that that is the end of the inquiry about a possible establishment violation?

Mr. McConnell: Yes. To use this Court's [own] words . . . , when a subsidy is distributed to a broad array of organizations, both religious and secular, on the basis of objective criteria, the fact that some of the aid may go to religious advocacy does not violate the Establishment Clause.

Examples might include income tax exemption for religious organizations, which must be related to good deeds, not beliefs or religion; or exemption for churches from (or special treatment of churches in) zoning laws, which must be based on architecture or a reward for the church's good deeds, for example, and not religion. Many would say, however, that these are just rationalizations. When Congress enacted a set of religious freedom acts following the *Smith* case, Congress didn't mince words: churches were to be exempt from zoning laws that interfered with their religious function because they were religious institutions, and not because they did good deeds or had interesting or unique architecture.

Question: On your criterion, then, if the State were to dispense funds for moral betterment, it could make direct cash payments to any organized religious group.

Mr. McConnell: Your Honor, if a group—

Question: Well, isn't the—

Mr. McConnell: I do not think—

Question:—consequence of what you just said? You said, if the level of generality is high enough so that we know the object is not a peculiarly religious object, that makes it okay.

Mr. McConnell: No, Your Honor, because in order to administer that category, money to morally uplifting groups, the Government would have to decide whether a religious group is in fact morally uplifting. I fully agree that such an inquiry on the part—

Question: Well—

Mr. McConnell:—of the Government is unconstitutional. Here, the only thing that the Government has to determine is—

The question catches McConnell up short. McConnell's argument would suggest, as the question does, that the answer is yes. That is, after all, the justification for tax deductions and exemptions for churches, in the minds of many people. Tax exemption is a cash contribution, or its economic equivalent: keep the $100 that you would otherwise have to pay in tax, without restrictions on how you use it.

Instead, McConnell tries to squeeze out by saying, in effect, that the answer would be yes except for the problem of judging whether a religious group is morally uplifting and thus entitled to the cash; this would be unconstitutionally intrusive into religion (violating free exercise). But his logic is wrong: the solution for the problem should be to include all churches and religious groups on the presumption that they are morally uplifting, in order to avoid intrusion—just like the result in *Rosenberger* should be, he argues, to include *Wide Awake* in the funding program because to judge whether the newspaper is too overtly religious and focused on proselytizing, rather than opinions on various questions from a religious perspective, would be to intrude on the belief system.

Why does McConnell feel compelled to try to squeeze out? Why not just answer that the morally uplifting money must also go to the churches? Perhaps it's because McConnell doesn't want to carry the baggage that such an argument would take on, for if he said yes, wouldn't he also have to say that religious high schools should receive the same government money as the public schools, else the government would be discriminating against religion in the program of compulsory education? It's hard to see how he could escape that conclusion. And he may well hold that belief. But he has a client whose claim is more limited. Win this one first, without carrying that burden, then he can turn to the next case and the next step.

But at least one Justice won't let him out of his bind, and presses McConnell *hard.*

Question: Let's make it a little easier. Instead of saying, as you were putting it, morally uplifting, those which simply espouse the pursuit of action based on moral grounds. One ought to act morally responsibly. That's the only criterion. That isn't going to require very much by way of inquiry, and I take it on your reasoning that direct cash payments could be made to any church group on that theory.

Mr. McConnell: Well, Your Honor, in [the earlier case dealing with access to rooms, not to funding],[5] the—

Question: Well [I know about that case]. What about *your* theory? Isn't it the case that on your theory the direct payments could be made?

Mr. McConnell: Your Honor, so much depends upon—it depends upon the practice with which such a category was administered. If, in fact, that meant that virtually anyone who espoused any view that was remotely related to the good life received money, I think that would be fine, but if in fact it meant that the Government was engaged in a searching, case-by-case inquiry, deciding this group promotes the moral life and this group doesn't, then that kind of selective funding I think would be unconstitutional, and religious groups could not be included, because then the Government would be putting its imprimatur upon particular religious views and saying these are good views.

---

5. *Lamb's Chapel v. Center Moriches Union Free School Dist.*, 508 U.S. 384 (1993).

But why wouldn't the answer be, in such a case, that the funding program would be unconstitutional and no one gets money, rather than, as McConnell says, the program would be fine but religious groups would have to be (i.e., constitutionally required to be) excluded and thus treated differently—discriminated against? In equal protection cases, the normal response to unconstitutional inequality when true equality can't be achieved is to strike the program down for everyone, not to excuse the discrimination. McConnell is trying to escape the questions about the implications of his argument, but the Court won't let him. The Justices bore in further, and McConnell seems to be getting a little shaky.

Mr. McConnell (continuing): Here, the only thing that's going on is that the Government has found that this is a student news, opinion, entertainment, or academic media group. That is not an entangling form of category.

Question: Mr. McConnell, would your theory mean that the . . . tax code [would be unconstitutional if it] provided that organizations engaging in religious activities would not be able to receive tax-deductible contributions?

Mr. McConnell: The—where the tax code has exempted—[where the tax code] provides tax exemptions for essentially the entire nonprofit charitable world, if there were an exclusion of charities that espoused religious views, I think that I would be here contending that that's unconstitutional.

The question was easy, and McConnell answered it clearly and directly. To say religious organizations must get benefit of charitable deductions and the like, just like all other charities, is hardly controversial, and it would hardly raise an eyebrow. After all, that's exactly what the tax law provides today. McConnell didn't have to answer the question about religious primary and secondary schools, about parents of children in those schools having to pay property tax for public education and also tuition to the religious school. Those would have been very sensitive questions. So McConnell got lucky. He stuck to his guns (where it wasn't painful to do so) and then quickly changed the subject to other and hopefully less nettlesome matters.

Mr. McConnell (continuing): Now, there are two ways in which the religious character of [the student group's] viewpoint might be considered relevant [to justifying the university's discrimination against them]. One is the university's position, which is [that] to draw the line between religious and nonreligious is not *viewpoint* discrimination [that violates the free speech guarantee, but is instead a subject matter category, like electioneering or commercial speech, that can be excluded]. Because it seems to me that [this argument] is plainly foreclosed by this Court's [recent and] unanimous decision [that government may not discriminate between religious and political activities in allocating public space], I would like to turn instead to the arguments not endorsed by the university today, but which were the basis of the . . . judgment below. That is—

We'll hear more about the university's argument about viewpoint or subject matter distinctions in relation to an exclusion of religious speech. The other, and more obvious, justification for excluding *Wide Awake* is, as the Justice's questions have already suggested, that to give funds directly to a religious organization for religious activities would violate the establishment clause, and thus the resulting discrimination against religion is valid because the discrimination against religion is required by the Constitution. The university made this argument from the very beginning of the case, and won on the basis of the argument in the federal circuit court. But the university elected not to pursue it in the Supreme Court. This would not stop the Court from considering the establishment clause argument, and even resting its decision on it, as we will see. But it raises the question of why the university gave up on that argument and instead decided to defend the funding program on the much weaker (for the university) free speech theory that discrimination against religious speech is not a content- or viewpoint-based discrimination that is presumptively unconstitutional under the free speech guarantee. The answer may never be known, but there is some evidence that the decision was the client's; that the state of Virginia and the university's board did not, for political reasons, want to take the position that funding religious speech would violate the establishment clause. If so, John Jeffries, who had prevailed on behalf of the university before and would follow McConnell in the Supreme Court oral argument, had been suddenly dealt a very difficult—indeed impossible—hand.

Question: Before you [turn to the establishment clause issue], may I just ask you one question about your understanding of the way the regulation would apply? Would funding be denied, as the regulation is written, to an organization espousing atheism?

Mr. McConnell: Your Honor, I think it would.

Question: What prevents the—are you saying the Constitution would prevent the university from deciding to teach Buddhism unless they also wanted to teach Hinduism, or the university's newspaper, edited by students, to decide that they want to print liberal articles but not conservative articles, or articles involving, say, Buddhists but not Hindus, or whatever? I mean, how does that interest in a university to edit, decide how it spends its money, or decide what's important for students to hear, how does that fit in to your First Amendment analysis?

Mr. McConnell: Well, Your Honor, absolutely fundamental to our position is the distinction between the Government's own speech, either through its employees or through grantees—

Question: These are State universities. I'm assuming State universities.

Mr. McConnell: Yes, but even with—Your Honor, even within the context of a State university, the State university is in some cases speaking itself, and in other cases it is providing a platform or a means for private speakers to be able to speak their own minds. That distinction is central to our position, and it is our view that the Free Speech Clause protects private speech where the content and viewpoint are initiated by the private speakers, that it protects private speech against viewpoint-based discrimination whether . . . the speech is religious or nonreligious.

Question: But maybe the Government wants to sponsor and speak through the views of private people but only on subjects that the Government wants spoken about.

Mr. McConnell: Yes, Your Honor.

Question: And the line is pretty hard to draw, isn't it?

Mr. McConnell: Your Honor, we absolutely agree that the university, that the Government, when it chooses to present its own message through private speakers by funding those speakers on account of their espousing the Government's message, that in those cases the Government's—the Government may take a viewpoint. It can espouse an antismoking campaign without funding a pro-smoking campaign.

Question: Is that possibly what's going on here?

Mr. McConnell: Absolutely not, Your Honor. The university has been completely clear that in its funding of student groups it means it does not endorse the groups, it does not agree with them, it doesn't even allow them to use the University of Virginia's logo. It has separated itself to the maximum possible extent from the content of these groups, and of course, the groups themselves that are funded—

Question: And a good idea, too, if you read some of them, right?

Mr. McConnell: I—

Question: But what they say that they're doing is, they're funding educational activities by students, and they don't want to fund non-educational activities. Why can't they do that? Do they have to fund every activity? I mean, why can't they?

Mr. McConnell: Your Honor, and they've made the further determination that writing a student newspaper is an educational activity. That is, the act of writing, editing, distributing, reading, engaging in ideas, is itself an educational activity, not because the content of the newspaper is educational, but because the activity of engaging in student journalism is itself educational. That's why you can have an animal rights oriented newspaper, and you can have a meat-eaters oriented newspaper on the same campus. It isn't that one of those views is better than the other, it's that the participation in this activity is itself educational.

Question: Mr. McConnell, what about the university's having in mind student cases that are coming up around the country, students who say . . . , "I don't want my activity fee to support something with which I disagree"? If this activity were to be supported, would the university not have to allow all the people who don't want their money to support a religious activity to get a deduction?

Mr. McConnell: Your Honor, the lower courts have been split on these questions, and some have said yes, but they have said yes with regard to controversial political speech, too, so that a person opposed to abortion is not required to contribute, or may get their portion of the student activity fee back that goes to the pro-choice campaign. There's been no distinction between controversial religious and political speech.

Now, other courts have upheld these programs and not allowed a right to refund on the theory that so long as the university is funding a broad array of viewpoints of all sorts that no student is being required to support any particular viewpoint, and that it's much like, you know, taxpayers supporting postal subsidies, or supporting public libraries that contain books that they don't agree with.

Question: Well, what about the student who says it isn't like the post office because when we're dealing with the Establishment Clause, this Court has recognized a right [under the Establishment Clause] that is not recognized in any other area, . . . where the taxpayer can challenge the use of her money to support a religious activity.

Mr. McConnell: Well, Your Honor, all the courts that have accepted this claim have in fact allowed students to object to controversial political claims, though all of the cases have involved secular speech. . . . In this context, religious and secular speech, it seems to me, are the same. Now, I don't know whether the university should be required to give refunds or not. I'd be perfectly content for objecting students to receive refunds if they object to some of the speech. The point is that the university may not use its power to skew the marketplace of ideas at the University of Virginia by favoring some viewpoints over others.

Question: Mr. McConnell, a new subject, and I know your time is about to expire. Is it your position that the State can never recognize that there may be a gray area where we're not sure that there's an Establishment Clause [violation] or not, and use that determination as a ground for withholding support from the activity?

Mr. McConnell: Your Honor, I wouldn't say never, but I would say that where citizens have a free speech or free press right, a constitutional right under the First Amendment, the university can't . . . defeat that right or deny that right on the basis of some nebulous fear of violating another provision of the Constitution [like the Establishment Clause]. Indeed, it is not at all clear to me why one clause of the Constitution should be read to trump the other clause to begin with. It seems to me much more sensible to take a step back and look at how the Establishment Clause and the Free Speech Clause and the Free Exercise Clause can be read as a consistent and harmonious whole, all of them designed to guarantee a neutrality between religion and its various ideological competitors in the marketplace of ideas.

I would like to reserve the remainder of my time for rebuttal.

Chief Justice Rehnquist: Very well, Mr. McConnell.

So McConnell finally gets to the establishment clause, but he said little more than his conclusion, which is that the establishment, free exercise, and free speech guarantees should be harmonized—by making the speech guarantee the dominant one, overriding the other two. Calling the establishment clause issue "nebulous" isn't helpful. The Court's opinions of late, to be sure, had been a bit confusing—a different establishment clause rule for public rooms and space than for public money going to religious activity or churches—but the decisions the Court reached in those cases had been decisive and clear, not nebulous, even if McConnell disagrees with them and thinks them intellectually and constitutionally weak in their reasoning.

But why harmonize the three guarantees the way McConnell says? Why not, instead, harmonize them by making the free exercise and establishment clauses dominant over the free speech guarantee; and then make the establishment clause override the free exercise clause when needed to maintain distance between the state and church, as the Court had done for over one hundred years since *Reynolds?* To do so wouldn't break any new ground.

Notably, the Court's opinions in *Reynolds* and *Everson* had dealt with history and purpose and the overriding meaning of religious freedom in the American Republic. McConnell's argument said nothing about these things: no history, no discussion of the purposes of the religion guarantees. Will equality alone foster or undermine the separation of church and state? Is active participation in politics by religious organizations compatible with the need in a diverse nation to base political judgments on at least nominally secular grounds? Can religious liberty thrive in a government openly influenced by religious organizations? Instead of addressing these questions, McConnell simply argues free speech theory under a different guarantee than the religion guarantees, thus avoiding religion guarantee issues and history and purposes altogether.

The Justices, in effect, let McConnell do so. They didn't ask about free exercise or establishment, except when it was too late, and they asked no hard questions of McConnell when he did make his brief, utterly conclusory statement about the establishment clause at the end of the argument. Why? Where were the *Everson* strict separationists? Was there none left on the Court in 1995? Did the unanimous strict separation view in *Everson* no longer have even one vote on this Court?

Chief Justice Rehnquist: Mr. Jeffries.

Mr. Jeffries: Mr. Chief Justice, and may it please the Court:

This case is not specifically about religion. It is about funding, and the choices that inevitably must be made in allocating scarce resources. Some funding decisions do not involve speech, but in a pubic university virtually all of them do. In public education, funding speech based on content is legitimate, routine, and absolutely necessary.

Under the university guidelines—

Question: But not based on viewpoint, I take it. You would agree with that.

Mr. Jeffries: I do. Under the university—

Question: So this boils down to whether this is a viewpoint case?

Mr. Jeffries: I do think that's exactly the heart of the question, and if I may just clear up one issue that was left over from the earlier colloquy, under the university's guidelines, the definition of political activity, which is defined to mean lobbying or electioneering, and the definition of religious activities are not exactly alike, but they raise precisely the same constitutional question. Imagine that students organized themselves in support of the President's reelection campaign, and published a Clinton reelection newspaper. That would be an electioneering activity. We would not fund it for that reason. Imagine that students lobby the State legislature to pass or defeat the balanced budget amendment. That would be a lobbying activity. We would not fund it for that reason. Students have a constitutional right to support the reelection of the President. They have a constitutional right to lobby the legislature. They have a constitutional right to advocate their religious beliefs. All of these cases present precisely the same free speech issue, and they stand or fall on that basis.

The intent of the guidelines is to allow in the political area a wide variety of [points of view], and to except two fairly narrow categories, electioneering, by which I mean publication devoted expressly to an election result, hence the Clinton campaign newsletter, and lobbying legislatures.

Question: Well then, suppose you have a newspaper that simply espouses the Republican point of view, or the Democratic point of view. Just as a more or less—liberal versus conservative, whatever you want to call it, but it has party identification. Is that permitted?

Mr. Jeffries: Liberal and conservative points of view are freely permitted. Indeed, all points of view are permitted. The question is, which are funded—

Question: Yes.

Mr. Jeffries:—and the exclusion from funding would be those activities so closely allied with an election result as to be found to be electioneering.

Question: So that some might say the Americans For Democratic Action, or something, a liberal group which consistently supports Democratic candidates but doesn't really electioneer for them, they could be funded?

Mr. Jeffries: Yes, sir, [they] would be eligible for funding.

Question: Now, why is that different from a group that is not trying to recruit people to a particular Christian sect, but simply espousing the truthfulness of certain Christian doctrines, just as this other group, while not trying to get you to vote for a particular candidate, is espousing the truthfulness of that candidate's position on a lot of issues? I don't see a distinction.

Mr. Jeffries: The guidelines make that distinction. My point in suggesting that these raise the same constitutional issue was to say that in all three categories, electioneering, lobbying, and religious activities . . . —[all of which are] activities which people have a constitutional right to engage in—the guidelines say [the University] nonetheless will not fund. If it's an unconstitutional action in refusing to fund religious activities under the Free Speech Clause, it must follow that it's equally unconstitutional to refuse to fund the Clinton campaign reelection newsletter or to refuse to fund students engaged in lobbying activities under the Free Speech Clause—

Jeffries' theory is strictly a free speech theory. His argument is that excluding religious speech—which involves proselytizing and speaking about a religion and its beliefs in a persuasive way, and does not include speaking about a political issue, like abortion, from a religious perspective—is no different from excluding political speech about a candidate or political lobbying by a student group. The latter exclusions are very common in most public university student activity fund schemes. If they are constitutional, Jeffries argues, so must the categorical (not viewpoint) exclusion of religious speech.

As a matter of general theory about the nature of the exclusion—viewpoint versus category, content, etc.—Jeffries is right. But it doesn't follow that the university is legally entitled to exclude religious speech as a category just because it has a justification for denying funding of electioneering or lobbying: keeping the university at arm's length from the partisan political process, therefore maintaining freedom of inquiry. What would the reason for excluding religious speech be? There are at least a couple of possibilities: avoiding confusion about the university endorsing a view on religion, or avoiding violation of the establishment clause. But these two arguments are really establishment clause arguments, which Jeffries can't make because his clients, the University of Virginia and the state of Virginia, apparently have discouraged him from making them. Could the university instead argue that religious speech is somehow inconsistent with the open forum for ideas in a university? It is hard to imagine doing so, as religion is taught and discussed at universities, and indeed it is arguably the central issue facing mankind.

So Jeffries has his work cut out for him. He can only argue that the exclusion of religious speech is made in general terms, so it should be permitted. But the first amendment prohibits government from outlawing talk about sex, or politics, or history, even if it does so in general terms unrelated to a specific sex act, or political question, or historical incident. Whether specific or not, it's still censorship by government unless there is a really good reason to support it. Jeffries is foreclosed by his client from offering one.

Question: I'm talking about different things. I'm talking about refusing to fund for religious publications simply the espousal of general ideas, without identification of a particular sect, without proselytizing, whereas in the political context, so long as you don't proselytize, so long as you're not electioneering, it's okay. Why is it—why is there that distinction?

Mr. Jeffries: Why do the guidelines make the distinction they make?

Question: You acknowledge that they make that distinction.

Mr. Jeffries: The guidelines—

Question: Now, you used to say the reason they make it is, the Establishment Clause made us do it, but you're not taking that position today, right?

Mr. Jeffries: Obviously, if the Establishment Clause forbids us from giving direct aid to religion, there is an end to the matter, but we do not stand on that ground. We take the following position. There is in this country a long and honored tradition of financial disengagement—again, this is a question of funding, not activities. There is a long tradition in this country of financial disengagement between church and State. We think it's entirely reasonable for the university to adhere to that tradition.

Well! Without the garb of establishment clause policy, this argument isn't worth the paper it's written on. Can one argue that certain subjects can be prohibited from being spoken about in a government forum simply in the interest of adhering to tradition? For many years there was a tradition in this country of not talking about sex; could a University prohibit talk about sex, or refuse to fund or provide space for that talk on the same terms that it does for, say, philosophizing, simply in order to maintain a tradition? My mother used to say (to no avail), "No arguing about sex, politics, or religion at the dinner table." She could do that, obviously. But would we let the government say that?

Question: This is not a church, though. I mean, if you're—you know, if your point were, we will not fund any church organization that publishes something, that's fine, but that's not what these guidelines say. It says, any organization that espouses that viewpoint. What's the term it uses?

Mr. Jeffries: With respect, Justice Scalia, the plaintiffs were not denied eligibility as a religious organization. They are not a church, and they were not denied funding on that ground.

Question: Yes.

Mr. Jeffries: They were denied funding because the publication of this magazine was found to be a religious activity, a conclusion that they have never contested.

Question: Because it manifests a particular belief in or about a deity, right?

Mr. Jeffries: Because it primarily manifests a particular belief in or about a deity, yes, sir.

Question: But that is different from lobbying and campaigning. Your premise that you're submitting to us is that because it is permissible to withhold funding from active campaigning in the political sphere, therefore it is permissible to hold—to withhold funding for abstract discussions of religious views, and it seems to me the two do not follow at all.

Mr. Jeffries: Well, in my judgment, Justice Kennedy, the cases on which the petitioners rely are quite consistently free speech cases. If the Court had meant to specify something special about religion, it probably would have relied on the Free Exercise Clause, so the inference which I made is that under the Free Speech Clause, lobbying, electioneering, religious activities are all protected, and all comparably protected under the Constitution.

Question: But the university can say that these are not educational activities, and draw the line there. But it doesn't follow that it can draw the further line that discussion of abstract views of religion is also prohibited. It seems to me that that's where your parallelism breaks down.

Mr. Jeffries: It may be misleading to think of the university's policy as refusing to fund a discussion of abstract views. The university refuses to fund religious activities. This magazine is a proselytizing activity. Basically, religious activity means worship services and prayer, or proselytizing, so there is little doubt that this magazine fits the university's guideline.

Question: Well, do you take the position that any discussion of religious views is proselytizing?

Mr. Jeffries: No, sir.

Here Jeffries is skirting the edge of the establishment clause issue, and with effect. If he were freed from his client's apparent insistence that the establishment clause not be mentioned in relation to university funding, his argument would be: (1) this is a religious activity, which means prayer, worship, and proselytizing, not discussion; (2) the university is not prohibiting or restricting religious activity by students or on campus, but is instead refusing to fund it; and (3) this it must do (or at least can do) in the interest of not giving government funds to support the practice of religion, lest that be an establishment of that religion and, as important, lest that religion become dependent on the government for support and therefore, in reality, no longer a religion answerable only to its God. Religious speech, he would argue, is different, not because the ideas are more or less pertinent or basic or important; nor because it attempts to persuade and convert; nor because it rests on faith rather than reason; but instead because to achieve and maintain religious freedom in a secular state, religious belief and exercise must be free from dependence on the government and must occupy their own independent realm. Because religious speech is in this sense very different from speech about politics or sex, it should be treated differently, especially with regard to government funding, and treating it differently should not be viewed as any form of discrimination. To treat different things the same is not to treat them equally.

Jeffries surely wants to make this argument. He made it in the court of appeals and won. He is probably chomping at the bit. So he skirts the edges, wades in a little, but can't take the plunge. That's too bad.

Question: That's all your guidelines say, manifests a particular view. If you primarily manifest a particular view relating to, in, or about a deity, you're out.

Mr. Jeffries: That constitutes a religious activity. Let me try to answer the rest of your question, if I may, Justice Scalia. In addition to the longstanding tradition of financial disengagement between church and State—in this particular area, we feel there's a very strong concern—[we feel that] by denying all religious activities university funding, we avoid having to choose among them. How would you choose among them?

Here Jeffries is making the same argument that McConnell did, but with a different conclusion. Jeffries is arguing that the problems of making comparative judgments about sincerity, purpose, and the like for various religions and religious practices, justify a rule treating them all the same by excluding them all. McConnell's argument, with the exception of the inconsistent argument he made about taxes, was that the same problems with making comparative judgments justify a rule requiring that they all be included (and thus not categorically treated differently than the nonreligious activities). The problem with Jeffries' argument, especially when divorced from the establishment clause, is that the result of excluding all religious activities discriminates against religion and punishes some activities that should be included. McConnell's argument errs on the other side by not treating religion differently, and is thus stronger. The only way to justify Jeffries' result is to argue that religious speech—or more specifically, proselytizing or preaching—is different from all other speech, and that argument must rest on the establishment clause, which he has been forbidden to rely upon.

Question: Is the giving of religious instruction a religious activity that calls—makes it outside the funding?

Mr. Jeffries: Our policy on that is exactly the policy reflected in the Religious Studies Department. We study—

Question: I mean, for example, if this magazine has articles in it that say Christianity and the five-legged stool, and then it says, for example, how you should lead a holy life, spread the Gospel, make social justice, follow the Holy Spirit, and pursue intellectual excellence, all of which are fine, but is that type of article the kind of article that falls outside funding, and why, precisely?

Mr. Jeffries: Funding decisions, Justice Breyer, are not made on the basis of articles or columns or particular essays.

Question: No, but I mean, the character of the magazine.

Mr. Jeffries: Yes, sir.

Question: If the magazine did not have such articles, but only said, we have a religious point of view involving certain social issues, certain educational issues. Would it then qualify for funding? I'm trying to get the distinction as to what makes it a religious activity and what doesn't—

Mr. Jeffries: The distinction—

Question:—in terms of this magazine.

Mr. Jeffries: On these facts, we think that distinction is clear. A magazine which is devoted in all of its content to proselytizing specific religious beliefs is a religious activity under the guidelines.

Question: I don't know what you mean by proselytizing. That's not what the guideline says. It says, manifests, promotes or manifests. Now, suppose you had a magazine that just said, we want to set forth the Christian or the Muslim or the Jewish point of view on social issues. It's called *Commentary.* You know—

(Laughter)

Mr. Jeffries: Let me answer that question this way. In a standard which depends significantly on the word "primarily"—as the university guidelines do—there are inevitably questions of degree, and there may well be close cases, and there may well be a line-drawing problem down the road. Now, I will say, we've not had that problem before this litigation. But in this case, the fundamentally, consistently, in the words of the Fourth Circuit, the "unflaggingly" religious character of the publication has never been contested or denied.

Question: Mr. Jeffries, suppose that a student newspaper decides that regular columns are good for the newspaper. Readers like them.

Mr. Jeffries: Yes, sir.

Question: And it said, we want good writers, and we want four regular columns, and they have a survey of the best writers, and one of them is a religious writer, a Christian writer, and that's all he writes about in the column. Can the university promulgate a guideline to withdraw funding by reason of the printing of that column?

Mr. Jeffries: We have not attempted to promulgate such a guideline.

Question: Can the university constitutionally do it under the First Amendment?

Mr. Jeffries: I doubt it.

Question: Why is this case any different?

Mr. Jeffries: We have—the standard, as I see it, under the decisions of this Court, is basically a standard of reasonableness. Public money cannot be a public forum. There cannot be a right of access to the budget of the University of Virginia.

Here Jeffries is making a new—and very treacherous—argument. But he's desperate. Public money, he says, cannot be a public forum . . . or else, he implies, there would be a right of access to the budget of the University of Virginia. The problems with this are legion. First, public money can be a public forum, if, and only if, the public authority chooses to make it so. If a city creates a program giving everyone who speaks at public high school graduations a $50 honorarium, the city can't withhold the $50 for a speaker whose ideas the city dislikes, or whose topic is unacceptable though it falls within the topics covered in the program. And the person who is wrongly refused the honorarium would have a "right of access" to the budget of the city to the tune of $50. If things get out of hand one year, the city can correct that situation in the future by withdrawing the program—the public forum it has created—for everyone. It can't do so selectively, however, for that would be to discriminate on the basis of viewpoint or content of the ideas expressed in violation of the free speech guarantee.

Now, Jeffries might respond that this isn't the whole story. The city could create a graduation speaker forum but explicitly exclude from speaking (and receiving an honorarium) any speaker who gives a sermon; religious speech of that nature—prayer, worship, proselytizing—can be excluded from a public graduation ceremony. Indeed, it must, constitutionally, be excluded, according to the Supreme Court. Why? Because such a speech would violate the establishment and free exercise clauses of the First Amendment. Free speech has absolutely nothing to do with it.

Again we see the disability under which Jeffries is struggling. But he must be careful. Saying public funds cannot be a public forum is simply not correct as a matter, strictly, of free speech law.

Question: But isn't there a difference between when the university decides, you know, what kinds of subjects to teach, say, in its Department of Religion, where it's putting out its own message, and where the university says, we're going to fund all sorts of student activities, and we're going to disassociate ourselves from their message?

Mr. Jeffries: Mr. Chief Justice, the university does not fund all sorts of student activities. They fund some broad categories, and there are other broad categories that are excluded. The funds we're talking about here are raised by mandatory fees. They're exactly like tuition and taxes. They're distributed by a budgetary process, by an official decision-making process, just like money raised from tuition and taxes.

Question: But they aren't devoted to espousing something that might be called the university's point of view, or the university's idea of what education should be.

Mr. Jeffries: That is entirely correct. They're not—well, the first part is entirely correct. They are not devoted to espousing a particular point of view. They are devoted—in funding, now, not access, they are devoted to those activities which in the judgment of the Board of Visitors are consistent with the educational purpose of the university, and there are several categories that are in, and there are several categories that are out, religion being one of the out categories.

Question: But according to [our earlier cases dealing with public space and rooms], where you're talking about student activities like this, you can't exclude religion.

Mr. Jeffries: Mr. Chief Justice, [those cases make] explicit reference to the fact that it is not intended to apply to funds.

Question: So you say providing space, or facilities and lighting and so forth—in doing that the university can't discriminate, but if instead of that it decides to make cash payments, it can?

Mr. Jeffries: That's exactly right, and the university does not discriminate in any way. These plaintiffs have full access to university facilities.

Question: Well, you could really help these people out and even the playing field by not distributing your student activity subsidies in cash, just provide printing presses for all these organizations. Then it would be okay to give these people what they want.

Mr. Jeffries: Justice Stevens [wrote in one of the cases] that if [space] were short, that is, if it needed to be rationed, that would warrant the university giving access on the basis of the content of speech. The distinctive fact about higher education, and about public education generally, is that owing to the demand at peak hours, classroom space always is in abundant supply after hours, so . . . there is no need to ration anything. It's a benefit that can be provided at practically no marginal cost.

Question: Well, what if the activity involves a controversial speaker and providing facilities to take care of that? That can cost a lot of money. I'm not sure that providing access to facilities is cost-free.

Mr. Jeffries: It has been practically so in our experience. I agree with—

Question: But it might not be.

Mr. Jeffries: Yes, ma'am, and I agree with Justice Stevens that if access needed to be limited either because of cost or because of a lack of physical space, that would present a very different case. Funding must—

Question: And you could say, because there's a shortage of space we're going to decide religious organizations are at the end of the line?

Good question. Again, without the establishment clause as ammunition, Jeffries is caught short. To say that if space is limited, some criterion—even one based on the content of speech—can be used, is quite a different thing than saying that *any* content category can be used, or that religion can be used as the category.

Mr. Jeffries: If there were a shortage of space that would present a—

Question: That's what *Widmar* stands for?

Mr. Jeffries:—a very different question.

Question: You're relying on Justice Stevens's separate opinion in *Widmar* for that?

Mr. Jeffries: For that point, I am.

(Laughter)

Question: I mean, I would have thought the First Amendment would indicate that if you have to restrict access it ought to be on some neutral ground. We're not going to provide access if to do so requires us to spend a lot of money.

Mr. Jeffries: And we do not restrict access, so to the extent that the concern is about access, these plaintiffs have no quarrel with us. This entire case involves the question of whether we write them a check.

Well. . . . A check is, for the student groups, access; so the university is, indeed, denying access through its policy. It can't slide out of the constitutional issue by claiming that it isn't denying access or doing anything that affects the student groups at all. Just as in so many other respects, with speech, money is access. The student group doesn't have the money to pay for the printing of its religious newspaper. With the university funds it will be able to do so. Can it fairly be said, in light of this, that denying money has nothing to do with denying *Wide Awake* access to the university for dissemination of its message to other students?

Mr. Jeffries (continuing): Now, Justice O'Connor, very early you asked me a question which I'd like to get to. I think it's the heart of the case. As I hear the petitioners, they more or less concede that in giving out scarce money, judgments must inevitably be made. Choices must be made, there must be priorities, so that the major ground of dispute here is their claim that the university's guidelines are guilty of antireligious viewpoint discrimination. That is not true. The university funds, not opinions or viewpoints, but activities. The university does not fund religious activities. The university does not fund antireligious activities. If there were a journal of antireligion, if there were a journal devoted primarily to denying the existence of a deity, we would not fund it, it would not be eligible for funding, and it would not be eligible on precisely the ground that *Wide Awake* is not eligible. If there were an anti-Christian newsletter devoted primarily to denying the tenets of Christianity, we would not fund it, it would not be eligible for funding, and it would not be eligible for funding on precisely the ground that *Wide Awake* is not eligible for funding.

How can this be squared with what Jeffries said early on: that *Wide Awake* was not funded because it was religious speech and activity, which he then defined, essentially, as "prayer, worship, and proselytizing." A journal of antireligion wouldn't do any of these. There is a difference between prayer, worship, and proselytizing, on the one hand, and theology (or antitheology) on the other. Jeffries finds himself out on a limb here, and he gets into very deep trouble at the hands of the Justices, especially Justice Scalia.

Question: What about secular humanism?

Mr. Jeffries: A journal devoted to secular humanism?

Question: Yes.

Mr. Jeffries: As far as I know from the name you've given it, that would be fine. I confess, I'm never sure that I know what secular humanism is. (Laughter)

Question: If secular humanism says, we take this position because all religion is rot, you wouldn't fund it.

Mr. Jeffries: If it were primarily devoted to the all-religion-is-rot position, it would qualify as a religious activity under the guidelines and would not be funded. My point in emphasizing this is to make a statement to you that the University of Virginia feels very strongly about. We are not picking out a religious point of view and trying to suppress it.

Question: No, but you're picking out theology. I don't know that you would try to justify the exclusion of some other area of thought, or discussion, or belief, by saying, we're excluding this entire area, both those who like it and those who don't like it.

Mr. Jeffries: Yes, we do exactly that, Justice Scalia, with respect, for example, to lobbying and electioneering. In all these areas, we do the same thing.

Question: Could the University of Missouri in *Widmar* have said, we're going to deny access to this religious group to these rooms, and we're also going to deny access to any antireligious group, but we're going to give it to everybody else?

Mr. Jeffries: Mr. Chief Justice, my understanding of the *Widmar* line of cases, which say that so long as they have a surplus of rooms, so long as there is no need to ration access to them, so long as everyone can be accommodated, those exclusions—

Question: Well, did the Court opinion in *Widmar* stress those facts?

Mr. Jeffries: . . . *Widmar* does say, and this is the majority opinion, "nor do we question the right of the university to make academic judgments as to how best to allocate scarce resources," which is what we're dealing with here.

Question: Could I go to a question peculiar to funds? Your opponents say that your argument there is specious, because you rely upon cases in which the Government is deciding, as it were, to speak for itself, and it can decide what speech to make, whereas the University of Virginia is not speaking for itself, it is funding the speech of others, and it is because of that distinction that it cannot make the distinctions that you draw. What is your response to that?

Mr. Jeffries: Justice Souter, the university pays my salary. It's not true that I represent in the classroom any particular university point of view, it's not true that I am a spokesman for a particular campaign, but it is certainly true that the university is not indifferent to what I do there. In other words, in the classroom there is a very broad range of educational speech that is funded, but that's not to say that all speech is funded. Exactly the same is true of the student activities fees.

Question: In effect you're saying, any subject-matter distinction can be made, and it doesn't matter at the point in time, or the point in the legislative process at which the Government says, "this is my speech" as distinct from "this is what I will pay for."

Mr. Jeffries: Any distinction can be made, so long as it meets this Court's standard of being reasonable and not an effort to suppress expression merely because public officials oppose the speaker's view.

Question: Suppose that there's a magazine put out by hobbyists, or by fraternities, and the magazine has some articles devoted to how wonderful it is to live at Theta Beta whatever, or how to build model airplanes, but several other articles have to do with issues on campus from the point of view of the fraternity, or issues on campus from the point of view of model airplane builders. Now, does that get funding, or not?

Mr. Jeffries: It is eligible to be considered for funding.

Question: Mr. Jeffries, if we don't accept your distinction placing this closer to the government choosing what subjects it wants discussed, and we do accept that it's Government facilitating speech of others, not its own choices, you—how would you address the establishment objection that you've assiduously stayed away from in your brief?

Suppose we reject your position on the free speech side of it?

One can almost hear Jeffries' sigh of relief. A Justice has asked him to make the establishment clause argument, so he must do so as an officer of the Court, even though his client appears to have instructed him not to rely upon it.

Question: Let me try to state as clearly as I can, since the briefs are so different in their emphasis on the Establishment Clause, what we think the relevance of that question is to this case. . . . From [Rosenberger's] point of view, the Establishment Clause is a grave problem, because there are many decisions of this Court stating that where religion is involved funding does matter, that it matters quite a lot. So petitioners are essentially coming to the Court and saying either that a lot of past Establishment Clause [cases] need to be distinguished within an inch of their lives, or they need to be overruled. That is, as you can tell from the exchange, including the exchange among religious amici, that is a controversial proposition, but it is only the first step in petitioners' argument. Petitioners not only want this Court to overrule Establishment Clause cases and permit Government to give direct aid to religious activities where other activities get such aid, petitioners want to go farther. They want to take a second step which is truly radical, to say that where other activities get Government aid, Government *must* fund religious activities. Petitioners want to go—

Question: You think that's a major step, a major additional step?

Mr. Jeffries: Oh, yes, sir.

Question: The step between providing a classroom and providing the money to rent a classroom you think is really a step off a cliff?

Mr. Jeffries: Access to a budget is a major step.

Question: But the classrooms are bought with budget money, certainly.

Mr. Jeffries: Yes, sir, and they are, once they're there, it is virtually cost-free to allow two classes or three classes as opposed to one or two, virtually cost-free. No practical significance to that.

Question: Well, that may affect the fisc. I can understand how those who are interested in a balanced budget may be concerned with that distinction, but I don't know how those who are interested in unconstitutional support of religion see a great difference between providing that assistance in cash or that assistance in some other—in some other means, whether it's cost-free or not.

Mr. Jeffries: May I try to identify the consequences? If, as petitioners claim, Government funding of speech activities must be accompanied by Government funding of religious activities, if that's true, all of public education as we know it is unconstitutional. Every public school in America at every level in every State does what we do. They fund speech—

Question: But of course the only justification for your using the word, religious activity, is because of the special way in which this regulation defines it. What we're talking about here is religious speech. That is different from religious activities and religious exercises.

Mr. Jeffries: Well, our definition of religious activity is stated in the guidelines that have been quoted to you. It includes activities, and the activity here is the publication of a magazine, and that involves religious speech. Maybe I'm missing your point.

Question: The only thing that's at issue here is religious speech, not religious exercise.

Mr. Jeffries: Justice Kennedy, you're drawing a distinction that I do not clearly apprehend.

Question: Well, if for example you have a Republican and a Democrat and an Episcopal minister all give exactly the same speech about the homeless problem, one from a Republican point of view, one Democratic, and one says I'm a minister and I have my own experience. The speeches are identical. You fund the first two but not the third?

Mr. Jeffries: All those may be published, and they all may be published in a newspaper which publishes lots of points of view.

Question: And isn't it the case that when you were using religious speech in this argument, and when Virginia is deciding what it means to fund, specifically when Virginia uses the word "manifest," aren't you, in each instance, talking about speech which does not merely explain a point of view, but espouses it, speech which in effect recognize[s] the difference between "this is a way of thinking" and speech which says "this ought to be your way of thinking"? Isn't that the distinction that is implicit in your entire argument, and in these guidelines as you read them?

Mr. Jeffries: Yes, sir, and as those guidelines are applied, they focus for the hallmarks of a religious activity of observances or proselytizing, which we do not wish to fund.

Question: Was there a finding of proselytizing intent as the basis for the—I don't find that anywhere in the record. I think manifest means manifest. Do you mean that it would be okay if this group said, we're not going to try to convert anybody, we just want to explain why Christian viewpoint provides certain consequences on a whole range of public issues?

Mr. Jeffries: The opening—

Question: Would that be accepted? The university will accept that publication?

Mr. Jeffries: It might be, depending on the facts more carefully defined. The magazine—

Question: Oh, but in theory, it would. I mean—

Question: You have to say yes if you're going to answer Justice Souter the way you did.

Mr. Jeffries: The only reason I haven't said yes is because I don't know enough about your hypothetical magazine to have a confident reaction to it.

Question: It may be tough to identify it as one or the other, but the distinction is a distinction that the university would honor, isn't it?

Mr. Jeffries: And that is—yes, sir, exactly.

Question: And the university would—who wrote these regulations for the university, then? The university would consider that—such a publication does not manifest a particular belief? It's whole basis is, Christianity provides these answers to a whole range of certain—that magazine does not manifest a particular belief?

Mr. Jeffries: I think the best answer I can give you is that the magazines in the record do manifest a religious belief. The letter from the editor in the inaugural issue says that its mission is to challenge Christians to live in word and deed according to the faith.

Thank you, sir.

Chief Justice Rehnquist: Thank you, Mr. Jeffries.

Things got a little confusing at the end, but it was clear that Jeffries was ready and anxious to make a strong establishment clause argument, based on the proposition that funding is different. He didn't get to explain why funding should be different—it allows the government to insinuate its way into religion and make religion dependent on it; it's an unmistakable manifestation of government support and preference, much more so than the ambiguous permission to use a room after hours. Justice Kennedy got in the way with a confusing question—confusing to Mr. Jeffries in particular. Justice Kennedy thought that the university's policy dealt strictly with exclusion of religious expression—speech only, not action—and thus raised a particularly grievous discrimination against speech that made the establishment clause funding problem irrelevant. But what else is religion but expression—through belief, through speech, through expressive action? The fact that all religion is a form of expression (unlike, say, soccer) can't be a reason for ignoring the establishment clause problems with funding. If all religion is expression and belief, under Kennedy's theory, we shouldn't have an establishment and free exercise guarantee at all. But we do. So Kennedy's question was a distraction only, but its price was Jeffries' inability to make the establishment clause argument more fully, as he had done so effectively in the district and circuit courts.

It's pretty clear that none of this would have made any difference in the outcome of the case, however. By this stage, it seems, the votes were lined up.

Chief Justice Rehnquist: Mr. McConnell, you have 1 minute remaining.

Mr. McConnell: Mr. Chief Justice, I'd just like to conclude with a practical observation about the real impact . . . on free speech of the Government's use of the power of the purse. Effectively, Ronald Rosenberger and his fellow students were enabled to put together a newspaper, and there's a carrot dangling in front of them, and the carrot has attached to it something about their speech, that they can address issues if they want to, but if they want to receive the carrot, they have to do them in a particular way. They have to censor their own religious viewpoints, they have to make sure that they don't quote from one book, the Bible. They could quote from others. They have to—

Question: I don't think that's what your brother is saying. I think what your brother is saying is, they cannot cross that line between saying "this is the Christian viewpoint" and "this ought to be your viewpoint." Now, that may be a tough line to draw. He certainly admits it. But that, it seems to me, is the only censorship that we're talking about.

Mr. McConnell: Your Honor, if their viewpoint were secular, they're certainly entitled to write a magazine saying, this is our viewpoint, and you should share that viewpoint. Animal rights groups are doing precisely that. Feminist groups are doing precisely that. Every other group is permitted to proselytize, which I'd just like to note is nothing but an ugly word for persuade, which is just exactly what the Free Speech Clause is designed to protect.

Question: They like the word manifest.

(Laughter)

Chief Justice Rehnquist: Thank you, Mr. McConnell.

The case is submitted.

(Whereupon, at 11:09 A.M., the case in the above-entitled matter was submitted.).

The Supreme Court's decision in the *Rosenberger* case did not come until the very end of the Term of Court, on June 29, 1995. The Justices, it seems, had a difficult time coming to a decision and writing an opinion in the case, but this is not surprising, given the difficulty of the issues presented and the utter lack of consensus on the Court about the correct interpretation of the establishment and free exercise clauses. This is borne out by the opinions in the case. There were four different opinions. Justice Kennedy wrote the majority opinion, in which Chief Justice Rehnquist and Justices Scalia, Thomas, and O'Connor joined. But Justices O'Connor and Thomas each had sufficiently different views of the correct reasoning in support of the Court's conclusion and the proper meaning of the Constitution that they felt compelled to write separate opinions clarifying their own views. Justice Souter, joined by Justices Stevens, Ginsburg, and Breyer, wrote a dissenting opinion. It was a 5-4 decision, in a formal sense, but it was really a 3-1-1 to 4 opinion. Ronald Rosenberger and *Wide Awake* had won, but it wasn't altogether clear why.

Justice *Kennedy* delivered the Opinion of the Court.

Wide Awake Productions (WAP) . . . was established "to publish a magazine of philosophical and religious expression," "to facilitate discussion which fosters an atmosphere of sensitivity to and tolerance of Christian viewpoints," and "to provide a unifying focus for Christians of multicultural backgrounds." WAP publishes *Wide Awake: A Christian Perspective* at the University of Virginia. The paper's Christian viewpoint was evident from the first issue, in which its editors wrote that the journal "offers a Christian perspective on both personal and community issues, especially those relevant to college students at the University of Virginia." The editors committed the paper to a two-fold mission: "to challenge Christians to live, in word and deed, according to the faith they proclaim and to encourage students to consider what a personal relationship with Jesus Christ means." The first issue had articles about racism, crisis pregnancy, stress, prayer, C. S. Lewis's ideas about evil and free will, and reviews of religious music. In the next two issues, *Wide Awake* featured stories about homosexuality, Christian missionary work, and eating disorders, as well as music reviews and interviews with University professors. Each page of *Wide Awake,* and the end of each article or review, is marked by a cross. The advertisements carried in *Wide Awake* also reveal the Christian perspective of the journal. For the most part, the advertisers are churches, centers for Christian study, or Christian bookstores. By June 1992, WAP had distributed about 5,000 copies of *Wide Awake* to University students, free of charge.

* * *

It is axiomatic that the government may not regulate speech based on its substantive content or the message it conveys. Other principles follow from this precept. In the realm of private speech or expression, government regulation may not favor one speaker over another. Discrimination against speech because of its message is presumed to be unconstitutional.

We conclude that viewpoint discrimination is the proper way to interpret the University's objections to *Wide Awake.* By the very terms of the SAF [student activity fee] prohibition, the University does not exclude religion as a subject matter but selects for disfavored treatment those student journalistic efforts with religious editorial viewpoints. We [therefore] hold that the regulation invoked to deny SAF support, both in its terms and in its application to these petitioners, is a denial of their right of free speech guaranteed by the First Amendment.

The Court of Appeals ruled that withholding SAF support from *Wide Awake* contravened the Speech Clause of the First Amendment, but proceeded to hold that the University's action was justified by the necessity of avoiding a violation of the Establishment Clause, an interest it found compelling. The court declared that the Establishment Clause would not permit the use of public funds to support "a specifically religious activity in an otherwise substantially secular setting." It reasoned that because *Wide Awake* is "a journal pervasively devoted to the discussion and advancement of an avowedly Christian theological and personal philosophy," the University's provision of SAF funds for its publication would "send an unmistakably clear signal that the University of Virginia supports Christian values and wishes to promote the wide promulgation of such values."

The governmental program here is neutral toward religion. There is no suggestion that the University created it to advance religion or adopted some ingenious device with the purpose of aiding a religious cause. The object of the SAF is to open a forum for speech and to support various student enterprises, including the publication of newspapers, in recognition of the diversity and creativity of student life. WAP did not seek a subsidy because of its Christian editorial viewpoint; it sought funding as a student journal, which it was.

The neutrality of the program distinguishes the student fees from a tax levied for the direct support of a church or group of churches. A tax of that sort, of course, would run contrary to Establishment Clause concerns dating from the earliest days of the Republic. The apprehensions of our predecessors involved the levying of taxes upon the public for the sole and exclusive purpose of establishing and supporting specific sects. The exaction here, by contrast, is a student activity fee designed to reflect the reality that student life in its many dimensions includes the necessity of wide-ranging speech and inquiry and that student expression is an integral part of the University's educational mission. The fee is mandatory—but the $14 paid each semester by the students is not a general tax designed to raise revenue for the University. The SAF cannot be used for unlimited purposes, much less the illegitimate purpose of supporting one religion. Our decision, then, cannot be read as addressing an expenditure from a general tax fund. Here, the disbursements from the fund go to private contractors for the cost of printing that which is protected under the Speech Clause of the First Amendment. This is a far cry from a general public assessment designed and effected to provide financial support for a church.

The Court of Appeals (and the dissent) are correct to extract from our decisions the principle that we have recognized special Establishment Clause dangers where the government makes direct money payments to sectarian institutions. The error is not in identifying the principle, but in believing that it controls this case. We do not confront a case where, even under a neutral program that includes nonsectarian recipients, the government is making direct money payments to an institution or group that is engaged in religious activity.

The error made by the Court of Appeals, as well as by the dissent, lies in focusing on the money that is undoubtedly expended by the government, rather than on the nature of the benefit received by the recipient. A public university may maintain its own computer facility and give student groups access to that facility, including the use of the printers, on a religion-neutral, say first-come-first-served, basis. If a religious student organization obtained access on that religion-neutral basis and used a computer to compose or a printer or copy machine to print speech with a religious content or viewpoint, the State's action in providing the group with access would no more violate the Establishment Clause than would giving those groups access to an assembly hall. The University provides printing services to a broad spectrum of student newspapers. . . . Any benefit to religion is incidental to the government's provision of secular services for secular purposes on a religion-neutral basis. Printing is a routine, secular, and recurring attribute of student life.

It is, of course, true that if the State pays a church's bills, it is subsidizing it, and we must guard against this abuse. That is not a danger here. . . . [T]he student publication is not a religious institution, at least in the usual sense of that term as used in our case law, and it is not a religious organization as used in the University's own regulations. It is instead a publication involved in a pure forum for the expression of ideas, ideas that would be both incomplete and chilled were the Constitution to be interpreted to require that state officials and courts scan the publication to ferret out views that principally manifest a belief in a divine being.

The judgment of the Court of Appeals must be, and is, reversed.

It is so ordered.

Justice Kennedy had written what can best be described as a very broad opinion narrowly couched. There is no establishment clause violation when the University of Virginia honors its duties under the free speech guarantee. Why? No real answer is given, no reasons offered why the establishment clause purposes must give way to the free speech guarantee when the issue concerns access by a religious group to state funding.

Indeed, is there any establishment clause violation in the case? If not, then there is no reason for the Court to state with such apparent certainty that the establishment clause must give way to the free speech guarantee. But the Court's opinion is studiously ambiguous on the establishment clause. There might be an establishment clause violation, Justice Kennedy implies, if money went directly to *Wide Awake,* but here the money was paid to the printer (on presentation of the bill to *Wide Awake*). Thus this case is like the classroom cases, involving access to physical space, not the money cases, which may, though the Court does not decide, raise a different question even under a neutral program.

Why does the majority equivocate? Perhaps because the Court will soon be faced with judging the constitutionality of voucher programs for private schools, where tax funds are given to parents of children attending private religious schools, or in which tax funds are given on a headcount basis directly to the religious schools for special education services. Also in the political air at the time were proposals that the government contract with faith-based providers of social service programs, paying the religious organizations directly. The Court would have to decide whether those programs are constitutional even though tax funds are channeled directly or indirectly to religious institutions without limits on their use. The majority chose not to, or could not, resolve the issues presented by direct cash payment programs, so it left that issue open and resolved the case on the ground that the university funds went to the printer, a way of looking at the case that hadn't been raised at any earlier stage and that was, frankly, close to an artifice.

Finally, the majority concluded that under free speech principles, the exclusion in the university program of religious speech (praying, proselytizing, worshiping) violates free speech because the exclusion is based on the content of religious speech and, indeed, on its (ardent, proselytizing) viewpoint. This conclusion is almost certainly correct, as long as the establishment guarantee is left out of the equation. That, however, is the rub. In the view of the courts below, and of the dissenters, the establishment clause question is the central question in the case because the demands of nonestablishment override any competing free speech claim.

Having reached all of these conclusions, however, the opinion still gives the impression of being mealy-mouthed—a little of this and a little of that, but we aren't saying anything very clearly, and certainly nothing "for sure." The Court instead relies heavily on narrow and technical factors, like the (unexplained) difference between a mandatory student fee to support specified activities and a tax placed in a "general tax fund." Is the social security "tax" not a tax because it is dedicated only to paying social security benefits? Can *Wide Awake* seek funding as a student journal, its editorial viewpoint notwithstanding? Might a religious public school seek state funding because it is a school, not because it teaches religion? Does it matter that a state university's money goes to the printer, not to the religious organization directly? Can a church seek state support for a new pulpit as long as the money is paid to the pulpit manufacturer? These are the narrowest of grounds, lacking even the pretense of explanation in terms of the purposes of the establishment and free exercise guarantees. But they serve their purposes: to gather the votes of five Justices whose own views are quite different; and to give the dissenters little purchase on the issues resolved by the majority.

For the concurring Justices the narrow factual distinctions are important. Justice O'Connor's view, for example, is that the establishment clause forbids government actions that appear to those who witness them to endorse religion or a religious belief. The question for her, then, is how the university's funding of *Wide Awake* would look. The observer, she says, should know that student fees ordinarily fund all sorts of ideas and activities and that no presumption of university agreement with any of them can reasonably be assumed. Moreover, the fact that the money goes to the printer makes unreasonable anyone's conclusion that the university endorses or favors *Wide Awake* because of its religious views.

Justice Thomas sees the establishment clause in very different terms than the majority or the dissenting Justices see it. For him, the fact that the money goes to religion as well as other activities itself satisfies the demands of the establishment clause. It doesn't matter, to him, whether the funds go directly to *Wide Awake* or to the printer, or whether they support religious training and education or secular training and education. Evenhanded assistance to religion, even in the form of direct funding, is permissible. Justice Thomas reads the historical record very differently from those who believe separation of church and state was the animating goal of the establishment clause. The clause, he believes, instead prohibits sectarianism—government preference for a religion, not any or all religions. Equal treatment of religion, not separation, is Thomas's principle. His reasons are explained in his opinion.

Justice *Thomas,* concurring.

I write separately to express my disagreement with the historical analysis put forward by the dissent. Although the dissent starts down the right path in consulting the original meaning of the Establishment Clause, its misleading application of history yields a principle that is inconsistent with our Nation's long tradition of allowing religious adherents to participate on equal terms in neutral government programs.

Even assuming that the Virginia debate on the so-called "Assessment Controversy" was indicative of the principles embodied in the Establishment Clause, this incident hardly compels the dissent's conclusion that government must actively discriminate against religion. The dissent's historical discussion glosses over the fundamental characteristic of the Virginia assessment bill that sparked the controversy: The assessment was to be imposed for the support of clergy in the performance of their function of teaching religion. Thus, the "Bill Establishing a Provision for Teachers of the Christian Religion" provided for the collection of a specific tax, the proceeds of which were to be appropriated "by the Vestries, Elders, or Directors of each religious society . . . to a provision for a Minister or Teacher of the Gospel of their denomination, or the providing places of divine worship, and to none other use whatsoever."

[M]ost schools at the time of the founding were affiliated with some religious organization, and in fact there was no system of public education in Virginia until several decades after the assessment bill was proposed. Further, the clearly religious tenor of the Virginia assessment would seem to point toward appropriation of residual funds to sectarian "seminaries of learning." Finally, . . . the dissent provides no indication that Madison viewed the Virginia assessment as an evenhanded program; in fact, several of the objections expressed in Madison's Memorial and Remonstrance Against Religious Assessments, focus clearly on the bill's violation of the principle of "equality," or evenhandedness.

James Madison's Memorial and Remonstrance Against Religious Assessments must be understood in this context. Contrary to the dissent's suggestion, Madison's objection to the assessment bill did not rest on the premise that religious entities may never participate on equal terms in neutral government programs. Nor did Madison embrace the argument that forms the linchpin of the dissent: that monetary subsidies are constitutionally different from other neutral benefits programs. Instead, [a]ccording to Madison, the Virginia assessment was flawed because it "violated that equality which ought to be the basis of every law." The assessment violated the "equality" principle not because it allowed religious groups to participate in a generally available government program, but because the bill singled out religious entities for special benefits.

Under any understanding of the Assessment Controversy, the history cited by the dissent cannot support the conclusion that the Establishment Clause "categorically condemn[s] state programs directly aiding religious activity" when that aid is part of a neutral program available to a wide array of beneficiaries. Even if Madison believed that the principle of non-establishment of religion precluded government financial support for religion *per se* (in the sense of government benefits specifically targeting religion), there is no indication that at the time of the framing he took the dissent's extreme view that the government must discriminate against religious adherents by excluding them from more generally available financial subsidies.

Stripped of its flawed historical premise, the dissent's argument is reduced to the claim that our Establishment Clause jurisprudence permits neutrality in the context of access to government *facilities* but requires discrimination in access to government *funds*. The dissent purports to locate the prohibition against "direct public funding" at the "heart" of the Establishment Clause, but this conclusion fails to confront historical examples of funding that date back to the time of the founding. To take but one famous example, both Houses of the First Congress elected chaplains, and that Congress enacted legislation providing for an annual salary of $500 to be paid out of the Treasury. Madison himself was a member of the committee that recommended the chaplain system in the House. This same system of "direct public funding" of congressional chaplains has "continued without interruption ever since that early session of Congress." The historical evidence of government support for religious entities through property tax exemptions is also overwhelming. As the dissent concedes, property tax exemptions for religious bodies "have been in place for over 200 years without disruption to the interests represented by the Establishment Clause." In my view, the dissent's acceptance of this tradition puts to rest the notion that the Establishment Clause bars monetary aid to religious groups even when the aid is equally available to other groups. A tax exemption in many cases is economically and functionally indistinguishable from a direct monetary subsidy. In one instance, the government relieves religious entities (along with others) of a generally applicable tax; in the other, it relieves religious entities (along with others) of some or all of the burden of that tax by returning it in the form of a cash subsidy. Whether the benefit is provided at the front or back end of the taxation process, the financial aid to religious groups is undeniable. The analysis under the Establishment Clause must also be the same: "Few concepts are more deeply embedded in the fabric of our national life, beginning with pre-Revolutionary colonial times, than for the government to exercise at the very least this kind of benevolent neutrality toward churches and religious exercise. . . ."

Consistent application of the dissent's "no-aid" principle would require that "a church could not be protected by the police and fire departments, or have its public sidewalk kept in repair." The dissent admits that "evenhandedness may become important to ensuring that religious interests are not inhibited." Surely the dissent must concede, however, that the same result should obtain whether the government provides the populace with fire protection by reimbursing the costs of smoke detectors and overhead sprinkler systems or by establishing a public fire department. If churches may benefit on equal terms with other groups in the latter program—that is, if a public fire department may extinguish fires at churches—then they may also benefit on equal terms in the former program.

Though our Establishment Clause jurisprudence is in hopeless disarray, this case provides an opportunity to reaffirm one basic principle that has enjoyed an uncharacteristic degree of consensus: The Clause does not compel the exclusion of religious groups from government benefits programs that are generally available to a broad class of participants. Under the dissent's view, however, the University of Virginia may provide neutral access to the University's own printing press, but it may not provide the same service when the press is owned by a third party. Not surprisingly, the dissent offers no logical justification for this conclusion, and none is evident in the text or original meaning of the First Amendment.

The constitutional demands of the Establishment Clause may be judged against either a baseline of "neutrality" or a baseline of "no aid to religion," but the appropriate baseline surely cannot depend on the fortuitous circumstances surrounding the *form* of aid. The contrary rule would lead to absurd results that would jettison centuries of practice respecting the right of religious adherents to participate on neutral terms in a wide variety of government-funded programs.

Thus, history provides an answer for the constitutional question posed by this case, but it is not the one given by the dissent. The dissent identifies no evidence that the Framers intended to disable religious entities from participating on neutral terms in evenhanded government programs. The evidence that does exist points in the opposite direction and provides ample support for today's decision.

According to Justice Thomas, the government can, consistent with the establishment clause, provide direct aid in the form of space or funding to religious organizations and activities pursuant to an evenhanded and generally applicable public program. That is all that needs to be decided in the *Rosenberger* case. Justice Thomas might, however, go further in another case, permitting a program of aid to religion as such, as long as it reflected a nonpreferential accommodation to religious belief and practice. In his view, the history of the establishment clause, properly understood, should not be read to foreclose either result.

But history is rarely certain. Like the Constitution's text, history, too, requires interpretation and choices. Even accepting Justice Thomas's interpretation of history, the fact that a practice is not prohibited by history doesn't mean that it should be permitted.

The dissent's burden, then, is to argue, first, that Thomas's interpretation of history is not the only or even the best one, and second, that there are good reasons grounded in the text and purposes of the Constitution to adopt a very different, separationist view of the establishment clause. The burden of making those arguments falls on Justice Souter.

Justice *Souter,* with whom Justice *Stevens,* Justice *Ginsburg,* and Justice *Breyer* join, dissenting.

[*Wide Awake*] is no merely descriptive examination of religious doctrine or even of ideal Christian practice in confronting life's social and personal problems. Nor is it merely the expression of editorial opinion that incidentally coincides with Christian ethics and reflects a Christian view of human obligation. It is straightforward exhortation to enter into a relationship with God as revealed in Jesus Christ, and to satisfy a series of moral obligations derived from the teachings of Jesus Christ. These are not the words of "student news, information, opinion, entertainment, or academic communication . . . ," but the words of "challenge [to] Christians to live, in word and deed, according to the faith they proclaim and . . . to consider what a personal relationship with Jesus Christ means." The subject is not the discourse of the scholar's study or the seminar room, but of the evangelist's mission statement and the pulpit. It is nothing other than the preaching of the Word, which (along with the sacraments) is what most branches of Christianity offer those called to the religious life.

Using public funds for the direct subsidization of preaching the Word is categorically forbidden under the Establishment Clause, and if the Clause was meant to accomplish nothing else, it was meant to bar this use of public money. Evidence on the subject antedates even the Bill of Rights itself, as may be seen in the writings of Madison, whose authority on questions about the meaning of the Establishment Clause is well settled. Four years before the First Congress proposed the First Amendment, Madison gave his opinion on the legitimacy of using public funds for religious purposes, in the Memorial and Remonstrance Against Religious Assessments, which played the central role in ensuring the defeat of the Virginia tax assessment bill in 1786 and framed the debate upon which the Religion Clauses stand:

> Who does not see that . . . the same authority which can force a citizen to contribute three pence only of his property for the support of any one establishment, may force him to conform to any other establishment in all cases whatsoever?

Madison wrote against a background in which nearly every Colony had exacted a tax for church support, the practice having become "so commonplace as to shock the freedom-loving colonials into a feeling of abhorrence." Madison's Remonstrance captured the colonists' "conviction that individual religious liberty could be achieved best under a government which was stripped of all power to tax, to support, or otherwise to assist any or all religions, or to interfere with the beliefs of any religious individual or group." Their sentiment, as expressed by Madison in Virginia, led not only to the defeat of Virginia's tax assessment bill, but also directly to passage of the Virginia Bill for Establishing Religious Freedom, written by Thomas Jefferson. That bill's preamble declared that "to compel a man to furnish contributions of money for the propagation of opinions which he disbelieves, is sinful and tyrannical," and its text provided "that no man shall be compelled to frequent or support any religious worship, place, or ministry whatsoever. . . ." We have "previously recognized that the provisions of the First Amendment, in the drafting and adoption of which Madison and Jefferson played such leading roles, had the same objective and were intended to provide the same protection against governmental intrusion on religious liberty as the Virginia statute."

* * *

The principle against direct funding with public money is patently violated by the contested use of today's student activity fee. Like today's taxes generally, the fee is Madison's threepence. The University exercises the power of the State to compel a student to pay it, and the use of any part of it for the direct support of religious activity thus strikes at what we have repeatedly held to be the heart of the prohibition on establishment.

The Court, accordingly, has never before upheld direct state funding of the sort of proselytizing published in *Wide Awake* and, in fact, has categorically condemned state programs directly aiding religious activity.

Even when the Court has upheld aid to an institution performing both secular and sectarian functions, it has always made a searching enquiry to ensure that the institution kept the secular activities separate from its sectarian ones, with any direct aid flowing only to the former and never the latter.

Reasonable minds may differ over whether the Court reached the correct result in each of these cases, but their common principle has never been questioned or repudiated. "Although Establishment Clause jurisprudence is characterized by few absolutes, the Clause does absolutely prohibit government-financed . . . indoctrination into the beliefs of a particular religious faith."

* * *

Since I cannot see the future, I cannot tell whether today's decision portends much more than making a shambles out of student activity fees in public colleges. Still, my apprehension is whetted by Chief Justice Burger's warning: "[I]n constitutional adjudication some steps, which when taken were thought to approach 'the verge,' have become the platform for yet further steps. A certain momentum develops in constitutional theory and it can be a 'downhill thrust' easily set in motion but difficult to retard or stop."

I respectfully dissent.

The *Rosenberger* decision had the potential profoundly to alter the meaning of the establishment guarantee, but it fell short of making a clear break from the past because the "majority" view was, in reality, only the view of three or, at most, four Justices. But the issues are nevertheless momentous. Two questions, in particular, seem most pressing.

The first question concerns what the dissenting opinion accurately describes as the core, nearly absolute, rule that public funding may not go directly to religious teaching or practice. This rule is at the heart of the disagreement between the majority and the dissenters. Why, apart from the historical materials (which are subject to different interpretations), should there be a special rule against direct funding of religion?

For Justice Thomas, and indeed for all members of the majority, such an absolute bar on funding is unnecessary. We are a religious people. Religion itself serves important public purposes, as reflected in the many religious traditions the country has passed on from generation to generation: "In God We Trust" on our coins; accommodations that foster religious practice, such as time off for religious holidays; the provision of police and fire protection for churches; property and income tax exemptions and deductions; and most recently voucher plans in schools, by which students are given public funds with which to select their own preferred school, including religious schools. Fostering of religion by government is a good idea, not a bad one. It strengthens religions and religious institutions, thus providing a public good, for religion is a primary source of American moral values and practices whose teaching is conducive to a peaceful and productive social order. The only risk with public funding would be its religiously selective distribution, assisting one religion or sect over others. Doing so would sow the seeds of true "establishment" by picking out a favored religion or a favored set of beliefs which, over time, could extinguish all others. The result would be lost religious choice and therefore a denial of the Constitution's demand that choices about religion be left free and in the hands of individuals, not government. But funding religion in an evenhanded way pursuant to a general program eliminates that risk.

The dissenters in *Rosenberger* believe that any direct funding of religion, even if equally available to all religions or to nonreligious and religious activities alike, is dangerous. Public funding of religious as well as secular schools; block payments to churches or religious organizations for the provision of social services, like AA; and payment of the cost of printing religious newspapers, or buying religious books for use in sectarian schools, is strictly prohibited by the establishment clause. Why? The dissenters, like the majority, think that we are a religious people, that religion is important and strong religious institutions are an important element of the social order. But they believe that the strength of religion depends on religion's independence, its occupation of the private rather than the public sphere. Funding of religious teaching and practices weakens religions, makes them dependent on secular government, saps them of spiritual and intellectual strength by requiring religious obedience to government as the quid pro quo of continued funding and support. The point of the establishment clause, they believe, was to protect religion from government influence on religious matters, just as it was also to protect secular government from religious influence. Religion cannot be free, and therefore religious liberty of the individual cannot be realized, without a rule that prevents the dependence of one on the other.

Both of these views have historical pedigrees and can find respectable intellectual and constitutional support. Both claim to serve the same goal—of strengthening religion and its value to the individual and the social and political order. Which view is in fact most likely to achieve that goal cannot be known with certainty. Choosing one or the other is an act of faith.

The second question raised by the *Rosenberger* case is related to what has just been said, so can be dealt with briefly. But it must be addressed expressly, for it defines the fundamental philosophical divide in establishment clause jurisprudence. The question is: what is the basic difference between equality and separation? Religious equality is the core establishment clause principle adopted by the majority; separation is the principle adopted by the dissenters. Equality and separation, in principle, are both compatible *and* profoundly inconsistent. An equality requirement that religion be treated the same as—not better than nor worse than—all other institutions or beliefs, enforces a kind of separation. A rule that religion can be helped as long as it is part of a larger, secular, universe of institutions or practices serves effectively to keep government at bay, foreclosing government intermeddling in the substance of religious belief, limiting the need for government to define what is religious, or to stake out a special claim for the importance of religion in achieving the secular ends of government. This relationship of "neutrality," as the Court has described it, combines an arm's-length relationship between church and state with an embrace. At best it is a subtle and difficult thing. Equality does not foreclose (indeed it may require) government support for religion. But in doing so it focuses on the *form* that support takes in order to achieve a limited kind of separation.

In contrast, the dissenting Justices' view of separation, perhaps best termed strict separation, means something more than the distance required by equality alone. It means, often, inequality, and also noninvolvement and strict independence. Separation places religion and the secular state in separate spheres: the secular state is the public sphere of politics, reason, and practical ends; religion is the private sphere of belief, faith, and individual commitment. Separation requires a clear rule by which the public sphere may not intrude into the private. Why? Because, to the separationist, protection of the private sphere is of great public value. It restricts the state's choice of ends and means: the state's acts must be public, its choices practical and reasoned (or, at least, democratic). Separation thus limits the power of the state and preserves the power of the private, including religion. But accomplishing this requires, often, that religion be treated differently, even unequally as judged by the secular standards of the public state. University funding of a pervasively religious newspaper must be prohibited, even though all other newspapers receive funding, for the provision of state funds to the religious newspaper would amount to intrusion of the public domain into the private, risking an embrace or even interdependence. Such direct financial assistance would ultimately cause the breakdown of the distinction between the public and private itself—the breakdown, as Jefferson put it, of "the wall of separation between church and State."

* * *

The Supreme Court confronted stark choices in the *Rosenberger* case. The Justices, perhaps, tasted the bitter pills that either choice serves up. But they didn't swallow. Instead, the majority drew back into the incoherence of current establishment clause law, and then reached outside the religion clauses to the free speech guarantee for a solution. In a sense the approach was a serviceable one, especially for a Court so riven and shattered. But the truce won't hold long, because the free speech clause has, on reflection, little to offer in such cases. Why are the religion clauses separately (and first) included in the First Amendment if their demands are subordinate to the later free speech guarantee? Why did the Constitution guarantee the individual right freely to exercise his or her religion—a right focused (the Court tells us) on freedom of religious belief and expression—if the free speech guarantee makes it redundant?

Religion *is* different. The Constitution's text says so as plainly as possible. It does not involve the secular and public stuff of political debate or commercial advertising or public policy. That's for the speech guarantee. The Supreme Court simply hasn't yet figured out why, or when, or how religion is different. Without answering those questions, the law of the religion guarantees can never be coherent.

STORY 8

Equality as a Sword: The Ghost of *Everson*

Locke v. Davey, 540 U.S. 712 (2004)

Joshua Davey was a talented and dedicated young man when he entered college in the fall of 1999. He was bound for the ministry. But he would not get there.

Joshua grew up in Spokane, Washington, raised in a family of modest means who valued education and made religion an important part of Joshua's upbringing. Joshua was a serious student in school and in his church. In the spring of 1999, he graduated as valedictorian of his high school class, headed for college the next fall. He had easily been admitted into his school of choice, Northwest College in Kirkland, Washington, a private college affiliated with the Assembly of God denomination. Joshua had earned a perfect 800 score on the verbal part of the SAT and had been awarded a National Merit Scholarship. In August 1999, he was also awarded a Promise Scholarship, a grant of $1,125 per year given by the state of Washington to help support college expenses of Washington students from low- and middle-income families who graduated in the top 10 percent of their high school class. The grant could be used to defray expenses in any accredited Washington college, private or public, religious or secular. In September, Joshua received a letter of congratulations from the governor and a certificate that he had been awarded the scholarship for the 1999–2000 and 2000–2001 academic years. He was not informed of any limitations on the use of the scholarship.

Northwest College was a devoutly religious school. On the admissions form applicants were required to "indicate that they have made a personal commitment to Jesus Christ as Lord and Savior and that they are willing to live by the community rules adopted by the College." Joshua Davey described the college's goal as being "to produce students who are . . . not only well educated, but also well equipped to serve God with their lives. . . ." Students were required to attend chapel three times a week and to take a certain number of courses in religion, such as History of the Bible, Evangelism, and Church Doctrine. The courses did not teach about religion. They taught religion. As Davey put it, "understanding the plan of redemption evident in both Testaments of the Bible as is intended by Northwest College requires taking the Bible as truth, as foundational. Whereas a purely academic understanding would not necessarily subscribe to the Bible as ultimate truth."[1] Students were also required in the first two years to take nonreligious courses in a variety of fields such as English, mathematics, science, history, and the like, much as any liberal arts college would require, and most students majored in such fields as psychology, nursing, business, English, and so on. When Davey first registered for classes in the fall of 1999, he declared his majors as business management and pastoral ministries, believing that "both [theology and business] would best equip me to be a member of the clergy."

The Washington Constitution provides that "no public money or property shall be appropriated for or applied to any religious worship, exercise or instruction, or the support of any religious establishment."[2] The Washington statutes contain a companion but more specific provision that "no aid shall be awarded to any student who is pursuing a degree in Theology."[3] In light of these prohibitions, the Washington State Higher Education Coordinating Board promulgated a policy limiting the scope of Promise Scholarships. On October 4, 1999, John Klacik, the associate director of the board, sent a letter to all college financial aid administrators clarifying an earlier, and broader, prohibition on Promise Scholarship recipients engaging in religious instruction, stating that "students who are pursuing a degree in theology are not eligible to receive . . . the new Washington Promise Scholarships." It fell to Lana Walker, the director of financial aid at Northwest College, to inform Joshua and three other students who had likewise declared a major in theological studies that their scholarships would be canceled. The cancellation could be reversed, however, if the students changed their majors or simply withdrew their declaration of a theology major, since students at Northwest were not required to declare a major until after their second year of college.

---

1. Unless indicated otherwise, quotations from documents and from Joshua Davey and state and college officers are taken from depositions in the case and of record in the Supreme Court.

2. *Washington Constitution,* art. I, sec. 11.

3. *Revised Code of Washington,* sec. 28B.10.814.

Walker scheduled an appointment with Joshua Davey on October 12. In her deposition, she described the meeting in some detail.

Question: At the time of the appointment . . . , was Mr. Davey . . . eligible for the scholarship?
Ms. Walker: Not according to the new criteria.
Question: If [Davey] had changed his major at that time to, for example, Business Administration, and solely Business Administration, would that have affected his eligibility for the scholarship?
Ms. Walker: Yes, with a caveat.
Question: What's the caveat?
Ms. Walker: I will share with you how I talk to students in this situation. I [say] to them, "if you plan to become a minister or to change your major to Religious Studies and you know that . . . you want to be a minister . . . or go into the ministry, you should not accept this award no matter what your major."
Question: Why do you say that?
Ms. Walker: I believe that it is the spirit of the law that I've interpreted in the State of Washington, [which] separates church and state. That is what they have meant, the founders of our [State] Constitution.
Question: So, this written State requirement that you cannot pursue a degree in Theology, in your situation is requiring a more, I guess I could say, conservative approach because of ethical implications; is that correct?
Ms. Walker: Correct.
Question: Within this context of ethical counseling, is there a faith-based component to that?
Ms. Walker: Yes. . . . [In other schools] students . . . may want to play the system. . . . When I counsel students, I talk to them as I explained previously. . . . And if they say to me, "I don't know if I want to be a minister, I don't know if I want to be a businessman," [then] I have faith in the student that they will be truthful with me in what they're doing in determining their major.
Question: At your mid-October appointment when you had the discussion with [Davey] and he had already declared a pastoral ministries major . . . , could he have retracted or rescinded that declaration and become an undeclared major at that point?
Ms. Walker: He could have, yes.
Question: Would that have made him eligible for the Promise Scholarship under the State criteria?

Ms. Walker: Yes.
Question: It is within the normal scope of your profession[al] duties to counsel students in this way?
Ms. Walker: Yes.

Davey explained his unwillingness to sign a new form to withdraw his theology major in the following way:

> [The new eligibility rule] confronted me with a serious dilemma: Should I change my religious beliefs that required me to study for the ministry? Worse, should I violate my religious belief regarding truthfulness by changing my course of study to a state-approved major, with the intent of switching back to the forbidden major once I had exhausted my Scholarship eligibility? Either way, if I signed that form I would have denied what I believe to be God's direction for my life, and would have had to violate my sincerely held religious beliefs. After much pondering and prayer, I refused to sign.

Davey said, "The Promise Scholarship restriction singles me out from other students like myself in terms of educational qualifications, and forces me to either choose to deny what I hold as sincere religious beliefs to pursue a degree in theology, or—either deny those beliefs at the expense of funding for which I would otherwise be eligible," and he decided to challenge the restriction in court. He brought suit in the United States District Court in Washington, where he lost. He then appealed to the United States Court of Appeals where, on July 18, 2002, the court reversed the district court, holding that Washington's denial of scholarship eligibility only because Davey pursued a degree in theology "infringes [upon] his right to the free exercise of his religion." The Higher Education Board's policy to that effect was stricken, and Davey was entitled to receive his scholarship.

The Circuit Court's decision not only struck the limitation on Promise Scholarships, but it jeopardized similar restrictions in other programs and, perhaps most important for the state of Washington, it cast serious doubt on the validity of Washington's constitutional provision enforcing separation of church and state. The state, therefore, chose to appeal Davey's case to the United States Supreme Court. The case had by then attracted major national attention, partly because of the serious questions it raised about separation of church and state, and also because of the potentially broad implications of the circuit court's decision. The Supreme Court accepted the case and set it down for oral argument on December 2, 2003.

* * *

Davey's case did, indeed, present fundamental and far-reaching questions about the meaning of religious freedom in the United States. It raised, specifically, the role of equality for religion under the First Amendment, and its use affirmatively—as a sword, not a shield—to require government to fund religious practices because other, nonreligious practices also received funding. The implications of such a use of "equality" were far-reaching—and potentially very, very expensive.

It will be recalled that in the *Smith* and *Rosenberger* cases, equality emerged as a central principle of the religion guarantees. Equality involves treating religion or the individual's religious exercise no worse than other institutions or individuals under a general law governing conduct or speech, like the student activity fee allocation system in *Rosenberger.* Likewise, in *Smith,* free exercise did not require that religious use of peyote be exempted from the general drug laws. But *Smith* also said that religion and religious exercise could be treated better than other institutions or individuals if the *political* branches of government deem such an advantage, or accommodation, an appropriate choice, as long there is no discrimination in favor of some religions over others. Thus, federal or state drug law exemptions for the religious use of peyote were approved in *Smith,* but discrete accommodations by the judicial branch in the name of the free exercise guarantee were foreclosed.

Davey's case involves the use of equality as a positive or affirmative right—a right to be included in general programs that exclude religion or religious exercise. Equality usually means two things: a right not to be treated worse than others (a negative right), and a right to be treated as well as others (a positive right). The issue of entitlement to inclusion of religion in a general program, of course, lies at the heart of the religion guarantees. As we observed in *Rosenberger,* this is a fundamental divide that distinguishes separationists, who believe in a general equality right to inclusion—and specifically the right to receive government funds—would conflict with the separation of church and state under the establishment clause, which often requires that religion be treated differently, and worse, than nonreligion in the interest of preserving separate and independent realms for public law and private faith.

In *Rosenberger,* of course, the Court's decision required the inclusion of the religious magazine in the university's student activity funding system, and thus it appears at first glance to be an example of positive equality, or a right to inclusion. But the constitutional basis for the positive right to inclusion in the funding system in *Rosenberger* was not just the free exercise clause, but also the First Amendment right to freedom of speech. By turning to the free speech guarantee, the majority in *Rosenberger* managed to avoid the positive right of equality under the religion guarantees, saving the question for a later day. The case in our story, *Locke v. Davey,* is that later day.

* * *

The Court that would hear oral argument in Davey's case was the same Court that had decided the *Rosenberger* case in 1995. The differences of opinion on the meaning of the religion clauses that had confounded a clear consensus in *Rosenberger* also remained. Nothing the Court had done in the intervening years made the lawyers' challenges in oral argument any easier: there were, it appeared, three clear votes in the conservative corner; three votes in the liberal, separationist corner; and three in the middle.

The lawyer representing Washington Governor Gary Locke was Narda Pierce, Washington's Solicitor General. Davey's side of the case was represented by two lawyers: Jay Sekulow, of Virginia Beach, Virginia, who was affiliated with the American Center for Law and Justice; and Theodore Olson, the Solicitor General of the United States, who had been granted time in oral argument to speak for the United States on behalf of Davey.

Chief Justice Rehnquist brought the proceedings to order at 10:11 A.M. on December 2, 2003.

Chief Justice Rehnquist: We'll hear argument now in No. 02–1315, *Gary Locke v. Joshua Davey.* Ms. Pierce.

Ms. Pierce: Mr. Chief Justice, and may it please the Court: To preserve freedom of conscience for all its citizens in matters of religious faith and belief, Washington's constitution limits the involvement of government. It limits both the ability to regulate religious activities and to fund religious activities.

Question: How—how many states have similar provisions in their constitutions or laws?

Ms. Pierce: It varies, Justice O'Connor, according to the particular provisions. This provision refers to not using public funds for religious instruction. We also have a provision that no public funds shall be spent at schools under sectarian influence. I believe it's something in the neighborhood of 36 states [that] have some provisions relating to use of public funds for religious instruction, but those vary.

Question: They were all adopted at about the same time, weren't these so-called Blaine Amendments?

Ms. Pierce: Your Honor, this is not the Blaine Amendment. The so-called Blaine Amendments are those that refer to use of public funds in schools under sectarian control. That's a different provision of the Washington constitution . . . that was required by Congress in the enabling act that provided for our statehood. The provision [involved in this case—barring the use of public funds for religious instruction—] was separate and apart, that was debated, that was added to Washington's constitution as a separate provision.

It was not in the original proposed constitution set before the framers. And during the course of that constitutional convention, that's where this language was added. And I know, referring to the Blaine Amendments, there's been much made in the briefs of whether or not those amendments stemmed from anti-Catholic motivation. There's certainly no evidence in Washington that there was any discussion, any evidence of anti-Catholic motive. In Washington, both article I, section 11 and article IX, section 4, which more directly stems from the Blaine Amendment [required by Congress, have] always been implemented in a non-discriminatory manner, prohibiting both the practice of any religion of any sort in our public schools, as well as any funding for private sectarian schools.

Question: But what if—what if a state prohibited only the study of theology from a Catholic perspective? Would that survive?

Ms. Pierce: No, Your Honor, we don't believe it would. But what the state has done here is prohibited public funds for religious instruction wherever it occurs.

This is a bit tricky and confusing. The provision initiated by Washington's founders prohibits funding any religious instruction. The Blaine Amendment, which Washington had to adopt as a condition of becoming a state, prohibited funding of sectarian schools. Congress has the power to place conditions on a state being admitted into the union, and the Blaine Amendment was one of those conditions that a large number of states admitted in the late nineteenth century had to adopt. The Blaine Amendment arose out of anti-Catholic sentiment in the nineteenth century. Its constitutionality today would be difficult to defend because it was, in the minds of most historians, aimed specifically at the Catholic Church.

Washington does not rely on the Blaine Amendment in the *Davey* case but instead relies on its own more general provision barring state funding of religious instruction, no matter the religion and no matter where it occurs—in private or in public schools, for example. The line separating the two provisions, however, is a subtle one, as the text of both apply to all religions, despite the different history and purposes. And Pierce says that Washington applies them both evenhandedly to all religions.

Pierce argues that Washington's own provision "preserves freedom of conscience for all of its citizens in matters of faith" by barring funding of religious instruction. It is thus not inconsistent with the general principle of separation of church and state voiced in *Everson:* "No tax in any amount, large or small, can be levied to support any religious activities or institutions." Washington's constitutional provision, however, presents a bit of a problem (in contrast to the language of the Blaine provision), because it is more limited to religious instruction and, as we will see, to the study of theology. Its narrowness presents a difficult balance for Pierce because the establishment clause is a broad and general principle. Washington has limited the funding restriction only to theological training. Why?

For the moment, however, the Court, through Justice Scalia, turns the inquiry to another aspect of Washington's policy: it applies just to theology, not philosophy. Is it thus discriminatory in that it prefers nonreligion to religion?

Question: It seems to me that if you say it does not violate the religion clauses to prohibit the use for any religious instruction whatever, you would also have to say that it does not violate the religion clauses to say no public funds shall be spent for Jewish theology studies. The state is not permitted to discriminate between religious sects, but it's just as much not permitted to discriminate between religion in general and nonreligion. So how can you possibly—I mean, if we say that you can do this, it seems to me, we have to say you can also prohibit Jewish studies.

Ms. Pierce: No, Justice Scalia—

Question: Why not?

Ms. Pierce:—I don't believe that follows. The line between funds for secular purposes and for religious purposes is a line that's been recognized by this Court in various funding cases and in reviewing government activities. It's a line that recognizes both the values of the Establishment Clause and the values of the Free Exercise Clause. Here, simply because the State of Washington is extending those values of the Establishment Clause beyond direct funding into indirect funding does not convert those values into hostility.

In response to Justice Scalia, Pierce is arguing that public funding for religion involves a special rule under the establishment clause. That clause may prohibit discrimination among religions, and between religion and nonreligion, as a general matter; but when it comes to public funding discrimination against religion in general, the state is required to preserve separation of church and state because direct funding of religious activities is likely to produce dependence of church on state. Pierce also argues, implicitly, that the threatened dependence from direct funding is not avoided by giving the funds to the individual student, like Davey, and allowing him to choose how to spend it—on religious training or on business training. This is an important distinction in some of the Court's decisions, notably the school voucher case upholding vouchers that could be used by the student to attend a religious school.

We will hear more about that question a bit later. For the moment, however, Justice Scalia wants to keep pressing the religion/nonreligion discrimination issue.

Question: [The policy is] treating religion differently from nonreligion. You can study anything you like and get it subsidized, except religion. Why is that not violating the principle of neutrality?

Ms. Pierce: It is treating religion different from a realm in which religion—religious belief or non-belief does not enter what we refer to as secular studies.

Question: You're making the—are you making the distinction between training in how to be religious, training as it were in the practice of some—of a religion that leads to the truth, on the one hand, and study about what people believe on the other hand? I thought that was the distinction, how to be religious versus what religions believe. Is that the distinction?

Ms. Pierce: Yes, Your Honor.

Question: Okay. So, I take it, then, if it that's the distinction, you would—you would agree that if Washington funded a school of atheism, but wouldn't fund a school like this one, that there would be a violation of one or both of the clauses?

Ms. Pierce: Yes, Justice Souter, because whenever you enter into the realm of faith or belief, whenever you try to affect someone's belief in that realm, that has been a particularly protected realm of individual conscience that becomes religious, whether it's non-belief or belief. It's when you—

Question: But it's the difference between being religious and studying religion. That's your line, isn't it?

Ms. Pierce: Yes, Your Honor, and I believe that's the Court's line. It's the line that's been drawn in many of the direct funding cases of this Court, to teach about religion—

Pierce has executed a sleight of hand. The state couldn't fund a school of atheism. Why? Because atheism is not a religious belief, it is a private "realm of individual conscience that becomes religious, whether it is non-belief or belief." This argument threatens to make all belief religious, and thus to extend the establishment prohibition to a prohibition against government's teaching ideology in general, whether atheism, capitalism, communism, patriotism, or positivism.

Justice Scalia pounces.

Question: Can—can you not study atheism under this statute? Suppose there is a course debunking, debunking all religious belief. Would that be prohibited? Would that be funded under this statute? I don't see any—any prohibition of the funding of that.

Ms. Pierce: Justice Scalia, I think when the statute is read in conjunction with Washington case law, that the definition—

Question: What does the statute say? I don't see how it can possibly apply to that. What does it say?

Ms. Pierce: Well, the statute says that no aid shall be awarded to any student pursuing a degree in theology.

Question: In theology.

Ms. Pierce: But—

Question: Now, is—is a degree in atheism a degree in theology?

Ms. Pierce: I believe it would be under the interpretation—

Why is Pierce taking this position? She has enough problems drawing the distinction between studying religion and studying "theology," which she seems to have claimed includes the study of a theology as the divine truth. But the scholarship program doesn't necessarily draw that line, and the state could more easily draw a line between teaching about or of religion on the one hand, and training in theology in preparation for the ministry on the other.

Question: That would be a question, would it not, for the state supreme court to decide? It may decide it needs to carry that limitation in order to be compatible with the Free Exercise Clause.

Ms. Pierce: Yes, Justice Ginsburg, and I think that the Washington Supreme Court would interpret it that way, not only to be consistent with the Free Exercise Clause, but to be consistent with its own state constitutional provision and its purposes, which is to not use public funds for instruction in the realm of faith and belief and—

Question: What cases do you cite for the proposition that you're asserting that the Free Exercise Clause or the Establishment Clause applies differently to discrimination between different religions than it does to discrimination between religion in general and nonreligion? The question is, assuming you are discriminating between religion and nonreligion, you can't study theology but you can study anything else, what is there in our cases that says that is okay, although it would not be okay to distinguish between Jewish studies or Catholic studies or Protestant studies and other studies? I don't know a single case that says the principle of neutrality somehow applies differently so long as you're discriminating against all religion than it does when you're just discriminating against one denomination. Did you have a case?

Ms. Pierce: Well, Your Honor, in the context of this Court's aid to education under the Establishment Clause, there's a distinction between providing materials, educational materials that are to be used in secular education, as opposed to those materials that might be diverted to religious, ideological education and—

Question: But that's—that's the Establishment Clause, isn't it?

Ms. Pierce: Yes, it is, Your Honor, and—and we believe the same—many of the same values underlie the Washington constitution. And we don't believe that the distinction is made invalid because it is extended to indirect funding and doesn't apply only to direct funding.

The relationship between the establishment and free exercise clauses is getting a bit confusing here. Joshua Davey claims that the state's discrimination violates his right to the free exercise of his religion. Washington, like the University of Virginia in *Rosenberger,* claims that providing the funding on equal terms with nonreligious activities would violate the establishment clause, and therefore that discrimination against religion (in general) is necessary and constitutional. The separation of church and state requires discrimination against all religion, not all philosophy. But if one doesn't find a broad requirement of separation in the establishment clause (Scalia and others don't), Washington's reliance on separation of church and state is misplaced and can't justify the discrimination against Davey.

This is the central question in the case. What values of the establishment clause (separation or neutrality) make discrimination necessary and constitutional?

Question: Well, I wanted to ask you about these values. As I understand, this student could have done exactly what he in fact did if only he did not declare a double major. He could have taken all of these religious perspective courses, if only he'd called his major business administration, which in fact it was because he had the credits for that, too. That would have been permissible. Is that correct, or am I incorrect?

Ms. Pierce: Well, the statute focuses on whether a student is pursuing a degree in theology and . . . and—

Question: If—suppose that he pursued a degree in business administration and yet, ancillary to that or as options, took all of these other courses. Could he have had the aid that he seeks?

Ms. Pierce: That could have happened, but it's an unlikely—yes, Your Honor, we think—

Question: All right. What is the state's interest in denying him aid simply because he declares a double major?

Ms. Pierce: I believe the reason the legislature has focused on the nature of the degree program is because it's an inherently religious program, and if they were to—

Question: What is the state's interest in denying him funds simply because of the way he labels the major he chooses, if all the other instructions, all the other elements of the case are the same? He takes all the same courses, he has all the same commitment as a Christian, and yet he's denied the relief in one case and given it—the subsidy in one case, and given it in the other. What is the state's interest in doing that?

Ms. Pierce: Justice Kennedy, I think the state's interest is not in that particular student, but in how you administer it overall. And the way the state administers it overall, in order to avoid a class-by-class, student-by-student determination, is to look at the degree programs that are inherently religious that have, or ask the universities actually to do that—

Ouch. Is Pierce admitting that the distinction in the law isn't the real one, but is just a rough approximation? That would be fatal to its constitutionality. But the real point is that the distinction in the law, as it is applied, is in fact between studying for a degree in theology and all other religious courses of study, whether they include the same courses that teach a religion, not just about religion. The distinction is between training for the ministry on the one hand, and being taught a religion on the other. For the state to support the training of ministers, she must claim, is a very different matter under the establishment clause, for the state would be insinuating itself deeply into what the training involves and who qualifies by approving the course of study and selecting the students to receive the scholarships. If the state selected the smartest and neediest students, would those necessarily be the criteria that the religion itself would use, as opposed to deeply religious, caring, devoted to others, articulate, and so on?

Justice Ginsburg tries to help Pierce turn to that question and away from religion versus nonreligion.

Question: May I ask you just to clarify what I thought was the purpose of this, was that the state has decided it does not want to fund the training of clergymen, and it cites a long history of that. And it's tried to be as accommodating as it can with that limitation. I mean, certainly if what you're doing is vulnerable, it would be no less vulnerable if the state said, well, we won't fund that school at all because it's an evangelical school.

Ms. Pierce: Justice Ginsburg, the focus is on the religious nature of the instruction. If someone had a career goal to enter the clergy and yet took a secular course of education, they would not be denied funding. Certainly one of the underlying values of our Freedom of Religion Clauses at the federal and state level is not to require people to support the promotion of a doctrine or religious belief with which they may not agree, and that, returning to Justice Kennedy's question, is . . . is the interest. The way it's implemented by Washington, and it has been by Congress and by other states in other contexts, is to look at that core course of study.

Pierce is on rough ground here. If Washington's purpose relates to "the religious nature of the instruction," then all students at Northwest College should be disqualified, because all must take a certain number of courses teaching evangelical Christianity. But the Washington law (as opposed to the Washington Constitution) just prohibits majoring in theology as training for the ministry. This more limited disqualification makes an utter shambles of the Washington law and of the establishment clause theory that Pierce uses to justify it.

The Justices are understandably confused.

Question: But we've decided in *Witters*[4] [where the Court upheld Washington's educational assistance to a blind student studying for the ministry] that it's unnecessary to [exclude studying for the ministry] to conform to the Establishment Clause.

Ms. Pierce: Yes, Justice Kennedy—

Question: So, after that, then what is the state's interest at this point? Is the state's interest in redefining the Establishment Clause?

Ms. Pierce: No, Your Honor, but the state has a different, although somewhat concurrent, scheme for religious freedom, and that involves not just avoiding a government endorsement of religion, which is what the Establishment Clause primarily turns on—

Question: But *Witters* said there is no endorsement.

Ms. Pierce: And . . . and—

Question: So you can't use that.

4. *Witters v. Washington Dept. of Services for the Blind*, 474 U.S. 481 (1986).

Ms. Pierce: No, and I'm not trying to.
Question: I still don't see what your interest is, and once you do define it, I want you to tell me if it's compelling.
Ms. Pierce: Okay. Washington's interest expressed in 1889 was to protect the freedom of conscience of all its citizens, and that included not compelling its citizens to provide enforced public funds to support the promotion of religious beliefs with which they may or may not agree. I think—

The interest is not avoiding state endorsement of religion in violation of the establishment clause, but the freedom of conscience of the citizens. Well! That's not exactly what the establishment guarantee is about; indeed, it smacks of hostility to religion. The state can fund deconstructionist philosophy because it doesn't clash with the conscience of the people, but it can't fund religion? Hardly. In contrast, the interest behind the establishment clause is keeping the state at a necessary distance from religion so that the State's actions or policies do not come to intrude upon and influence religious beliefs, tenets, and canons, and vice versa. This interest can much more easily be linked up to the state's distinction between religious courses or even individual training in a religion on the one hand, and training for the ministry in a religion on the other.

Question: Does that mean that the state can decline to provide fire protection to churches and synagogues?
Ms. Pierce: No, Your Honor, and that distinction has been made.
Question: And Washington doesn't do that, does it?
Ms. Pierce: It does not decline that—
Question: So that general public benefit is extended to both religious and nonreligious institutions equivalently, and people don't get upset about that, do they?
Ms. Pierce: No, Your Honor. I think providing the essential services that include people as part of our civilized community has been distinguished from other kinds of funding when these questions are asked.
Question: Well, Washington's position, I take it, is that, although it . . . it will certainly put out the fire in the church, it won't spend money for the purpose of persuading people that they ought to be inside the church. Is that the . . . the point you're making?

Pierce still has a problem, since the scholarships are not prohibited to students who take courses, even lots of them, in a religion, even when the courses *teach* the religion. Indeed, as Pierce has admitted earlier, if Davey enrolled in all of the religious courses—training in a religion—but did not major in the religion and/or have the intention to take the courses as training for the ministry, but instead did so in order to become a better Christian businessperson, he would not have been denied the scholarship under the interpretation given the law in its actual application. This is the distinction that Pierce must avow and defend, yet she seems not to want to make it. Why?

Ms. Pierce: Yes, Justice Souter. There is a distinction there and it's a distinction that's been made in a variety of contexts, but—

Question: And you're saying that even though it would not offend the Establishment Clause if the state did provide this sort of funding, there is still, I think your point is, there is still an area within which it has a choice, even though that choice may not be determined by the Establishment Clause?

This is a softball question, but a tricky one. If not non-establishment, what is the state's interest? It simply cannot be the consciences of the people, which can hardly be seen as all benign, and in any event people's consciences—i.e., ideological or moral preferences—cannot serve as a justification for a law that would otherwise violate a substantial constitutional right, like equal treatment for religion. And if the interest were just "conscience" of the people as taxpayers, would spending money for a war that people conscientiously objected to be a violation?

Washington's provision is a *religion* provision. Pierce must get back to that, and away from conscience in general. She really must say that the state's interest is in non-establishment of religion, and for authority she can quote directly from the *Everson* case, which articulated the meaning and purposes of the establishment clause. To be sure, by 2003 the Supreme Court had badly bruised the *Everson* articulation, but could the Court really say that a state following the Court's own established and longstanding interpretation, which has not been expressly overruled, would be acting unconstitutionally?

The question before Pierce, however, is whether the state of Washington has, in effect, a range of discretion to define "non-establishment" for itself, even if not the same way as the Court would define it under the First Amendment.

Ms. Pierce: Yes, Your Honor, [the State exercised its own judgment on non-establishment,] because the purpose of the state constitution, which of course, when it was adopted in 1889, was not viewed as greater than the Establishment Clause, it was viewed as the only protection for religious freedom at the state level, since it wasn't until 1947 that the Establishment Clause was held to apply to the states. And to return to your question, Justice Souter, the distinction between providing police and fire services to an organization and providing funding to assist in the educational purpose of that organization was made [in an earlier decision admittedly involving] very different circumstances, but for similar reasons, this Court held that textbooks could not be provided to segregated schools because that would aid the discrimination of those schools in violation of—

Question: Well, isn't that an Establishment Clause issue? It's been litigated under the Establishment Clause, right—providing textbooks or other aid to religious schools? Those have been Establishment Clause challenges, and we . . . determined that the Establishment Clause is not violated by giving aid to the blind, which is used then to study for the ministry, right?

Ms. Pierce: Yes, Justice O'Connor, and that's because under the Establishment Clause, the question is, is the government endorsing religion? Under Washington's article I, section 11, the question is, is—are public funds being used for the promotion or—of religious belief or disbelief and—

Pierce is getting herself into deeper trouble. She cites a race discrimination case only to be "reminded" by the Justice that the establishment clause cases have gone the other way. She then shifts the question back to conscience-promoting religious belief *or disbelief.* The question is not whether Washington's aid to Davey endorses religion—it doesn't under the Court's decisions—but whether it *promotes belief or disbelief.* What is the difference between promoting and endorsing? Doesn't an endorsement promote, and a promotion endorse? And how is the state promoting if it just gives money to the student under a general program and lets the student decide? If school vouchers were constitutional because the child has his or her own choice, the Promise Scholarship would hardly seem to be a promotion. This is where the Court goes next.

Question: Ms. Pierce, may I ask you a question there on how you draw the line? Because I want to get clear on one thing. Is my understanding correct that this clause that we are dealing with here, and nothing else for that matter in the Washington law, forbids the state from paying—we'll call it a tuition voucher here—that is going to a sectarian school like this one, so long as it's not being used for theological education? In other words, going back to Justice Kennedy's question, if this same student said, I want to study business and I want to study it at this sectarian school, there would be no impediment in Washington giving him the voucher or whatever you call it and letting him spend it at this sectarian school? Is that correct?

Ms. Pierce: That's true at the higher education level.

Question: Okay. But isn't it also true he could even take the same courses and [receive support] as long as he didn't declare his major until he was a junior?

Ms. Pierce: Your Honor, the statute says pursuing a degree in theology, so I think it should be properly read and is properly read by Northwest College as a student who is, during the academic terms that are funded, working toward that degree in theology.

Question: But I . . . I just want to be sure I understand how it works, in response to Justice Kennedy's inquiry. Is it not true that he could have taken all or most of the religious courses he did take if he'd only declared a different major or postponed the time when he declared his major? Which has a double aspect. On one hand, as Justice Kennedy points out, the state interest doesn't seem all that compelling there, but on the other hand, the burden on him is also pretty slight, because all he had to [do] was just manage his curriculum a little differently. And I just want to know, am I correct that he could have taken either all or substantially all of the religious courses and qualified for the scholarship if he just declared a different major?

Ms. Pierce: You're partially correct, Justice Stevens. I think he could have taken some of the same religion courses. I don't think just simply declaring your major later is what meets the purpose of the statute. The statute says are you pursuing—

Question: Wasn't he counseled—wasn't he counseled specifically by the school to be honest?

Ms. Pierce: Yes, Justice Ginsburg.

Question: And not try to hide what his purpose was, which he was perfectly open about? And, of course, if—if you take a whole bunch of religious courses, it may be they can't be counted for some other major other than the—the theology [major].

Ms. Pierce: Yes, Justice Ginsburg. Well, the theology degree, Your Honor, does require, I believe at Northwest, 125 credits, and 79 of those credits are required to be in various Bible and theological courses, so I think it is—it would be possible, but unusual, for another student to have those same courses and not being pursuing a degree in theology.

Question: Could we go back to Justice Kennedy's second part of what he was asking, because it's bothering me, too. I think it's absolutely well-established, whether there's a case or not, that people have thought it's different when what the federal government or state government says is, what we have here is a secular program, we're paying for secular programs, whether it's schools or social services or any one of a million things, or if it were to say, well, it's a Baptist program, but not a Catholic program.

I think if they said the second, they'd have to pass [very] strict [constitutional] scrutiny as far as their reasons are concerned. [If it were a secular program], so far I don't think they would have to pass anything like that. What do we judge that distinction on the basis of? What kind of a test?

Ms. Pierce: Justice Breyer, I believe it is a rational basis test [which is very deferential to the state], that is, it is a neutral line, it's a recognized line between the secular that does not involve the realm of belief and faith, and a religious that does.

Question: Rational [basis?] You think there's a difference in free exercise if what the state says is "we are burdening the free exercise of all religions," as opposed to "we are burdening the free exercise of one particular religion." You think there's a different . . . a different standard? Again, I would ask for the case that—that suggests that.

Ms. Pierce: [T]his case involves application of public funds in a funding program, and we believe that the principle [is] that a state's decision not to fund the exercise of a fundamental right is not a burden on that right, it's not an infringement on that right. All that the State of Washington has done here is decline to fund theology studies, Justice Scalia.

Question: Certainly in our—in our *Rosenberger* case there was a rational basis for what the University of Virginia did, but we held it violated the Free Exercise Clause.

Ms. Pierce: Yes, Mr. Chief Justice, and the purpose of the public forum principles that were applied in *Rosenberger* are to protect the open public forum. There the Court specifically acknowledged that that was a forum for the publication, for the expression of ideas, and that the expression of those ideas in that open public forum would be incomplete if certain viewpoints were excluded. But certainly the purpose of the Promise Scholarship is not to open a public forum.

Question: You think a [mere] rational basis suffices for the state to prohibit this student from declaring one of his legitimate majors? [Rational basis means the law is sloppy and ill-fitting. Here the Washington Constitution prohibits support for religious instruction, but the law restricts only majoring in theology with the intent to enter the ministry. The law, in short, is vastly underinclusive.]

Ms. Pierce: We believe—yes, Your Honor, we believe there is a rational basis to not fund religious instruction wherever it occurs, including a theology course.

Question: Is it essentially your position that not everything that is compatible with the Establishment Clause, not everything that the state could do under the Establishment Clause, it must do under the Free Exercise Clause? And if that's your position, how do you define the space in between those two where the state has a choice?

Ms. Pierce: That is our position. We don't think states should be in constitutional pincers where whatever they're allowed to do under the Establishment Clause [they are] required to do, particularly given the history that states have come to their own path to religious freedom. And I think applying the various principles on when you burden the exercise of religious freedom leads you to the latitude in this area. That's all that the state has done, Mr. Chief Justice. Here, not providing funding does not infringe—

Chief Justice Rehnquist: Thank you, Ms. Pierce. You're reserving your time.

The question at the end was a softball. But it was logically confusing, as was much of Pierce's argument. If the question is free exercise versus nonestablishment, shouldn't the individual liberty of free exercise control? Here the funding wouldn't violate the establishment clause if it were seen as a voucher, giving the individual a free choice and not involving a state endorsement of any choice. Under this view, Pierce would lose. She had to argue that the establishment clause prohibits funding even with individual choice. That's a case she didn't make.

It is now Joshua Davey's turn. His argument is that discriminating against him in the Promise Scholarship program violates his right freely to exercise his religion; that there is no establishment clause violation; and that even if there were, the free exercise right should control.

Mr. Sekulow: Mr. Chief Justice, and may it please the Court: In the free exercise context, this Court has held that the minimum requirement of neutrality is that a law not discriminate on its face. In this particular case, Josh Davey applied for the grant when he was notified by the state that he was qualified and accepted in the program in August. At that point he enrolled at Northwest College, which is an accredited and eligible institution. He declared his major, the dual major, at that point in business administration and the pastoral ministries degree.

The state decided that in fact there would be a prohibition put in place on pursuing a degree in theology, and the state has interpreted that to mean pursuing a degree in theology from a religious perspective.

The check, Justice O'Connor [referring to her earlier question of Ms. Pierce], is sent to the student [at the college]. The school gets the check and hands it to the student. It's not written to the school. The school cannot use [it] for any expenditure. The school merely verifies that the student's enrolled. The check then goes to the student. It can be used for any—

Question: So it wouldn't violate the Establishment Clause, but I guess what we're addressing is whether there's a free exercise violation.

Mr. Sekulow: Right.

It is not altogether clear that the Promise Scholarship would satisfy the establishment clause, but the Court has often said that a general program of assistance that goes to the student, who is then free to use it for education or service in a secular or religious environment, does not trigger establishment clause scrutiny because the public funds go to the individual rather than directly to the religious organization and thus the individual is free to exercise his or her own preference, including a preference for religion. It serves the individual's free exercise interests. This has been the basis upon which the Court has held that religious groups (like a practicing religious student organization) cannot be forbidden to use school rooms after the end of the school day, if those rooms are available to nonreligious groups (like the chess club). It is the basis upon which the Court had recently approved school voucher plans in Ohio in the *Zelman* case. And this is the basis upon which the Justice surmises that the case involves a claimed free exercise violation.

The distinction based on the recipient of the aid is a clear but thin one, however. For example, in *Rosenberger* a majority of the Justices (the dissenters and Justice O'Connor) were not moved to ignore the establishment clause by the fact that the university paid the printer. For Justice O'Connor, the distinction between a nonsectarian (the printer) and a sectarian (*Wide Awake*) recipient was relevant only to deciding whether the funding program would be reasonably viewed by outsiders as a government endorsement of religion. For her, establishment clause scrutiny still applied even though the religious actor was not the recipient of state funds.

Even accepting the Justice's surmise and Sekulow's agreement, it should also be said that the free exercise claim is a thin one, too. The argument would essentially be that the failure of the state to fund Davey's own religious choice is a denial of his right freely to exercise his religion. But the free exercise clause has never been understood to give individuals a right to state-subsidization of their religious activities. The state has no obligation to reimburse people for their tithes, or to provide free transportation to religious schools. In the latter case, the state may, but need not, do so, as the Court decided in *Everson*.

In contrast, the issue in the *Davey* case is not the right to state funding as a general matter, but the more limited right not to be excluded from funding in a general program for which Davey qualifies but for his religious activity. Davey's claim, in other words, is that the equality principle underlying the Court's recent religion decisions confers an affirmative right to inclusion in such general programs, not just a right not to be discriminated against by, for example, an evenhanded law that includes religious acts, and from which an individual seeks exclusion. And as we have seen in *Smith* and in *Rosenberger,* the affirmative inclusion claim triggers establishment clause scrutiny on the ground that separation of church and state forecloses government from funding religious activities and institutions.

So the case cannot easily be reduced to the free exercise clause, even in light of the majority opinion (plurality, really) in *Rosenberger,* which, it will be recalled, turned to the speech guarantee to find an affirmative right to inclusion.

Question: How does this violate the student's right to free exercise of religion? Maybe it's more expensive to go to school, but why does that violate his free exercise of religion right?

Mr. Sekulow: Joshua Davey has the free exercise right to pursue a degree in theology. The question here is the burden that's placed on it. Of course, two responses. With regard to the actual burden, here a general benefit was available to a student and a religious classification was utilized to deny the student access to those funds. He met the criteria.

Question: Well, let me ask you this. Suppose a state has a school voucher program such as the Court indicated could be upheld in the *Zelman* case. Now, if the state decides not to give school vouchers for use in religious or parochial schools, do you take the position it must, that it has to do one or the other? It can have a voucher program, but if it does, it has to fund all private and religious schools with a voucher program? Is that your position?

Mr. Sekulow: No. The state—

Question: Well, why not? I mean, why wouldn't it follow from what you are saying today?

Mr. Sekulow: For this reason. The state can set neutral and eligible criteria for admission as an eligible institution. Here it was accreditation. Now, if the religious school, the school that was affiliated with the religious denomination met the general neutral eligibility requirement, and there were no countervailing Establishment Clause problems, yes, then it should—

Question: I . . . I don't know what you mean. The state says all schools were going to have a program to give vouchers for use in all schools of a certain grade level, assuming the teachers are qualified to be teachers. Can they refrain from making that program available for use in religious schools?

Mr. Sekulow: I would think not.

Question: So what you're urging here would have a major impact, then, would it not, on voucher programs?

Mr. Sekulow: Well, it would. I think a voucher program could be established that has a neutral criteria and if the private schools meet that criteria, including the private religious schools, and there is no countervailing Establishment Clause problem, I wouldn't see any reason—

Question: Surely, the state can decide to fund only public schools.

Mr. Sekulow: Absolutely.

Question: And it's only when it starts funding some private schools that you get into the religious question.

Mr. Sekulow: That's correct.

We're into the thick of it now. First, as Sekulow does and must admit, a voucher program for all public and private accredited schools could not, under his theory, discriminate against religious schools by excluding them from the program. Those schools would have an affirmative right to equal treatment—a right to be included in the program. The *Rosenberger* decision was ambiguous on the constitutional stature of such a religion clause right (as opposed to a free speech right), but its acceptance by a majority of the Justices would not be surprising in light of both *Smith* and *Rosenberger,* as well as the many cases guaranteeing religious groups access to public spaces if the spaces are available generally to the public.

But the implications of such a right are far greater in the funding—and especially in the school voucher—setting. Two implications appear to be very much on the Justices' minds, both financial in part. First, there are many private religious schools, and they may be much better schools than the public schools, especially in large urban centers with large minority populations. The financial implications of a right to inclusion for religious schools could thus become a great deterrent to the spread of voucher plans. The second implication is even greater and much more costly. If discrimination against religious schools in voucher plans can't be justified, how can a state justify discriminating against religious schools in its general school funding system? Will funding for public education, which by definition excludes accredited religious schools, be held unconstitutional under Sekulow's equality principle?

While in the ivory tower it may be said that the Constitution's demands shouldn't be overridden by their cost—jury trials cost a lot, for example, as does the right to counsel paid by the state for those who cannot afford a lawyer—the Justices are not just oracles. They are also practical, wise, and prudent people who are aware of the limits on their power, and thus of the economic and social consequences of their decisions. The implications of

Davey's claim, therefore, surely have their attention and may well contribute to their individual votes in the case. More about that later. For now, the Justices just agonize over them.

Question: But I'm . . . I'm concerned—but you say if they [include] any private school they must . . . support all religious schools as well. They could not just say we will [include] all private schools except sectarian schools?

Mr. Sekulow: I don't think they could do that.

Question: That's the issue here? Even though there are quite a few state laws and constitutional provisions around the country that provide just that, aren't there? So the decision here could have very broad impact, I assume.

Mr. Sekulow: Interesting, Justice O'Connor, and, admittedly, this is a bit of a moving target because state policies change, but there are approximately [37] states that have this type of amendment. Twenty-five of those states have programs of aid that do not have a discriminatory basis upon religion. It's given to any accredited—

Question: Mr. Sekulow? May I ask you the question that I asked Ms. Pierce, because I think this is really what the case turns on. Is there any space between what . . . a state is permitted to do, what it's permitted to fund under the Establishment Clause, and what it *must* fund under the Free Exercise Clause, and if so, what fills that space? You've been candid in saying voucher: no. If you are going to give to any private school, you can't leave out the parochial schools. You certainly said that about this program.

Mr. Sekulow: Yes.

Question: Suppose the state would say, we are going to fund professional education, lawyers, doctors, architects, engineers, but we're not going to fund people who are in a divinity program. Would that qualify, or would that fall also?

Mr. Sekulow: Well, I think a program that were to just limit it to specific professions would not necessarily have to go towards theology. For instance, in a lot of states there is a shortage of nurses right now. And if the state were to adopt a program to fund education for nurses that included public and private schools, they don't have to bring theology—

Question: No, but my program includes all professions, save one, and that is ministry.

Mr. Sekulow: Well, if it [were] as you described it, I would be here arguing the same point in this context. The idea that you would list all of the professions and then say "we are going to fund everything [except] those students studying theology" would be [a] religious classification, and I would think unless the state could establish its compelling governmental interest—

Question: As I understand your answer to Justice O'Connor, if we decide in your favor, we necessarily commit ourselves to the proposition that an elementary and secondary school voucher program must include religious schools if it includes any other private schools. It seems to me that your case can be resolved on a much narrower issue than that. Here we have a . . . a college student who is being required to surrender his conscientious beliefs by declaring a major which otherwise would have been completely funded by the school, and I just don't see any interest in doing that. It seems to me a very severe violation of religious conscience. I think that's quite different from an overall neutrality principle, which would foreclose this Court on the voucher issue.

Mr. Sekulow: Well, I agree, Justice Kennedy. I don't think the Court has to go that far here.

Question: But certainly that's what you're arguing. I mean, your . . . your brief and your presentation certainly urge us to go that route. Let's assume that all the public schools and all the private schools, including all religious private schools, are accredited in whatever way the state accredits them, and that the criterion, apart from religious education, is simply that the ultimate recipient of the voucher has to be an accredited school. It seems to me, following Justice O'Connor's question, that the argument that would be made in any case in which a state says we will allow a voucher to be spent in a private school, but not a private religious school is the same argument that Justice Kennedy was suggesting a moment ago, and that is that the religious student must somehow surrender a conscientious belief and go from a religious school and seek to be enrolled in a nonreligious private school or a public one to get the voucher. And I don't see why that argument would not be just as applicable there as the argument that you are making here.

Mr. Sekulow: It's their major. In this context, the way the program is implemented within that hypothetical and within the facts here, here students can take these very same courses in religion that Josh Davey—

Question: Well, that may show that the state draws a kind of a funny line. Maybe it was a bad job of line drawing, and I have to admit, I'm not quite sure why they draw it the way they do, but on the basic proposition that the state raises as its position here, that it will not fund ministerial education or education in how to be religious versus funding other kinds of training, the argument, it seems to me, from the Free Exercise Clause would be the same in the voucher case as the argument that you are making here.

Mr. Sekulow: If in fact the programs were put forward this way with the accreditation as you suggested, and there is no countervailing Establishment

Clause issue and the eligibility issue of the school is met, yes, I wouldn't see the justification to exclude a particular major here in this particular case, a submajor from a religious viewpoint.

There are two related arguments being explored here: first, that discrimination against religion is invalid; and second, that discrimination against those who major in theology is invalid. In response to Justice Kennedy, Sekulow argues that the second argument would be a narrower ground for invalidating the law, though he freely admits that the underlying equality principle is the same. He is right as a matter of logic and common sense. If discrimination against training for the ministry is impermissible, then surely discrimination on the basis of other less central religious criteria—like the religious affiliation of an accredited school—would also be invalid.

Question: Well, how many states . . . have voucher programs which allow students to go to any private school, you know, an elite academy, but not allow them to go to religious schools?

Mr. Sekulow: Twenty-five states have voucher-type programs that have no restrictions at all as long as it's an accredited institution, so that's usually the standard. They can go to any school that's accredited. There are some states, and it's about a half-dozen, Justice Scalia, that actually have this prohibition for religious education, and even within some of those states, the programs are inconsistent.

Question: But am I correct or incorrect that the state would fund a student who majored in literature at an institution [that] was sectarian and had instructors who taught literature from a religious perspective?

Mr. Sekulow: Yes.

Question: Well, but the state is saying—I don't know if we can escape the broader ground—the state's saying, look, we understand that, you know, applying our standard there'll be all kinds of anomalies that you can get. Maybe this case is one. But what we're doing by and large is to say, we don't want to spend too much of our state money in this program, we'll do it subsidiary, you know, the odd example doesn't matter, but people who major in philosophy are [un]likely to become priests or at least spend a lot of time studying theology. If they major in theology, or they spend a lot of time studying theology, that's going too far. So this is, like many administrative lines, a very crude effort to identify those people who are taking too much of their time in totally religiously oriented matters. Now, of course that's unconstitutional if we accept your argument that the state must treat the religious study the same way as any other. That's your broad ground.

But if we reject the broad ground, I don't quite see at the moment how we can accept the narrow one, which turns on these details of the administrability of the line.

Mr. Sekulow: Well, let me address the latter, if I might, Justice Breyer. Those details matter because the line drawing [which is] crude [occurs in] the context of the Free Exercise Clause. There is no countervailing Establishment Clause issue here. There is only one exclusion. It's not even, Justice Ginsburg, a situation with a number of majors. It's one.

Question: Certainly, you are not standing here to tell us that, oh, if they were more restrictive, if they said we're simply not going to fund scholarships to students who go to sectarian schools, that that might be all right. I mean, you don't want to win on the ground [that the state] was too generous in what it did fund.

Mr. Sekulow: Well, two responses. First, on the issue of the state and [its] obligation, to [characterize our claim] as the state being required to fund Joshua Davey's education, I think is . . . is a miscast[ing] of the issue. The state has decided to develop a scholarship program that's very broad-based and in that program they have given the student the ultimate choice of where they could go to school as long as it's within Washington state and accredited and literally they can major in any major except for one, and that is a theology exclusion.

Question: Wouldn't it be any better if they said, you can go to any school except a church school?

Mr. Sekulow: No. I think it would raise the same problem. But it's not to say that the state universities don't teach courses in theology and religion. There's a listing of the courses offered at the University of Washington, and it covers a broad array of religious courses—

Question: You don't know of any case that says that the less significant the interest the state has, the more latitude it has in discriminating against religion. You don't know of any case that said that?

Mr. Sekulow: No. That . . . that would—

Question: I hope you don't.

Mr. Sekulow: No. And hopefully this won't be that one.

(Laughter)

Question: May I ask you a broader question? A number of the briefs discussed the breathing space between the Establishment Clause and the Free Exercise Clause. Do you take the position, or just what is your position on whether or not there is such a breathing space?

Mr. Sekulow: The play in the joints, as it's referred to.

Question: Yes.

Mr. Sekulow: I think the play in the joints gives the state broad flexibility in establishing the programs or not establishing a program at all, but to use the play in the joints to not accommodate religion but rather to target religion as an exclusion I think is a misuse in my view of what the Court has at this point—

Question: But do you go so far as to contend that any violation, any time there is no violation of the Establishment Clause that then the Free Exercise Clause would necessarily kick in? [Can you] give me an example of a case where the state can say we know we can give this funding to religious schools if we want to, but we don't want to? Can you give any example where that would be legitimate in your view of free exercise?

Mr. Sekulow: Sure, Justice Ginsburg. The Center Moriches School District in the *Lamb's Chapel* [case, where the school was precluded from refusing religious groups access to otherwise open spaces in the school.] This Court held that they were not required to open their facilities up at all. The State of Washington could develop programs for specific majors.

Question: So let me just say what I think your position is. I think your position is that, although certain religious funding may not violate the Establishment Clause, it does not follow that the state must fund it. But if the state has a general program for funding instruction, and this is religious instruction, it's got to fund religious instruction and there's no middle ground, there's no play in the joints there. Is that correct?

Mr. Sekulow: [T]hat would be our position, that once you have gone into the private schools and the school meets the neutral secular criteria, our view would be at that point the state should be equal and not target out religion for an exclusion, which is precisely the viewpoint neutrality issue that we think should apply and, of course, within the free exercise context, the minimum requirement of neutrality is [that a] law not discriminate on its face. This one does. If there are no further questions, thank you, Mr. Chief Justice.

Chief Justice Rehnquist: Thank you, Mr. Sekulow. General Olson, we'll hear from you.

Mr. Olson: Mr. Chief Justice, and may it please the Court: The Promise Scholarship program practices the plainest form of religious discrimination. It disqualifies the one course of study that is taught from a religious perspective. The clear and unmistakable message is that religion and preparation for a career in the ministry is disfavored and discouraged.

Question: Well, but of course, there's been a couple of centuries of practice in this country of not funding religious instruction by tax money. I mean, that's—that's as old as the country itself, isn't it?

Mr. Olson: Well, yes, it is. But there is the other tradition that is as old as the country itself, is the free exercise component of the religion clauses, which this Court has said repeatedly mandates neutrality.

Question: But how is his free exercise chilled at all? Can't he practice his religion just as he always would and become a minister? He just has to pay for it.

Mr. Olson: [W]ell, Justice Stevens, [what about] the individual [who] was disqualified in Tennessee from being a member of a delegate to the Constitutional Convention because he was a minister? [This Court struck down that disqualification, which involved no money at all.] [T]he Court would have come out the same way, I submit, if it said that ministers will not have their expenses paid, but everybody else will.

Question: But you're still not addressing the question of how his freedom to practice the religion he wants to practice is impaired at all.

Mr. Olson: Well, he can practice it, but he practices it at a price. Studying of theology as the—

Question: He practices it without a subsidy.

Mr. Olson: He practices it without the same subsidy that is made available to every other citizen except someone who wants to study to be a minister. If it [were] discrimination against a minister in the case involving Tennessee, this is a discrimination against a person who aspires to be a minister. He is given less of an advantage than all—

Question: So you take the position there's no breathing space between the [establishment and free exercise clauses]?

Mr. Olson: Well, there may be breathing space, especially with respect to the Establishment Clause area, where this Court will not find entanglement or endorsement under certain programs that may not be required, but what this Court has said is that distinguishing—that discriminating against Catholics and discriminating against people who are religious generally and even people who are antireligious generally violates the twin components of equality and neutrality that are mandated by the religion clauses.

Olson is hanging tough here. His position is that discrimination against religion in a general program can never be justified by the establishment clause, and thus is never constitutional. But this is a tough pill to swallow, and the Justices are deeply concerned.

Question: What is your response to the following concern that's been brought up a few times but I'd like you to address it directly. This case is perhaps a small matter of a distinction that doesn't make all that much sense, but makes some. But the implications of this case are breathtaking, that it would mean if your side wins, that every program, not just educational programs, but nursing programs, hospital programs, social welfare programs, contracting programs throughout the governments would go over, you'd have to go over each of them and there would be a claim in each instance that they cannot be purely secular, that they must fund all religions who want to do the same thing, and that those religions, by the way, though it may be an excellent principle, may get into fights with each other about billions and billions of dollars, which is something about which I have written, which you know. All right. So, I'd like you to address that.

Mr. Olson: Yes, Justice Breyer. It is not a major step at all in this Court's jurisprudence to say that those funding programs for medicine, doctors, nurses, cannot distinguish and not discriminate against a person who decides to [be] a Catholic nurse or a Catholic doctor. If money is made available for individuals in the Medicare program, to exclude people that want to go to religious hospitals for their heart surgery would violate the Free Exercise Clause.

Question: So do you agree, do you take the position that if we affirm the court of appeals and accept your position, that the Court is committed on the school voucher issue if, say, a school voucher program excludes parochial schools?

Mr. Olson: It would depend, I suppose, on how the program was structured. There may be a difference, for example, with respect to funding that's associated with institutions, as opposed to individual conscience. [But this case] is the plainest form of religious discrimination because the person who wants to believe in God or wants to have a position of religious leadership is the one that's singled out for discriminatory treatment. The Court has said before that religious tests for governmental benefits violate the Free Exercise Clause. This is a religious test.

Question: May I ask you—What are the practical implications? Just a sentence on the practical implications. Is it as far-reaching as my tone of voice suggested?

Mr. Olson: I would say that it is not as far-reaching as the—the sense of doom that your question suggested.

(Laughter)

Question: Maybe a good thing I'm not . . . don't—

Mr. Olson: The idea that this country when it provides tax exemptions or cash to citizens to educate their children, cannot single out for discriminatory treatment the Catholic or the religious person is not far-reaching. [I]t may have been far-reaching at the time, and thank heavens [it was].

Question: General, may I ask you this question? I mean, the whole argument for neutrality comes down to an argument, I think, about the following distinction. Washington says, look, there is a line to be drawn, not between funding Catholics and Protestants or atheists or what-not. The line to be drawn is the line between funding education about a religion, and on the other hand, education that says, this belief is valid, and you ought to go out and persuade other people to hold this belief. They say, that is the distinction we are trying to draw. Why is that distinction invalid under a neutrality criteri[on]?

Mr. Olson: For the reason that the same argument was rejected in the *Rosenberger* case, that the notion of—

Question: But . . . the opinion in *Rosenberger* said these people are not proselytizing. And the distinction that they are drawing is a distinction between believing in proselytizing on the one hand, how to do it, why it's valid, and instruction on what people believe as a fact on the other. And *Rosenberger* is an authority for the rejection of that distinction?

Mr. Olson: I respectfully submit that it is, that the students in *Rosenberger* [who] were publishing those articles were publishing articles that advocated belief in God.

Question: Oh, look, you're writing my dissent. I—[Laughter]—I agree, but I couldn't get four colleagues to agree with me on that, and they went off on—on another—another course.

Mr. Olson: Yes, but the Court went on to say that this was a free exercise violation as well as a First Amendment [speech] violation. The other point that I think is very, very important with respect to that, if the state starts to distinguish between discussion of a subject and proselytizing, the entanglement problem [i.e., involvement of the state in determining the validity and importance of religious beliefs and practices] is going to be enormous. The program will have to be looked at to see how persuasive it is. We know today that—

Question: If that argument is good, why do we even bother with the criterion of direct funding of religion? Because we could have drawn the line there.

Mr. Olson: No, because the line has been drawn by individuals, individuals making genuinely free, independent choices to make a dispensation. It's like the Court's example in those cases of an individual receiving a check and then deciding exactly how to spend it so there's a great difference between those kind of cases. This is no different than the example that Justice Scalia raised as providing fire protection or—or providing tax deductions. Thank you.

Olson parries the last question by holding to the Court's own distinction between state funds going directly to the religious activity or institution, and funds being instead given to the individual who is then free to make his or her own choice about how (religious or not) to spend them. Giving the funds to the individual allows his or her choice to be characterized as an exercise of religious freedom, and the establishment clause problem evaporates because the state is not making intrusive decisions about religious doctrine or belief, nor is it giving money to a religion for religious activities. Instead, it is giving money to a general class of recipients—needy and able students—only some of whom will choose to spend it for religious education, and most of whom won't. This is a clear and principled distinction that can be made consistent with the policies of both religion guarantees.

But does it go far enough? What about faith-based providers of government services, a program that now exists (and, of course, is being challenged in court)? If a church successfully bids on a contract to provide substance abuse counseling and assistance, the federal funds will be paid directly to the church without any limitation on where and how they are used. This wouldn't satisfy Olson's requirement that the funds go to the recipient rather than the religious institution or activity. Could such programs only be done through voucher arrangements? That would be a big change, and an administratively difficult one. And it is not clear why such a change should be required under the establishment clause. If a tax exemption for a church is the economic equivalent of a subsidy, then isn't a voucher program pretty much the equivalent of a direct payment or subsidy for the religious school?

For Olson, this is a question he prefers to leave for another day, as it needn't be decided to resolve Joshua Davey's case in his favor.

Chief Justice Rehnquist: Thank you, General Olson. Ms. Pierce, you have three minutes remaining.

Ms. Pierce: This Court has accorded the states wide latitude in funding decisions for the states to make their own policy judgments. Here, all the state has done has been to decline to fund religious instruction wherever it occurs, including in a theology degree program. We have not overstepped our bounds by imposing an unconstitutional condition on Mr. Davey as a recipient. In the overall picture, we're not suppressing—

Question: It . . . it . . . it *will* fund religious instruction. So long as he doesn't major in theology, he can take the same courses and get . . . get instructed in religion, can't he?

Ms. Pierce: Yes, Justice Scalia, that—

Question: So what you say is just not true?

Ms. Pierce: Yes, Justice—well, that can happen in a rare circumstance. We believe that there's a good reason to use that—

Question: Everybody who takes a theology course has to major in theology? I don't think it's rare at all. Probably most of the students at Northwest College take theology courses. It's—it's a religious institution, and that's perfectly okay, and the state is willing to fund that.

Ms. Pierce: That's what the statute permits now. Some justices of our state supreme court have expressed the same question whether that is possible.

Chief Justice Rehnquist: Thank you, Ms. Pierce. The case is submitted.

Pierce just got butchered by Justice Scalia. But she asked for it. What she said about the Washington law "is just not true," as Justice Scalia observed. The scholarship program's exclusion is limited, in fact and practice, to those students studying for the ministry or some other professional theological vocation. Pierce may not like that, but she can't deny it. Indeed, she agreed with that description at least twice in her argument. Moreover, such a limited program provides her with her strongest argument, that there is a difference between state support for studying and learning theology, and state support—and thus involvement—in the training of ministers.

In the end, however, her persistent mischaracterization of the Washington scholarship program, and the very bumpy ride she experienced in oral argument, didn't make any difference in the outcome. Sekulow and Olson had the cleaner and more coherent theory and defended it admirably in a difficult oral argument before a worried and slightly confused Court. But the prettiest theory and the best argument rarely determine the outcome of cases. When February 25, 2004, rolled around, Pierce "won" the case despite herself.

The Court's majority was an odd amalgam: the liberal and separationist Justices (Stevens, Souter, Ginsburg), the middle group (O'Connor, Kennedy, Breyer), and the Chief Justice, who wrote the opinion. It was Chief Justice Rehnquist's job to find some common ground among all the disparate views in the seven-Justice majority. That proved to be an immensely difficult, and ultimately confounding, job.

Chief Justice *Rehnquist* delivered the opinion of the Court.

The Religion Clauses of the First Amendment provide: "Congress shall make no law respecting an establishment of religion, or prohibiting the free exercise thereof." These two Clauses, the Establishment Clause and the Free Exercise Clause, are frequently in tension. In other words, there are some state actions permitted by the Establishment Clause but not required by the Free Exercise Clause.

This case involves that "play in the joints" described above. Under our Establishment Clause precedent, the link between government funds and religious training is broken by the independent and private choice of recipients. As such, there is no doubt that the State could, consistent with the Federal Constitution, permit Promise Scholars to pursue a degree in devotional theology, and the State does not contend otherwise. The question before us, however, is whether Washington, pursuant to its own constitution, which has been authoritatively interpreted as prohibiting even indirectly funding religious instruction that will prepare students for the ministry, can deny them such funding without violating the Free Exercise Clause.

Davey urges us to answer that question in the negative. He contends that the program is presumptively unconstitutional because it is not facially neutral with respect to religion. We reject his claim of presumptive unconstitutionality. In the present case, the State's disfavor of religion (if it can be called that) is [mild]. It imposes neither criminal nor civil sanctions on any type of religious service or rite. It does not deny to ministers the right to participate in the political affairs of the community. And it does not require students to choose between their religious beliefs and receiving a government benefit. The State has merely chosen not to fund a distinct category of instruction.

Justice Scalia argues, however, that generally available benefits are part of the "baseline against which burdens on religion are measured." Because the Promise Scholarship Program funds training for all secular professions, *Justice Scalia* contends the State must also fund training for religious professions. But training for religious professions and training for secular professions are not fungible. Training someone to lead a congregation is an essentially religious endeavor. Indeed, majoring in devotional theology is akin to a religious calling as well as an academic pursuit. And the subject of religion is one in which both the United States and state constitutions embody distinct views—in favor of free exercise, but opposed to establishment—that find no counterpart with respect to other callings or professions. That a State would deal differently with religious education for the ministry than with education for other callings is a product of these views, not evidence of hostility toward religion.

Even though the differently worded Washington Constitution draws a more stringent line than that drawn by the United States Constitution, the interest it seeks to further is scarcely novel. . . . Most States that sought to avoid an establishment of religion around the time of the founding placed in their constitutions formal prohibitions against using tax funds to support the ministry. The plain text of these constitutional provisions prohibited any tax dollars from supporting the clergy. . . . That early state constitutions saw no problem in explicitly excluding only the ministry from receiving state dollars reinforces our conclusion that religious instruction is of a different ilk.

Far from evincing the hostility toward religion, we believe that the entirety of the Promise Scholarship Program goes a long way toward including religion in its benefits. The program permits students to attend pervasively religious schools, so long as they are accredited. As Northwest advertises, its "concept of education is distinctly Christian in the evangelical sense." It prepares all of its students, "through instruction, through modeling, [and] through [its] classes, to use . . . the Bible as their guide, as the truth," no matter their chosen profession. And under the Promise Scholarship Program's current guidelines, students are still eligible to take devotional theology courses. Davey notes all students at Northwest are required to take at least four devotional courses, "Exploring the Bible," "Principles of Spiritual Development," "Evangelism in the Christian Life," and "Christian Doctrine," and some students may have additional religious requirements as part of their majors.

In short, we find neither in the history or text of article I, section 11 of the Washington Constitution, nor in the operation of the Promise Scholarship Program, anything that suggests animus towards religion. Given the historic and substantial state interest at issue, we therefore cannot conclude that the denial of funding for vocational religious instruction alone is inherently constitutionally suspect.

If any room exists between the two Religion Clauses, it must be here. We need not venture further into this difficult area in order to uphold the Promise Scholarship Program as currently operated by the State of Washington.

The judgment of the Court of Appeals is therefore reversed.

The two dissenters, Justices Scalia and Thomas, had an easier job to do. They didn't have to navigate around the shoals of conflicting views on equality and separation. They could just state their own, and then tear at the majority opinion for its confusing and often inconsistent logic and, of course, for the deeply unfortunate result it reached.

Justice *Scalia,* with whom Justice *Thomas* joins, dissenting.

We articulated the principle that governs this case more than 50 years ago in *Everson:* "New Jersey cannot hamper its citizens in the free exercise of their own religion. Consequently, it cannot exclude individual Catholics, Lutherans, Mohammedans, Baptists, Jews, Methodists, Non-believers, Presbyterians, or the members of any other faith, because of their faith, or lack of it, from receiving the benefits of public welfare legislation."

When the State makes a public benefit generally available, that benefit becomes part of the baseline against which burdens on religion are measured; and when the State withholds that benefit from some individuals solely on the basis of religion, it violates the Free Exercise Clause no less than if it had imposed a special tax. That is precisely what the State of Washington has done here. Davey is not asking for a special benefit to which others are not entitled. He seeks only equal treatment—the right to direct his scholarship to his chosen course of study, a right every other Promise Scholar enjoys.

The Court's reference to historical "popular uprisings against procuring taxpayer funds to support church leaders," is therefore quite misplaced. That history involved not the inclusion of religious ministers in public benefits programs like the one at issue here, but laws that singled them out for financial aid. For example, the Virginia bill at which Madison's Remonstrance was directed provided: "[F]or the support of Christian teachers . . . [a] sum payable for tax on the property within this Common-wealth, is hereby assessed." Laws supporting the clergy in other States operated in a similar fashion. One can concede the Framers' hostility to funding the clergy specifically, but that says nothing about whether the clergy had to be excluded from benefits the State made available to all.

No one would seriously contend, for example, that the Framers would have barred ministers from using public roads on their way to church.

The Court does not dispute that the Free Exercise Clause places some constraints on public benefits programs, but finds none here, based on a principle of "play in the joints." I use the term "principle" loosely, for that is not so much a legal principle as a refusal to apply any principle when faced with competing constitutional directives. There is nothing anomalous about constitutional commands that abut. A municipality hiring public contractors may not discriminate against blacks or in favor of them; it cannot discriminate a little bit each way and then plead "play in the joints" when hauled into court. If the Religion Clauses demand neutrality, we must enforce them, in hard cases as well as easy ones.

What is the nature of the State's asserted interest here? It cannot be protecting the pocketbooks of its citizens; given the tiny fraction of Promise Scholars who would pursue theology degrees, the amount of any citizen's tax bill at stake is de minimis. It cannot be preventing mistaken appearance of endorsement; where a State merely declines to penalize students for selecting a religious major, "[n]o reasonable observer is likely to draw . . . an inference that the State itself is endorsing a religious practice or belief." Nor can Washington's exclusion be defended as a means of assuring that the State will neither favor nor disfavor Davey in his religious calling. Davey will throughout his life contribute to the public fisc through sales taxes on personal purchases, property taxes on his home, and so on; and nothing in the Court's opinion turns on whether Davey winds up a net winner or loser in the State's tax-and-spend scheme.

No, the interest to which the Court defers . . . is a pure philosophical preference: the State's opinion that it would violate taxpayers' freedom of conscience not to discriminate against candidates for the ministry. This sort of protection of "freedom of conscience" has no logical limit and can justify the singling out of religion for exclusion from public programs in virtually any context.

The Court makes no serious attempt to defend the program's neutrality, and instead identifies two features thought to render its discrimination less offensive. The first is the lightness of Davey's burden. The Court offers no authority for approving facial discrimination against religion simply because its material consequences are not severe. [But] even if there were some threshold quantum-of-harm requirement, surely Davey has satisfied it. The First Amendment, after all, guarantees free exercise of religion, and when the State exacts a financial penalty of almost $3,000 for religious exercise—whether by tax or by forfeiture of an otherwise available benefit—religious practice is anything but free. The Court distinguishes our precedents only by swapping the benefit to which Davey was actually entitled (a scholarship for his chosen course of study) with another, less valuable one (a scholarship for any course of study but his chosen one). On such reasoning, any facially discriminatory benefits program can be redeemed simply by redefining what it guarantees.

The other reason the Court thinks this particular facial discrimination less offensive is that the scholarship program was not motivated by animus toward religion. The Court does not explain why the legislature's motive matters, and I fail to see why it should. If a State deprives a citizen of trial by jury or passes an ex post facto law, we do not pause to investigate whether it was actually trying to accomplish the evil the Constitution prohibits. It is sufficient that the citizen's rights have been infringed. [As we said in *Lukumi*,[5]] "[It does not] matter that a legislature consists entirely of the purehearted, if the law it enacts in fact singles out a religious practice for special burdens."

It may be that Washington's original purpose in excluding the clergy from public benefits was benign, and the same might be true of its purpose in maintaining the exclusion today. But those singled out for disfavor can be forgiven for suspecting more invidious forces at work. Let there be no doubt: This case is about discrimination against a religious minority. Most citizens of this country identify themselves as professing some religious belief, but the State's policy poses no obstacle to practitioners of only a tepid, civic version of faith. Those the statutory exclusion actually affects—those whose belief in their religion is so strong that they dedicate their study and their lives to its ministry—are a far narrower set. One need not delve too far into modern popular culture to perceive a trendy disdain for deep religious conviction.

Today's holding is limited to training the clergy, but its logic is readily extendible, and there are plenty of directions to go. What next? Will we deny priests and nuns their prescription-drug benefits on the ground that taxpayers' freedom of conscience forbids medicating the clergy at public expense? This may seem fanciful, but recall that France has proposed banning religious attire from schools, invoking interests in secularism no less benign than those the Court embraces today. When the public's freedom of conscience is invoked to justify denial of equal treatment, benevolent motives shade into indifference and ulti-

---

5. *Church of Lukumi Babalu Aye, Inc. v. Hialeah*, 508 U.S. 520 (1993). *Lukumi* involved a city ordinance making certain kinds of animal slaughter a crime. The Court found that, while generally applicable on its face, the law was targeted: it "sought to suppress ritualistic animal sacrifices of the Santeria religion." Because of its express purpose to "single out a religious practice for special burdens," the law violated the establishment clause.

mately into repression. Having accepted the justification in this case, the Court is less well equipped to fend it off in the future.

I respectfully dissent.

* * *

What should we make of the *Davey* case? One might well be excused for scratching one's head in confusion. Just as a principle of equality was about to emerge full bloom, it wilted. Yet the decision can be no comfort for the separationists, Stevens, Souter, and Ginsburg, for while it is clear that Washington may follow a strict separation path, it is not entirely clear why—and, in any event, it's clear that Washington need not do so. The votes that shifted from the *Rosenberger* case were Chief Justice Rehnquist and Justices O'Connor and Kennedy, who authored *Rosenberger.* The Chief Justice and Justice Kennedy, at least, were unlikely to have changed their minds about the religion guarantees. Might the implications of a full-blown equality principle, with its powerful affirmative edge, have given them pause?

Before stepping back and trying to take full stock of the Davey decision, it is worth itemizing what the opinion contained and what it decided, piece by piece. The first noteworthy item is the majority opinion's complete, and surely conscious, silence on the *Rosenberger* decision. The case wasn't so much as cited in the text of the opinion, and it was cited in just two footnotes, once simply for a historical reference and once to dismiss the First Amendment speech analogy by stating that the scholarship in *Davey* was not a forum for speech, which would invoke serious free speech scrutiny. While that doesn't mean that free speech is not still an issue in the case, it is clear that the majority rejected such a claim (which Davey had made) by ignoring it. The message the Court was subtly conveying is that *Rosenberger* was a speech case and therefore has nothing to do with Davey's discrimination claim. That message had to be subtle, however, because the four dissenters in *Rosenberger,* all of whom rejected the first amendment analysis, joined the majority opinion in *Davey.*

Davey, then, was a religion case, pure and simple. Thinking about *Davey* as a religion case, and then thinking about the meaning it gives to the equality principle, yields a surprising result. The rejection of Davey's claim of discrimination against religion means, logically, that whatever equality means in the religion guarantee setting, it does not mean a right not to be treated worse because of religious practice (negative equality) or a right to be treated the same as nonreligious actors (affirmative equality). Without either form of right, equality doesn't amount to much—certainly it isn't the powerful tool argued for by Justices Scalia and Thomas in *Rosenberger* and stated strongly by a majority of the Justices in *Smith.*

It seems unlikely, though, that equality has been so quietly and even offhandedly sapped of its strength, replaced by a full principle of separation of church and state. Instead, the Court appears to dabble in a little of this and a little of that: when it comes to core religious practices, state assistance can, but need not, be precluded in the interest of non-establishment—to prevent government insinuating itself into core religious beliefs and practices. When the practices are outside the core, or concern religious institutions' non-central tenets and rites, equality is a strong force that prohibits their exclusion from general government programs and requires their inclusion under the free exercise clause.

But there are a number of problems with the core/non-core distinction, even apart from its difficulty of application. First, it is a strange rule that treats religious acts closest to the core of the free exercise liberty as least deserving of protection, yet treats non-core activities as most deserving of protection. Second, the Court must, though it doesn't, explain how training for the ministry is less core than proselytizing through a religious magazine in *Rosenberger.* If they are the same in terms of their core religious nature, then *Rosenberger* should have been decided differently, or at least it should have explained how the speech right could override such a strong interest in avoiding government funding of core religious practices (as the University of Virginia had argued in *Rosenberger*). It is hard, I think, to rank training for the ministry as any more "core" than proselytizing (or teaching the Word, which is what ministers do, after all). Surely, if government tax support for such core activities as preaching the Word were what the core of the establishment guarantee was aimed at, as the majority opinion in *Davey* says, then the drafters of the Constitution would not have followed it with another (free speech) guarantee that swallowed it up. *Rosenberger,* in other words, simply can't be ignored, and probably can't be made consistent with *Davey.*

Accepting *Davey* as written, however, there is yet another serious problem. The reason Davey's core free exercise right to engage in training for the ministry is rejected is the establishment clause—the need, with core religious practices and beliefs, to keep government separated from religion by denying government the ability to fund core practices. This is clear enough, and seems to be what the Court's opinion says. But the quite limited problem in the *Davey* case was Washington's ability to pursue such a policy of separation, which the Court affirms. There is no establishment clause problem with Washington changing its mind, or other states following different courses and extending their general scholarship programs to all qualified recipients, even those who are studying in preparation for the ministry. If Washington can exclude them because including them would amount to the state funding core religious activities and thus insinuate government too much into core religious practices and beliefs, then it should follow that if Iowa, for example, decided on its own to fund ministerial training as part of a merit scholarship program, Iowa would be acting unconstitutionally in violation of the establishment clause. It is no answer to this logical and principled dilemma to say that this is just the "play in the joints" between nonestablishment and free exercise, for the play in the joints explaining Iowa's problem would be in the establishment clause alone. There is, in short, no joint in which to have any "play."

In the end, the Court runs out of grounds for its decision, and reverts, finally, to the claim that there is no "hostility" toward religion reflected in Washington's policy. But can this distinction really be made to work? Can it be said that the University of Virginia's policy, based on its understanding of the establishment clause, reflected (or was born of) hostility toward religion? That would be a difficult case to make. More to the point, when asked about the reason Washington's constitutional provision was included in the first place, and why it continues to be strongly supported, Narda Pierce answered that "Washington's interest expressed in 1899 was to protect the freedom of conscience of all its citizens, and that included not compelling its citizens to provide enforced public funds to support the promotion of religious beliefs with which they may or may not agree." If you think about it, that sounds like a reason grounded expressly in citizens' hostility toward religion.

None of these specific points and arguments in the opinion reveals much, except the apparent lack of consistent principle underlying it. Does this prove that, when faced with the prospect of state funding for religious schools or state scholarships for ministers, the Court simply blinked, carving out an exception into which it could duck for the moment? No. But there is reason to be a bit skeptical.

At best we can say the opinion was a bit inconsistent, uncertain, and disappointing. Strangely enough, that may be fitting, in a way. In the fall of 2003, after graduating from Northwest College and just before his case was to be argued before the Supreme Court, Joshua Davey entered the Harvard Law School. "I'm very excited," he said. "It's obviously very exciting to be part of a Supreme Court case."

Religion in America

"The life of the law," said Justice Oliver Wendell Holmes, "is experience, not logic." With the Constitution of the United States, it is the Supreme Court that gives life to the law. Accordingly, this book is not just an inquiry into the meaning of religious liberty. It is also a study of the Supreme Court of the United States. Vague and evocative at best, the religion guarantees of non-establishment and freedom of exercise represent the Supreme Court's, not the Constitution's, idea of religious liberty.

The Supreme Court, it is often said, must base its decisions on principle—on the logic and reason of the history and text and purposes of the Constitution. To fail to do so is to fail to exercise its power properly and within necessary limits. The Supreme Court is an unelected and frankly elite body blessed with life tenure and thus insulated from the political branches. Compromise, expediency, and public passion belong in the legislative and executive halls, not in the marble palace that is the Supreme Court building. There, in the Court's house, reason and logic, publicly revealed in opinions, must reign.

In its unfolding religion jurisprudence the Supreme Court has been largely true to this commitment to logic and reason. It has also, and more recently, been deeply divided. Yet the deep divisions have largely focused on competing ideas of the text's meaning, its history, and its purposes—competing ideas, it should be said, that are each equally tenable, given the uncertainties and apparent inconsistencies in the First Amendment's language: "Congress shall make no law respecting an establishment of religion, or prohibiting the free exercise thereof."

Logic and reason, in other words, have generally marked the Court's decisions, though they have competed at a fundamental level. Is the separation of the secular and the religious, of the realms of reason and faith, of church and state, the primary of the two religion guarantees? Is this because without strict separation, religion cannot be independent, answerable only to its God, and thus the individual's freedom to pursue his or her religious convictions would be but a hollow promise? Or is the individual's liberty to exercise his or her religion the primary of the two guarantees? Is this because freedom in America exists at the individual, not the institutional (church, for example), level? Churches are, after all, but a collection of like-minded individuals, and without the energy of individual acts of religious conscience, churches would ossify and ultimately expire. Can individual liberty on matters of religion flourish in an environment when the state can discriminate against an individual's religious ideas and actions, denying them an equal place in the secular order?

These, at base, are the two competing and principled visions of religious liberty in America that are now vying for dominance among the Justices of the Supreme Court. They are fundamentally conflicting visions: one focusing on the institutions of religion (church versus state), the other focusing on the individual (freedom of conscience in religious belief and exercise). Given that these views arise from conflicting core premises, they cannot easily be reconciled—at least not in logic or reason or principle. This is why Chief Justice Rehnquist observed at the beginning of his opinion in the *Davey* case that the religion clauses are "frequently in tension."

Holmes's assertion that experience, not logic, is the life of the law is not a rejection of principle and reason as necessary justifications for, and limits on, the exercise of nondemocratic judicial power. It is instead an observation on the limits of logic. Logic, unrestrained, has a certain hydraulic power about it, a power that drives inevitably to the absurd. We experience this in our daily lives. Discrimination is unequal and bad, but not grades in school or higher pay for better work. The country's foreign policy should be governed by principles of freedom and equality and democracy, but not in our dealings with OPEC countries or our trade with China.

It could be argued that when principles and logic approach their tolerable limits—when they threaten, if extended further, to produce absurd results—the Supreme Court should step aside and leave the rest of the problem to the elected, political branches. Justice Scalia's opinion in *Smith,* the peyote case, can be seen as doing just that by foreclosing judicially crafted exemptions from general laws in the interest of religious liberty, but at the same time encouraging the legislative and executive branches to accommodate to religion by granting exemptions or providing support if they so choose. Government can draft religious objectors to fight in war, but it can also exempt them from that duty. Government can enforce the liquor laws by requiring churches to have licenses for communion, but it need not. Washington could include Joshua Davey in its grant program, but it need not. Ewing Township could have declined to pay for bus transportation for children attending religious schools, but it could also choose the opposite course.

These examples illustrate one way in which the Court can make concessions to Holmes's experience. Stick to logic but let the other branches of government smooth the hard edges by contributing experience and compromise and expedience when logic runs its course. In many ways this is the methodology used by the conservative, accommodationist wing of the Court, the Chief Justice and Justices Scalia and Thomas, abetted by the middle-grounders, Justices O'Connor, Kennedy, and Breyer. It is a view that could be described, in this setting at least, as judicial restraint. It could also be described in less glowing terms, such as pragmatism in the face of public or legislative resistance, or practical limits on the Court's capacity to enforce its own decisions, or cowardice. All of these terms, too, have been used to describe the Court's decisions.

Another way to acknowledge the contribution of Holmes's experience is to bring that experience into the matrix of the Court's own decisions. Holmes's statement implies this result by saying that the life of the law is experience. Experience occupies a place alongside logic and reason in the Court's job of making law as it interprets the Constitution. John Marshall, the most respected Chief Justice in the history of the Court, said in *Marbury v. Madison,* the seminal 1803 case that identified the Court's—and the judicial branch's—function under the Constitution: "It is emphatically the province and duty of the judicial department to say what the law is."[1] When a case comes to the Supreme Court, the Court must decide it, not slough it off to others (which, of course, would indeed be a decision). This is the stuff of fulsome judicial authority, resting on the premise that, at least with the Constitution, the job of interpretation and enforcement must rest with the judicial branch since the consequences of a case will often be visited upon the conduct of the legislative and executive branches. Without judicial supremacy on the meaning of the Constitution, the legislative and executive branches could simply go about "amending" the Constitution any time they wished.

This is the vision of judicial authority that has animated the Supreme Court on or off (but mostly on) throughout its roughly 225-year history, and it is the vision that animates the liberal side of the Court: Justices Stevens, Souter, and Ginsburg. It is John Marshall's vision of an independent check on the other branches of government—on their inevitable tendency to seek to ex-

1. *Marbury v. Madison,* 1 Cranch (5 U.S.) 137 (1803).

pand their power. In more common and less flattering terminology, this is the stuff of judicial activism. The necessity, indeed the solemn duty, of deciding cases inevitably leads over time to the expansion of the judicial branch's domain. And the legitimacy—the duty, according to Holmes—of bringing experience, not just logic and reason, to the table of judicial decision making, obliges the Court to seek answers beyond the reason and logic revealed in the history, text, and original purposes of the Constitution. Concepts like "evolving standards of decency" and "fundamental to ordered liberty" become the criteria for judicial decision when, as with the religion guarantees, the text, history, and purposes of the Constitution provide no answer.

This is, it must be said, an overly simplistic portrayal of the Court's tortuous journey through the inner workings of the religion guarantees. And it is wrong to assume that restraint is always the stuff of conservative justices and activism the stuff of liberals, even in the religion setting. After all, it was Justice Hugo Black, in *Everson,* who built the wall of separation and then proceeded to open a gate through it, in the process leaving much room for action by the political branches of government. It is as if he said, "Here is the principle and logic, but it is not our job to decide every question at their outer boundaries." And it was Justice Scalia who said, in *Smith,* that a general law that incidentally burdens religious liberty is never unconstitutional, leaving the mess his rule created to the political branches. Can one imagine the Supreme Court hewing to that absolute logical rule if a city were to enforce its liquor laws against churches offering communion, or if students practicing their religion on an important religious holiday were made truants, or if churches and their contributors were made subject to the McCain-Feingold campaign finance law because their beliefs and expression of them have political consequences? Justice Scalia might not blink at such results, but it is a safe bet that other Justices on the conservative side of the Court or in the middle ground would intervene in the name of religious liberty in recognition of the fact that the *Smith* rule would otherwise be taken to its logical, and absurd, consequences.

This, of course, is precisely what Chief Justice Rehnquist did when faced with the conflict between non-establishment and religious liberty in the *Davey* case. The equality principle of religious liberty would, in his view, be taken to an absurd extreme, writing the interest in maintaining any separation between church and state completely out of the Constitution if states were required to fund the training of ministers. For the Chief Justice, religious liberty may be primary over separation, but it doesn't extinguish it. There is a tension that must be acknowledged and accommodated, and the political branches—including the political branches of the state of Washington—have a role to play in such cases. In *Davey* the majority acted consistently with *Everson* and *Smith* by leaving room for political judgment to be made. It was Scalia, the author of the *Smith* opinion and dissenter in *Davey*, who violated his own rule and acted out the judicial activism role in the process.

* * *

It is widely declared in academic circles today that the law of the religion guarantees is a mess, undergirded by deeply conflicting premises, marked by judicial uncertainty, and freighted with detailed and technical distinctions. At one level, at least, it is hard to avoid this conclusion. How can school prayer be distinguished from "God Save This Honorable Court," or the teaching *of*, not teaching *about*, evolution in public schools, to the exclusion of the Genesis story? How can the religious exemption from compulsory education for the Amish be distinguished from the failure to exempt polygamy for the Mormons or ceremonial use of peyote for the Native American Church? This is the work of a Court at sea, in over its head.

But there may be a different perspective on the Court's work, one that does not try to justify all of the Court's decisions, but one that nevertheless yields a more sympathetic understanding of the Court's efforts. It begins with an important observation. Whatever they mean, the religion guarantees operate at two levels: at the institutional or structural level in the case of non-establishment; and at the individual and libertarian level in the case of free exercise. They are not like ships passing in the night, but rather like ships following the same general course but that occasionally meet, requiring one to give right-of-way to the other. To put it in Chief Justice Rehnquist's terminology, the religion guarantees are not strictly separationist, nor, after *Davey*, are they completely accommodationist. They are both, and separation and accommodation are "frequently in tension." Strict separation fully applied can yield hostility to religion. Accommodation taken too far can amount to a preference for religion.

The "mess," in other words, is not (entirely) the result of indecision or the work of a Court in transition. It is, instead, inherent in the very nature of the religion guarantees. Both matter. Neither can be completely satisfied without sacrifice of the other. Confusion and messiness at the intersection of the two—an area of give and take, as Chief Justice Rehnquist described it hopefully in the oral argument in *Davey*—is textually inevitable and, if we are to follow the Constitution, desirable. The balance between non-establishment and free exercise, *not* the existence of both, is what divides the Court most clearly at its extremes, the liberal separationists and the conservative accommodationists.

But to focus only on these two sets of views would be to miss another and perhaps larger issue: when the two guarantees conflict, and principle and reason, prudently applied, cannot explain their reconciliation, who should decide? This Court has generally taken it upon itself to make those decisions. It has done so in cautious, narrow, and often technically inconsistent ways, thus giving rise to suspicion that the God-fearing, law-abiding, peaceful Amish are preferred over the stranger and more assertive Mormons because of who they are, not what they wish to do. This is what Holmes's "experience" yields when experience is not leavened by reason, text, and logic.

But has the Court chosen the right course in doing so? Can the Court really decide, in the way we expect it to decide, whether a December display of a Menorah and a Christmas tree are any differently religious than a display of a crèche? Is this more than we can reasonably ask a Court to do, and more than those who wrote the Constitution ever had in mind? It is entirely possible that the real fight on the Court, and the real source of confusion, results from disagreement over the role, if any, a necessarily text- and history-bound judicial branch can play in setting the rules for religious freedom and the relationship between secular government and religious beliefs and institutions. It may just be that areas of messiness and ambiguity are inherent in the very idea of religious liberty in an organized society.

We are, as the Supreme Court has said on a number of occasions, "a religious people." That may simply mean that questions of religion—who are we? how do we explain the condition in which we live? what is our place in the unfathomably larger scheme of things?—are on our minds. Answers to these questions, at least for those who claim to have found them, are truly acts of faith and belief. And for many Americans, they are acts of obedience to a higher, supernatural power. How can obedience to God be reconciled with obedience to human institutions, including most notably the authority of the secular state—an organized way of living together in a social order that has within it, particularly in America, a remarkable diversity of belief and faiths, both religious and nonreligious?

America has committed itself to a society in which churches—the institutional forms of faith in a "known" higher power—coexist with one another and with all other institutions and people. The coexistence is not just a concession, but also a belief that a richer social order will result. But coexistence takes hard work. It is not easy to construct a system in which competing and mutually inconsistent, if not hostile, religious belief systems can live together, respecting the others' right to exist while denying their truths. At the same time, the place of the individual person's religious freedom—whether to believe or not, what to believe, how to act—must be strongly guaranteed. Religion consists not of churches or doctrines or texts, but of beliefs of individual, free-willed people.

Without individual religious freedom to contend with, government could simply compose the rules of coexistence of churches and institutional religions and enforce them by force: no trespassing; no use of force; no disobedience of general laws, and the like. Under such a regime, churches would take their rightful place in the social order, play out their social roles, and persist. This would be stasis, but little more.

Religious belief, however, is a living and changing thing, an ongoing quest. Its life and breath comes from the mind and imagination of people, not churches. If the individual's freedom of religious belief and its exercise are to be protected and, indeed, encouraged, then churches become living organizations, themselves changing, waning, growing, redefining themselves over time. A regime consisting simply of rules of obedience backed by force will not do if creativity and changing beliefs and forms of belief are to be fostered, as they must be in a society that protects, first and foremost, the freedom of the individual in matters of conscience and belief. Instead, what is needed is a social and legal order that can adapt itself to changing circumstances, that can preserve space for evolution of religious institutions at the hands of religious people, that can leave the needed "play in the joints," and that can live with a certain degree of ambiguity, loosening the legal and social constraints at the appropriate times and in the appropriate ways. Such a government cannot be hostile to religion. It cannot be simply "neutral," in the sense of being indifferent, treating religion just like anything else. It must, instead, facilitate religion, leaving it room to live or die, grow and change, on its own. But in facilitating religion, government can't intrude and mustn't control. It must keep to its distinct and secular sphere. Religion and government do not occupy mutually exclusive spheres: they often overlap. When they do, each must respect the distinct prerogatives and responsibilities of the other. This is where the "tension" implicit in the religion guarantees lies. Resolving the tension necessarily involves negotiation and compromise—ambiguity and play in the joints—but it cannot mean conceding authority to the other.

Such a system is messy: informed by general principles but operated by the demands of practicality and uncertainty, marked by atomized, perhaps even idiosyncratic, choices. It is no real surprise that the Supreme Court's jurisprudence looks much the same. Is this a good or bad state of affairs? It probably depends—on whether one is a believer or not, first and foremost; or on whether one is a middle-grounder, still and perhaps always thinking and searching, suspending belief. But in truth, this state of affairs has its own grand virtue. It accounts for, or has been produced by (or both) a peculiarly

American culture and religious tradition. America is the most religiously diverse, religiously preoccupied, and religiously free country in the world—indeed, in all of human history. We are religiously disputatious yet respectful; we are firm and fixed in our own beliefs, until they change; we are distrustful of institutions and their power, including churches and the rules they issue, yet we love them too, often too much; we frequently profess belief in an omnipresent God who guides events and governs our actions (even influences the outcome of sporting events!), yet we follow the rules laid down by the secular state. We are able embrace two inconsistent ideas at the same time.

This, I think, is why religion is free in America.

Suggested Reading

Articles and Books

Audi, Robert, *Religious Commitment and Secular Reasoning* (2000).

Audi, Robert, and Wolterstorff, Nicholas, *Religion in the Public Square* (1997).

Behe, Michael, *Darwin's Black Box: The Biochemical Challenge to Evolution* (1996).

Carter, Stephen L., *The Culture of Disbelief: How American Law and Politics Trivialize Religious Devotion* (1993).

———, "The Resurrection of Religious Freedom?" 107 *Harvard Law Review* 118 (1993).

Chemerinski, Erwin, "Do State Religious Freedom Restoration Acts Violate the Establishment Clause or Separation of Powers?" 21 *University of California–Davis Law Review* 645 (1999).

Choper, Jesse, "Defining 'Religion' in the First Amendment," 1982 *University of Illinois Law Review* 579.

Cogan, Neil H. ed., *The Complete Bill of Rights: The Drafts, Debates, Sources, and Origins* (1997).

Cord, Robert L., *The Genesis of the Establishment of Religion Clause* (1982).

Darwin, Charles, *The Origin of the Species* (1859).

DelFattore Joan, *The Fourth R: Conflicts Over Religion in America's Public Schools* (2004).

Eisgruber, Christopher L., "The Vulnerability of Conscience: The Constitutional Basis for Protecting Religious Conduct," 61 *University of Chicago Law Review* 1245 (1994).

Esbeck, Carl H., "A Constitutional Case for Government Cooperation with Faith-Based Social Service Providers," 46 *Emory Law Journal* 1 (1997).

Feldman, Noah, "The Intellectual Origins of the Establishment Clause," 77 *New York University Law Review* 346 (2002).

Fraser, James W., *Between Church and State* (1999).

Garvey, John H., "Another Way of Looking at School Aid," 1985 *Supreme Court Review* 61.

Gey, Steven G., Brauer, Matthew J., and Forrest, Barbara, "Is It Science Yet? Intelligent Design Creationism and the Constitution," Florida State University College of Law, Published Law Research Paper No. 125 (2004).

Glenn, Charles L., *The Ambiguous Embrace: Government and Faith-Based Schools and Social Agencies* (2000).

Green, Steven K., "The Ambiguity of Neutrality," 86 *Cornell Law Review* 692 (2001), *reviewing* Charles L. Glenn, *The Ambiguous Embrace: Government and Faith-Based Schools and Social Agencies* (2000).

Greenawalt, Kent, *Private Consciences and Public Reasons* (1995).

Hamburger, Philip A., "A Constitutional Right of Religious Exemption: An Historical Perspective," 60 *George Washington Law Review* 915 (1992).

Jefferson, Thomas, *A Bill for Establishing Religious Freedom* (1786), in Neil H. Cogan ed., *The Complete Bill of Rights: The Drafts, Debates, Sources, and Origins* (1997).

Jeffries, John, and Ryan, James, "A Political History of the Establishment Clause," 100 *Michigan Law Review* 279 (2001).

Johnson, Philip, *Darwin On Trial* (1991).

———, *Reason in the Balance* (1995) (creationism/intelligent design).

Kurland, Phillip, *Religion and the Law* (1962).

Larson, Edward J., *Summer for the Gods: The Scopes Trial and America's Continuing Debate Over Science and Religion* (1995).

Laycock, Douglas, "'Nonpreferential' Aid to Religion: A False Claim About Original Intent," 27 *William and Mary Law Review* 875 (1986).

———, "Theology Scholarships, The Pledge of Allegiance, and Religious Liberty: Avoiding the Extremes but Missing the Liberty," 188 *Harvard Law Review* 155 (2004).

———, *The Remnants of Free Exercise,* 1990 *Supreme Court Review* 1.

———, "The Underlying Unity of Separation and Neutrality," 46 *Emory Law Journal* 43 (1997).

Levy, Leonard W., *The Establishment Clause: Religion and the First Amendment* (1986).

Lupu, Ira C., "Reconstructing the Establishment Clause: The Case Against Discretionary Accommodation of Religion," 140 *University of Pennsylvania Law Review* 555 (1991).

———, "The Increasingly Anachronistic Case against School Vouchers," 13 *Notre Dame Journal of Law Ethics and Public Policy* 375 (1999).

———, "Where Rights Begin: The Problem of Burdens on the Free Exercise of Religion," 102 *Harvard Law Review* 933 (1989).

Madison, James, *Memorial and Remonstrance Against Religious Assessments* (1785), in Neil H. Cogan ed., *The Complete Bill of Rights: The Drafts, Debates, Sources, and Origins* (1997).

Mansfield, Harvey C., Jr., "The Religious Issue and the Origin of the Constitution," in Robert A. Goldwin and Art Kaufman eds., *How Does the Constitution Protect Religious Freedom?* (1987).

Marshall, William P., "In Defense of *Smith* and Free Exercise Revisionism," 58 *University of Chicago Law Review* 308 (1991).

McConnell, Michael W., "The Origins and Historical Understanding of Free Exercise of Religion," 103 *Harvard Law Review* 1410 (1990).

———, "The Supreme Court's Earliest Church-State Cases: Windows on Religious-Cultural-Political Conflict in the Early Republic," 37 *Tulsa Law Review* 7 (2001).
Pennock, Robert T., *Intelligent Design Creationism and Its Critics: Philosophical, Theological, and Scientific Perspectives* (2001).
Perry, Michael, *Religion in Politics: Constitutional and Moral Perspectives* (1997).
Pfeffer, Leo, *Church, State, and Freedom* (1967).
Post, Robert, "Law and Cultural Conflict," 78 *Chicago-Kent Law Review* 485 (2003).
———, "Cultural Heterogeneity and the Law: Pornography, Blasphemy, and the First Amendment," 76 *California Law Review* 297 (1988).
Sherry, Suzanna, "*Lee v. Weisman:* Paradox Redux," 1992 *Supreme Court Review* 123.
Smith, Steven D., *Foreordained Failure: The Quest for a Constitutional Principle of Religious Freedom* (1996).
———, "Non-establishment under God? The Nonsectarian Principle," 50 *Villanova Law Review* (2005).
———, "The Pluralist Predicament: Contemporary Theorizing in the Law of Religious Freedom," http://ssrn.com/abstract=559129.
———, "The Rise and Fall of Religious Freedom in Constitutional Discourse," 140 *University Pennsylvania Law Review* 149 (1991).
———, "Symbols, Perceptions, and Doctrinal Illusions: Establishment Neutrality and the 'No Endorsement' Test," 86 *Michigan Law Review* 266 (1987).
Stone, Geoffrey R. "Constitutionally Compelled Exemptions and The Free Exercise Clause," 27 *William and Mary Law Review* 985–996 (1987).
Strossen, Nadine, "'Secular Humanism' and 'Scientific Creationism'; Proposed Standards for Reviewing Curricular Decisions Affecting Students' Religious Freedom," 47 *Ohio State Law Journal* 333 (1986).
Tushnet, Mark V., "'Of Church and State and the Supreme Court': Kurland Revisited," 1989 *Supreme Court Review* 373.

Cases

Abington School District v. Schempp, 374 U.S. 203 (1963).
Sherbert v. Verner, 374 U.S. 398 (1963).
Board of Education v. Allen, 392 U.S. 236 (1968).
Lemon v. Kurtzman, 403 U.S. 602 (1971).
Lynch v. Donnelly, 465 U.S. 668 (1984).
Wallace v. Jaffree, 472 U.S. 38 (1985).
Edwards v. Aguillard, 482 U.S. 578 (1987).
Zobrest v. Catalina Foothills School District, 509 U.S. 1 (1993).
Mitchell v. Helms, 520 U.S. 793 (2000).
Good News Club v. Milford Central School District, 121 S.Ct. 2093 (2001).
Zelman v. Simmons-Harris, 536 U.S. 639 (2002).

Index

RANDALL P. BEZANSON is the David H. Vernon Distinguished Professor of Law at the University of Iowa. His books include *How Free Can the Press Be?; Speech Stories: How Free Can Speech Be?; Taxes on Knowledge in America: Exactions on the Press from Colonial Times to the Present; Libel Law and the Press: Myth and Reality;* and *Taking Stock: Journalism and the Publicly Traded Newspaper Company.*

The University of Illinois Press
is a founding member of the
Association of American University Presses.

Composed in 10.5/13 Adobe Minion
with Helvetica Neue display
by Type One, LLC
for the University of Illinois Press
Designed by Dennis Roberts
Manufactured by Thomson-Shore, Inc.

University of Illinois Press
1325 South Oak Street
Champaign, IL 61820-6903
www.press.uillinois.edu